COLORADO STATE PARKS

A Complete Recreation Guide

Philip Ferranti

THE
MOUNTAINEERS

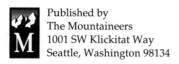

Published by
The Mountaineers
1001 SW Klickitat Way
Seattle, Washington 98134

0 9 8 7 6
5 4 3 2 1

Published simultaneously in Canada by Douglas & McIntyre, Ltd., 1615 Venables Street, Vancouver, B.C. V5L 2H1

Published simultaneously in Great Britain by Cordee, 3a DeMontfort Street, Leicester, England, LE1 7HD

Manufactured in the United States of America

Edited by Kris Fulsaas
Maps and book layout by Gray Mouse Graphics
All photographs by the author
Cover design by Watson Graphics
Book design and typography by The Mountaineers Books

Cover photographs by the author except as noted: clockwise from upper left, *State Forest State Park* (Photo by Bruce Hill), *Roxborough State Park*, *Golden Gate Canyon State Park* (Photo by Bruce Hill), *Eleven Mile State Park*
Frontispiece: *Swift-moving South Boulder Creek rushing through Eldorado Canyon State Park*

Library of Congress Cataloging-in-Publication Data
Ferranti, Philip, 1945–
    Colorado state parks : a complete recreation guide / Philip Ferranti.
        p. m.
    ISBN 0-89886-469-0
    1. Outdoor recreation—Colorado—Guidebooks.   2. Parks—Colorado—Guidebooks.
    3. Colorado—Guidebooks.   I. Title
    GV191.42.C6F47   1996
    917.88'0433—dc20   95–49792
                                                                          CIP

CONTENTS

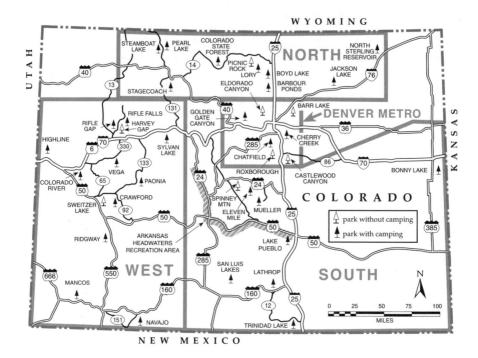

APPENDICES   196

INDEX   203

Hikers descending into Castlewood Canyon on the Inner Canyon Trail

PREFACE

Modern Colorado and a Re-creational Philosophy

▲Colorado is changing. Population shifts over the past ten years are bringing an influx of people into the Rocky Mountain states and Colorado. Denver, Boulder, Colorado Springs, Grand Junction, and other cities are expanding to include the newcomers. The Colorado State Parks department recognizes that these changes necessitate a balance between providing "a spectrum of safe, quality outdoor recreation experiences for visitors while effectively managing the natural resources . . ."

But there is an additional concern. Some argue that the stress and fast-paced culture America has created is taking its toll on the stability of all Americans. Are we losing touch with the natural world? Are we divorcing ourselves from accessing our deeper selves, replacing the experiential contact nature gives us with media-generated images of reality? If we are losing our civility, how can we regain it? Where are those quiet places, free from urban noise, marketing pressures to buy-buy-buy, and violence?

What most of us can use in today's world is a clear set of values and priorities that, when practiced, ensures our true growth as persons . . . human beings with character and a sense of "home" within. It can no longer just be a matter of "recreational escape or stimulation," but of true re-creation of our best selves.

We sometimes forget just how close a developed recreational area is to where we live. Especially during summer, when the daylight hours are extended, it might be a good idea to "treat" ourselves to a beautiful, quiet outing, alone or with friends, at some nearby state park, city/county park, or national forest area. Returning to nature is a valuable part of anyone's personal program for well-being.

John Muir suggested that we "climb the mountains and get their good tidings. Nature's peace will flow into you as sunshine flows into trees." And the Colorado State Parks division, steward of the land, lakes, and wildlife areas, offers forty gorgeous opportunities to renew oneself and rest in nature's peace. Less than 40 miles from Denver are seven state parks offering wetlands and lakes, canyons and colorful rock formations, subalpine hiking trails and fabulous boating, swimming, and fishing. Visitors can quickly exit the convention centers and seminar meeting rooms and avail themselves of the nature experiences virtually at their front doorstep. The rest of the state parks offer similar re-creation opportunities. The good tidings are always there. We just have to take the time to listen . . . and re-create.

In my travels throughout Colorado, I came across many people who knew of great places to visit, hike in, fish at, etc. I was surprised, however, to find that these same individuals often were unfamiliar with the state parks located in their own "backyards." I wrote this book, in part, because I have spent many summers in Boulder, Colorado, enjoying many visits and hikes in the state parks found nearby. It is my hope that this book will serve as an invitation for Coloradians to see the many recreational treasures near where they live and, thus inspired, to travel across the state and discover the parks on the "other side of the Rockies!"

Some of the parks are located close enough to each other that two parks can be seen in one day, or, if you are camping for several days, two or three parks might be explored. I am always excited to see the reactions on people's faces whom I have taken with me on my visits to Colorado's state parks. "Oh, I never knew that this was here! And such a beautiful place!" Unlike the treasures of old, Colorado's state parks are not buried in some obscure place . . . they are everywhere throughout the state and within easy reach of most urban areas. But no treasure can be enjoyed if it is not found. Let this book, then, serve as a guide to the many fulfilling outdoor experiences awaiting those who find the natural treasures that are the Colorado state parks.

ACKNOWLEDGMENTS

I have written this book with the help of many dedicated people who are on the staff of the Colorado State Parks department. Laurie Mathews, director of Colorado State Parks, first supported my enthusiasm about writing this recreational guide to the state parks, then directed me to Antonette DeLauro, director of public affairs, who supplied me with valuable information and encouragement. Deborah Duke, art director for Colorado State Parks, assisted me with map and photo information and resources, which have contributed greatly to the quality of information found throughout this book.

So many park managers, rangers, and other staff at all the state parks took time out from their demanding work schedules to offer valuable insights: Craig Bergman (Lory State Park); Mike Severin (Jackson Lake State Park); Carol Leasure (Golden Gate Canyon State Park); Wayne Olsen (Stagecoach State Park); Dave Uphoff (Bonny Lake State Park); Tom Macedo (Lathrop State Park), who offered special information about the Spanish Peaks and the park's visitors center murals; Bob Miller (Ridgway State Park); Chris Foreman (Highline State Park); Augie De Joy (Eleven Mile State Park); Heather Poe (Cherry Creek State Park); John Merson (Lake Pueblo State Park); Randyll Rivers (Boyd Lake State Park); Richard Fletcher (Colorado River State Park, Island Acres), who allowed me to photograph the park even though it was closed due to flooding; Roxanne Martin and Todd Farrow (Steamboat Lake State Park); Dave Bassett (North Sterling Reservoir State Park); Ron Dellacroce and Danielle Jenzen (Colorado State Forest)—Danielle, thanks for the thoughtful call from Ranger Lake to the Colorado State Forest Ranger Station on my behalf; Tim Metzger (Eldorado Canyon State Park); Linda Williams (Roxborough State Park). So many others offered a helping hand . . . I dedicate this book to you all, stewards of the beautiful, natural treasures of the Colorado State Parks system.

Thanks also go to the staff at The Mountaineers Books: Margaret Foster for her guidance and support and Christine Clifton-Thornton for her personal input, as well as Kris Fulsaas for her insightful editing.

Picnicking at Picnic Rock State Park

INTRODUCTION

Over 12 million people annually visit and enjoy the state parks of Colorado. Recreation is not confined to summertime swimming, boating, warm-weather nature walks, hiking, and the like. Colorado offers year-round recreational opportunities. The autumn season encourages visitors to view the spectacular fall colors of a wide variety of trees, especially the famous aspen. Tranquil lakes and their surrounding wetlands offer solitude. Hiking in the fall quickens the spirit, as the crisp air and azure clear skies stimulate our senses and permit us to more effortlessly climb to those higher elevations we sometimes struggle with during the hot summer months. Wildlife make their last appearances before heading south.

Winter at the state parks is a celebration of all that snow offers the outdoor enthusiast. Miles of spectacular cross-country skiing draw visitors into evergreen forests, over once-verdant meadows, and onto spectacular vista overlooks. Snowtubing allows one to mimic the antics of otters frolicking through the snow, while ice-skating opportunities abound at nearly every lake. Even anglers can challenge themselves with ice fishing . . . although patience seems to be in greater demand with this sport!

Spring and the first thaw brings brave boaters out to test whatever new craft they may have purchased during the winter. Camping can be especially nice during a mild spring, with temperatures sometimes rising into the 70s. Birds returning from wintering in the south renew the promise of life that is emerging once again to claim the land and give bird-watchers all the challenge they could hope for. Fishermen can again line the shores or take to their boats and go for the big one! The flowers and emerging foliage surprise and delight both eye and nose and hint of the great wildflower displays of summer yet to come.

The natural treasures found in Colorado's state parks offer recreational enjoyment year-round. Each season yields its own special pleasures and only asks that we come and discover for ourselves what each park has to offer . . . snowcapped mountains, sylvan beauty, serene lakes, and majestic vistas.

HISTORY OF THE STATE PARKS

In its stewardship of natural resources, Colorado began to establish state parks in 1957 with the creation of the State Parks and Recreation Board. The first state park to open was the reservoir at Cherry Creek State Recreation Area . . . just miles from the first gold strike at this same Cherry Creek area almost 100 years prior! Thus the land and its natural and recreational treasures have supplanted the mineral wealth upon which much of modern-day Colorado was first built.

Most of Colorado's state parks were established, then, since the 1960s, making these parks relatively young and somewhat unique among western states' park systems. Another noteworthy facet of Colorado's state parks is that, from the incorporation of Eleven Mile State Park in 1960 to Jackson Lake State Park in 1965 to North Sterling Reservoir State Park in 1992, many were formed around existing reservoirs. Thus, park development often followed natural resource development, connecting park formation to the economic activities of hydroelectric power, agricultural irrigation, and urban water supply.

Until 1972, the Game, Fish and Parks Department managed the state park system, but in that year was separated into the Colorado State Parks within the Department of Natural Resources. A Board of Parks and Outdoor Recreation was also established, which became responsible for real estate, information and education, resource management and visitor services, comprehensive recreation coordination, public safety, business management, and planning and development . . . a mission and scope that the Colorado State Parks still accepts today.

Since then, Colorado State Parks has grown rapidly, until it now oversees almost 160,000 land acres and over 46,000 surface acres of water. Nearly 3,000 campsites are available throughout thirty-one of the parks, with many parks offering both modern and backcountry camping; group camping is available at eight parks. The other ten parks are day-use only, with facilities for picnicking, fishing, boating, and hiking.

State Parks and Education

Colorado State Parks has taken a dynamic role in fostering an appreciation and understanding of the state's natural heritage throughout the entire population of Colorado, but especially with its youth. Over 3,700 interpretive programs were conducted during a recent year, covering topics ranging from outdoor survival, animal tracking, astronomy, dinosaurs, weather, and wildlife identification to boat safety and ecosystem studies. There were guided nature walks, survival weekends, campfire programs, field trips, and classroom demonstrations. Anyone interested in participating in these programs can contact the Colorado State Parks office or the park you plan to visit (see appendix A).

Colorado State Parks conducts wildlife observation programs throughout the

Signage at the Muskrat Run Nature Trail

state park system, in partnership with the National Partners in Watchable Wildlife, while also producing and distributing related brochures statewide. School children of Colorado are, from an early age, directly experiencing the rich mix of animal and plant life surrounding them. They are taught skills in how to approach and identify wildlife without posing a threat.

New seasonal interpreters are being hired to further develop these already successful programs. Groups of school children are welcomed to visit the parks and their nature centers, learning from trained naturalists and rangers about the ecosystems at each park. Students are even hired as seasonal employees to assist in this educational mission. And it is a hands-on approach all the way. Students actually build trails, participate in field biology projects, and take an active role in preserving Colorado's rich natural heritage. The outdoor survival schools and boating safety programs help build personal confidence for each participant. Real skills that students can apply to their recreational experience become part of what it means for each individual to "enjoy nature."

Volunteer programs complement the learning process by offering teens the chance to work in the parks, do trail patrols, and serve as staff at visitors centers. The underlying and guiding principle behind this effort is a simple one: what you truly know about and enjoy, you will preserve.

Since 1984, Colorado State Parks has worked as a partner with Volunteers for Outdoor Colorado to encourage and provide volunteer opportunities statewide. This organization sponsors hundreds of projects, including national river cleanups, trail rehabilitation and construction, restoration projects, backcountry ranger programs, and environmental education. For further information on this organization, see appendix A.

A Look Toward the Future

Colorado State Parks is emerging from a steady, sustained period of spectacular growth. With new funding, the agency is planning an ambitious rehabilitation and renovation program for all forty state parks under its management. This updating process will include purchasing new lands to be incorporated into existing parks; building new facilities such as campgrounds, visitors centers, boat ramps, and picnic sites; and expanding the watchable wildlife and interpretive programs where possible. Some parks will see the addition of informative slide shows that highlight the scenic and diverse recreational offerings found in that particular park.

Because Colorado has such a wealth of public lands that might be developed into new recreational resources, Colorado State Parks is examining the possibility of new land purchases that might become future state parks. In the past, the Bureau of Land Management, the U.S. Forest Service, and the federal government have enjoyed a close partnership in releasing land to the state of Colorado, which in turn has entrusted the Colorado State Parks with the land's development. The future suggests that this process will continue.

In the near future, a proposed Mount Evans Recreation Area is planned to be built, developed, and jointly managed with other agencies. Mount Evans (14,264 feet) is one of the most accessible and beautiful alpine-tundra environments in Colorado. The scenic Mount Evans Highway is the highest paved roadway in North America! It allows visitors of every ability to experience directly a real alpine setting and to access an extensive trail system. Plans call for extending a recreational boundary 0.5 mile on either side of the Mount Evans Highway, to the top of the peak itself. When plans are completed, a world-class environmental center near Echo Lake will offer programs, exhibits, and tours about the Mount Evans area.

This center will also help instill realistic outdoor ethics. Staff will offer visitors the chance to learn something about the Mount Evans area, its geology, wildlife, climate, plant life, wetlands, alpine tundra, and history.

Hiking trails may be extended to the Mount Evans Wilderness Area trail system, and fishing will be available at Echo Lake. The Division of Wildlife, along with the U.S. Forest Service, will offer a series of educational exhibits explaining safe ways to interact with the nearby wildlife, where the best opportunities exist for viewing the wildlife in the area, and how to interpret the Watchable Wildlife signs planned for the trails. The hope is that, as visitors come into close contact with a real high-country and alpine environment, they will carry this newfound appreciation to all the other many outdoor recreational experiences found throughout Colorado's high country.

ABOUT COLORADO'S STATE PARKS

History shows that from the discovery of gold in 1859 at Cherry Creek near Denver to about 1920, Colorado enjoyed a fabulous mining boom in precious metals. The common perception was that as the gold and silver fields played out, Colorado would lapse into a more balanced economy, the bulk of its natural treasures spent. Nothing could be further from the truth.

Since the end of World War II, visitors have steadily "rediscovered" the real and timeless wealth of Colorado: its pristine natural beauty, etched in dozens of soaring mountain ranges; stately western mesas and plateaus; wild and raging rivers; countless mountain streams; expansive forests of Douglas fir, blue spruce, pine, and aspen; brilliant wildflowers; colorful rock formations; abundant wildlife; and scenic vistas that never seem to end. Colorado has been blessed with some of the most spectacular scenery on earth. Even the red soil that inspired the Spanish explorers to name the state Colorado (which means "red" in Spanish) offers a stunning and attractive contrast to the lush green trees and grass.

Colorado's Water Resources

Water has always been a precious commodity in this somewhat dry state, where the rainfalls and snowpack might be heavy, but the challenge has always been to capture, store, and conserve this precious resource. Because Colorado is landlocked, the people of this state value their mountain lakes, rivers, and streams and the fishing, swimming, and boating that they offer. The Colorado State Parks has recognized this relationship between Colorado's people and their water; many of the important reservoirs statewide have been developed into beautiful recreational parks. Of the forty Colorado state parks, thirty-two are developed around a body of water and water-based recreation.

However, the importance of water-based parks goes beyond their obvious recreational value. The lakes and reservoirs serve as needed habitat for wildlife, thereby giving the Colorado State Parks a meaningful role in the stewardship of riparian habitat. It is estimated that although riparian habitat makes up less than 3 percent of Colorado's total land, it is used by almost 90 percent of all wildlife in the state!

Riparian refers to life along the water's edge. Plants and wildlife that live along banks of rivers, streams, or lakes or in marsh conditions make up the "riparian ecosystem." Whether it is the cottonwood-, grass-, and bush-lined rivers and lakes of Colorado's eastern plains or western plateaus, or the forest- and meadow-surrounded mountain lakes, riparian wetlands are often the sites that the State Parks agency has carefully developed.

Blue heron feeding in a marsh

Wetlands serve many functions in the life cycle of an ecosystem. Wetlands clean and filter water that flows through it, including heavy metals and chemical pesticides. They store water, thereby helping to prevent flooding, as well as replenish the underground aquifer depleted by irrigation and well systems. And, ultimately, wetlands provide food and habitat for the wildlife that is so dependent on this resource.

In light of the importance that wetlands and riparian habitat play in the total "life" of Colorado, the Colorado State Parks work closely with all natural resource agencies to protect, conserve, and in places develop the lands and water resources placed in its hands. Through thoughtful legislation, education, and responsible resource management, Colorado State Parks continues to add value to the priceless natural treasures entrusted to it.

Colorado's Topography

Flying from east to west over Colorado allows you to see the "crown" of Colorado's natural beauty, the dominant geological feature influencing every aspect of the state . . . the Rocky Mountains. To understand Colorado, one must appreciate how these mountains affect the ebb and flow of geological events, weather, and the diverse ecosystems found throughout the state, as well as the interconnectedness of the Rocky Mountains with all the other natural formations making up the state.

The eastern third of Colorado is made up of the Great Plains, vast expanses of prairie sweeping down from the Rockies and extending out into the adjoining states of Kansas and Nebraska. Much of the soil and rocks found on the plains were deposited by forces of erosion wearing down the Rocky Mountains over millions of years. Almost every river, stream, or creek found in this section of the Great Plains was born in the high, snow-filled valleys of the Rockies.

The Rocky Mountains, occupying the central third of the state, are a collection of often famous individual mountain ranges known as the Southern Rocky Mountains. Ranges like the San Juans, Sangre de Cristo, Sawatch, Flat Tops, Mosquito, and Front Range have each given their unique character to what most of us know as "The Rockies." The geological history of the Rocky Mountains includes at least two births.

The first creation of the Rocky Mountains occurred over 300 million years ago. The land was thrust upward until a broad range of mountains, perhaps even higher than the present-day Rockies, was formed. Eroded at the rate of 1 inch per 1,000 years, they eventually disappeared. Remnants of the Front Range give mute testimony of these ancestral mountains. The second formation of the Rockies began perhaps 70 million years ago, and is still going on. Uplift has often been pronounced, with the Continental Divide in some places along the Front Range being only 25 miles from the Great Plains.

The present-day Rocky Mountains dominate Colorado. Over 75 percent of the United States' area above 10,000 feet is found in Colorado, which also has the highest average altitude (6,800 feet) anywhere in the fifty states. The Rockies boast fifty-three peaks over 14,000 feet. This fact alone accounts for a cult of alpine enthusiasts . . . climbers dedicated to summiting every "fourteener" in the state. Almost 70,000 hikers a year summit one or more of these mountains.

A frequent topographical phenomenon in the Rockies is a mountain grassland surrounded by forest, known as a "park." Park grasslands are broad, flat, and often extend for 30 to 50 miles. At higher elevations, the forests are composed of Douglas fir, ponderosa pine, aspen, lodgepole pine, and Engelmann spruce.

Running along the north–south axis of the Rockies is the Continental Divide. Waters flowing down the western slope of the divide make their way into the Pacific Ocean: from the Colorado Rockies to the Gulf of California via the Colorado River and its tributaries. The eastern-slope waters flow into the Mississippi—via the Arkansas, Rio Grande, and North and South Platte Rivers—before eventually emptying into the Gulf of Mexico. Thus most of the hydrographic activity in Colorado emerges from or is influenced by the Rocky Mountains.

Traveling further westward to the remaining third of Colorado, one begins to see the Rockies slowly fade into the down-sloping canyons, mesas, and plateaus known as the Colorado Plateau. The forces uplifting the Rocky Mountains helped lift these basin lands west of the Rockies, while the Colorado River and its tributaries scoured and carved the colorful canyonlands reaching away from Colorado and into the great desert highlands of Utah.

Thus the uplifted Rocky Mountains in the center of the state greatly affected all the topography to the immediate east and west. Taken in their entirety, the Rocky Mountains are indeed the golden crown sitting atop Colorado . . . more valuable than all the precious ore ever mined out of this great state. However, the jewels of this crown, the Colorado state parks, are the focal points of the diverse natural beauties and recreational opportunities found in every corner of Colorado.

The Rockies and Colorado's Weather

The Rocky Mountains also play a central part in most of the weather throughout Colorado. The high elevation of the Rockies causes temperatures to be lower throughout the year than in most other states. Colorado's thinner atmosphere is less able to block out ultraviolet light, so sunburn happens more readily than on the beaches of Miami. Air heats up and cools down faster than at lower elevations. Outdoor enthusiasts need to remember that cool mountain air does not necessarily mean cool skin temperatures or freedom from the effects of solar radiation.

The Rockies also control much of the precipitation that occurs throughout Colorado. In winter, the moist air from the Pacific is blocked by the Rocky Mountains, causing massive amounts of rain and snowfall as the air rises, cools, and condenses. In the late spring and fall, moist air from the Gulf of Mexico sweeps upslope on the eastern side of the Rockies and falls mostly as rain, both along the Front Range (the first north–south range of the Rockies one meets as one travels west from the Great Plains), and further out into the sweeping prairie grasslands.

Colorado is blessed during the summer with "dramatic" weather caused by warm moist air rising over the higher elevations and condensing into those infamous late afternoon downpours. These storms are often blown out into the plains by early evening. I am always awestruck by the majestic beauty of those towering white and gray thunderheads boiling up over the plains, fading into soft reds and

Colorado bison feeding on open range

pinks, then deep purples, as the evening draws on, the sky often swept by erratic discharges of brilliant lightning and echoes of distant thunder.

These sometimes predictable, sometimes surprising weather patterns impact the recreational decisions visitors make when considering which state park to visit. Twice within several years it snowed someplace in Colorado on the Fourth of July, allowing skiers to have one final go at the slopes! The high-plains state parks tend to enjoy warm, sunny summer days . . . perfect for swimming, boating, and fishing. During the mid- to late summer "monsoon" season, late afternoon or early evening thunderstorms can be the order of the day, with strong winds blowing down from the western Rockies. At places like Spinney Mountain and Eleven Mile State Parks, these same winds in late afternoon make for exciting sailboarding and challenging sailing. Further west, at Rifle Gap and Harvey Gap State Parks, the same, strong westerly winds can add to (or detract from) the recreational experience. Visitors traveling to Colorado State Forest need to be aware that the elevation at that park ranges from 8,000 feet to 12,000 feet.

If you are coming from a balmy 85 degrees Fahrenheit at Denver, remember that the temperatures in the high country will not be anywhere near that. It is a good habit when visiting any state park to call ahead for weather and temperature conditions—research the five-day forecast in the area you plan to visit, and call the park for up-to-date information (see appendix A). Knowing the statewide weather patterns and their seasons will add to your recreational enjoyment.

Scenic Byways

Colorado's Scenic and Historic Byways Commission has identified key touring routes in the state for their exceptional scenic, historic, cultural, recreational, and natural features. These have been designated as Scenic and Historic Byways, and they pass directly by at least twelve of the state parks. Visitors to the state parks are offered the treat (and another great reason for traveling to the parks) of driving roadways surrounded by majestic mountains or serene lake and river valleys. For more information about Colorado's Scenic Byways, ask the Colorado Tourism Board (see appendix A) for the "Discover Colorado" brochure.

A sampling from the north-central area of the state might include the fabulous Highway 14, which follows the thundering Cache la Poudre River west for almost 75 miles on the way from Interstate 25 to Colorado State Forest. Another real treat is County Road 129, which takes you north from US Highway 40 through the beautiful Yampa Valley, along the Elk River, as you approach Steamboat and Pearl Lake State Parks. The surrounding mountains balance and frame the grassy farmlands and horse ranches with majestic relief. The drive to Sylvan Lake south from Interstate 70 along West Brush Creek Road offers forests of aspen carpeting the lush mountainsides. Further west, visitors to Rifle Falls, Rifle Gap, and Harvey Gap State Parks driving north from Interstate 70 on Highways 13 and 325 enjoy canyon valleys and Swiss-like farmland, complete with those famous Rocky Mountains to accent the skyline.

In the southwest corner of the state, the incredibly scenic San Juan Skyway (US 160, CO 145, US 550) competes for top honors as the state's most beautiful drive. The diversity of towns found along the way include the old western town of Durango, just east of Mesa Verde National Park and the Cortez area, famous as a depository of Anasazi Indian culture and history. North of Durango are Silverton and Ouray, Victorian mining towns which still wear their heritage with grace and beauty. Telluride, the famous ski resort in winter and host to jazz, film, and bluegrass festivals in summer, completes this incredible loop. Along the way you can

West Elk Mountain Range

visit Mancos State Park, just northeast from the town of Mancos, and Ridgway State Park, located 4 miles north of the town of Ridgway.

Finally, the West Elk Loop located just south of Glenwood Springs makes a wide circle that includes Crested Butte and Gunnison, and passes right through Paonia and Crawford State Parks . . . how's that for front door service! The scenic byways are almost extensions of the parks themselves, inviting you to the recreational opportunities at road's end. Almost every state park reaches out to touch visitors long before they ever arrive. Driving to the Colorado State Parks, then, offers plenty of immediate recreational/scenic benefits.

PARK AMENITIES

The amenities at Colorado's state parks are continually being improved and new ones added. Castlewood Canyon, along with Mueller and Roxborough State Parks, offers beautiful slide shows highlighting the facilities, and other parks are on-line to develop their own slide shows in the near future. Check with each park or regional office to discover what is available at the park you plan to visit.

Day-Use Areas. All of the state parks offer day-use areas, which combined consist of over 1,500 picnic sites and 150 boat ramps, almost 500 miles of hiking trails, and over 700,000 square feet of swim area; many also boast laundry facilities and dump stations. Visitors and nature centers are found at fourteen parks, with most offering interesting and varied interpretive programs.

Campgrounds. Camping at state parks is readily available, with over 3,000 campsites statewide. Most developed campsites accommodate both tents and RVs. These sites generally include a visitor services center with flush rest rooms and showers. Electrical hookups are located at fifteen of the parks, with more planned for the near future. Group campsites are available at many of the parks and can accommodate up to 100 people. Primitive camping sites are located in twenty-eight areas, and in some places even rugged backcountry camping sites are available. Check with your destination park to see what facilities exist. Reservations can be made a maximum of 90 days and a minimum of 3 days in advance. For information about camping reservations, see appendix A.

Handicap Facilities. Colorado State Parks provides park accessibility to the physically challenged. Its aim is to make each park as barrier free as possible. All new facilities are built with maximum accessibility in mind for all levels of ability. Please check with each park facility you plan to visit for the particulars regarding the accessibility of any facility (also see appendix B). The Wilderness on Wheels Foundation (see appendix A) shares this same mission of providing natural recreational areas that are accessible to the physically challenged.

Marina Facilities. Marina facilities, which can be found at most parks that are water-based, include boat rentals for sailboats, motorboats, water skis, rafts, and boating supplies.

Fishing. Fishing is a popular activity at most of the state parks. Park rangers will answer any questions concerning fishing at their facility. However, the Colorado Division of Wildlife brochure entitled "Colorado Fishing Season Information and Wildlife Property Directory" is a must. Another brochure every fisherman should have is titled "Gold Medal Waters." This highlights eleven areas that have "high-quality aquatic habitat, a high percentage of trout 14 inches or longer, and the potential for trophy trout fishing and angling success." Some of the gold medal waters include Blue River, the Colorado River, the Gunnison River, and Spinney Mountain Reservoir . . . one of Colorado's own state parks. "Colorado's Fishing Hot Spots" lists nine Colorado state parks as "hot" fishing holes. Visits to the state parks will reward fishermen with scenic surroundings, well-stocked waters, and hopefully many catches.

Water Sports. Colorado State Parks also offers what few other states do . . . three designated river-rafting "parks" offering entry areas into some of the nation's most famous waterways, including the Colorado River, the headwaters of the Arkansas River, and the wild and raging Cache la Poudre River. The combined riverfront miles that these parks offer measure into the hundreds. Besides rafting and boating of all kinds, these river parks and recreation areas offer miles of prime fishing waters, and numerous camping opportunities for people to enjoy a beside-the-river experience.

Hiking. Colorado's state parks offer over 500 miles of hiking trails, with access to additional trails close by in dozens of major wilderness areas, state forests, national forests, land administered by the Bureau of Land Management (BLM), and national parks. The State Trails Program assists in the maintenance and oversight of over 200 trails. Colorado State Parks publishes a series of well-documented trail guide/maps showing the major trail systems at key areas around the state. The series is called "Urban Trails in Colorado," and includes such titles as: Western Slope and Mountains, Denver Metro Area, North Front Range, and South Front Range. These can be picked up at state parks or visitors centers, or by calling Colorado State Parks (see appendix A).

Another very useful publication also available from Colorado State Parks is the Colorado Trails Resource Guide. This resource is a must for every hiker. The guide lists almost all trails support groups statewide; all federal, state, and local government agencies; clubs and organizations; biking, equestrian, and off-highway vehicle groups—complete with addresses and phone numbers. When visiting any state park, ask any staff person about nearby hiking opportunities, phone numbers, and the like. Many rangers and staff are avid hikers and are quite familiar with the trail systems on which their parks border.

The Colorado Trail, a proud, home-grown 470-mile trail stretching from Denver to Durango, is one such trail system that can be accessed from some of Colorado's state parks. Hikers visiting the state parks at Mueller, Eleven Mile, Spinney Mountain, Navajo, and Mancos Lake find themselves within miles of being able to reach the Colorado Trail. There is even a connector trail leading from Mancos State Park to the Colorado Trail's terminus at Durango. Most of these sections are long backpacking stretches for which hikers need to be adequately prepared. Hiking just this one trail is as good a way as any to see a sampling of Colorado's best scenic vistas, forests, and (when you're hiking the length of the Colorado Trail) never-ending mountain ranges. Most bookstores and map shops have literature or maps on this fantastic trail.

Equestrian Facilities. At a few parks, horseback riding concessionaires are available, but many of the parks allow you to trailer your own horses in and enjoy the miles of scenic trail and sweeping vistas. During my travels to all the state parks, I came across many single or groups of riders, and those I chatted with agreed that Colorado's state parks offer real opportunities for equestrian adventure. Lory State Park even boasts a premier cross-country jumping course. In each park's description in this book, more detail on amenities and programs is presented.

Dunes Campground and group picnic area at Jackson Lake State Park

Rock Climbing. Rock climbing has been taken to an art form at Eldorado Canyon State Park. This facility draws technical climbers from all over the world to test their skills on "The Bastille," "The Wind Tower," "Hawk-Eagle Ridge," and several other challenging rock climbs. Along with rock climbing, Eldorado offers beautiful canyon views for picnicking and hiking.

Wildlife Viewing. Want something more serene? Barr Lake State Park hosts one of the largest concentrations of bird life in the United States. The park's pride and joy is a wildlife observation station/gazebo that offers close-up views of one of the few pairs of nesting bald eagles found along the entire Front Range.

PARK GUIDELINES AND REGULATIONS

State parks are open year-round, weather permitting, and attempts are made to keep at least some campsites open during the fall and winter months, again, weather permitting. Hours of operation are generally 5:00 A.M. to 10:00 P.M. in the day-use areas, and, when they are open, campgrounds are open 24 hours a day.

Noise. Quiet hours in campgrounds are generally from 10:00 P.M. to 6:00 A.M. During these hours, all generators, loud radios, or other loud noises that may disturb the peace are prohibited. It is especially annoying to have driven many miles for the tranquillity offered by a park setting, only to find loud and irresponsible people nearby.

Pets. All pets must be kept on a leash no longer than 6 feet. Pets are not permitted in certain areas such as the Wildlife Refuge at Barr Lake State Park, at Roxborough State Park, outside the developed facilities area at Mueller State Park and Wildlife Area, at Harvey Gap State Park, or on swim beaches.

Even where dogs are permitted, owners have a responsibility to ensure that no other person, pet, or wildlife is endangered by their animal. A dog or cat unleashed

Flowers alongside marshlands

in a wilderness area, or in parks where wildlife is common, invites itself to be a meal for a hungry predator or may kill or chase smaller wildlife. In Colorado, law enforcement officers are authorized to destroy dogs seen chasing wildlife and fine the pet owners.

Motorized Vehicles. Motor vehicles must obey all normal street traffic regulations, park only in designated areas, and drive only on designated roads. Never is a motor vehicle allowed on the same trails used by hikers, bicyclists, or horseback riders.

State Parks administers boat, snowmobile, and off-highway vehicle registration as well as its Commercial River Outfitters licensing program. Interested boaters are encouraged to contact the state park they intend to visit (see appendix A) for more information concerning regulations. (See also the Safety section later in this chapter.)

Swimming. The freshwater lakes and reservoirs at the state parks are especially beautiful places to swim in. Soaring mountains and forests provide quite a scenic backdrop for any water sport! However, some basic rules apply. Swimming is permitted only in designated areas and is regulated so that boaters and anglers using the water concurrently are not in conflict. Swimmers are not permitted to build a fire on any swim beach, or fish from any swim beach. Children twelve years of age and under are not allowed on a swim beach unless accompanied by an adult. Swimmers in state parks or recreation areas are required to swim only in areas designated for swimming use.

Fires. As in most recreational areas, fires are permitted in grills or fire rings, which are provided in picnic and camping areas and placed where the possibility of creating a wildfire is minimized. Contained barbeques and hibachis are also allowed. No one is allowed to burn a fire in a careless manner, to leave a fire unattended, or to fail to completely extinguish any fire on Colorado State Parks land.

No fireworks are permitted in any state park, except special displays approved by the director.

Garbage. Glass containers are not permitted on swim beaches, and all littering is strictly forbidden. People need to be especially careful about leaving fishing lines and six-pack plastic rings in the water. These pose a hazard to people and wildlife.

Fishing. One of the most important fishing regulations are that anyone fifteen years of age or older must possess a valid fishing license to fish or take frogs, crustaceans, or mollusks from Colorado waters. Fishermen are especially advised to know both the daily bag limits and the possession limits for each species caught. The Colorado Division of Wildlife (see appendix A) publishes a comprehensive brochure entitled "Colorado Fishing Season Information and Wildlife Property Directory," a must-have for every fisherman.

Wildlife. Another area of concern when visiting the state parks is the possibility of encounters with wildlife and the effects both on them and on the visitor. Wildlife is just that . . . wild. Basic rules of common sense dictate that animals should never be harassed, chased, captured, domesticated, or (in most cases) fed. Most wildlife problems stem from improper feeding of animals. In fact, it is illegal to feed deer, bighorn sheep, mountain goats, antelope, and elk in the state parks. Garbage cans and other waste areas in campgrounds or in backcountry campsites need to be covered and sealed in such a way that wild critters do not think they have been invited to dinner!

When driving in the backcountry, be watchful for animals crossing the road. Especially at night, deer and other wildlife are out and about. Deer crossing signs are placed in areas where deer are often present, so do slow down when you come to these signs.

At some of the Front Range parks or on the plains, visitors often encounter those cute little animals known as prairie dogs. These animals like to stay in their habitat—dog towns—and people should avoid feeding or disturbing them.

Almost all Colorado snakes are harmless, and even benefit humans because of their appetite for harmful rodents. Rattlesnakes are sometimes encountered in the wild, but not often. This species is poisonous. The best rule of safety is to look where you walk, sit, or reach. If you do see a snake, back away slowly and give it an escape path.

SAFETY

Because boating, fishing, and swimming comprise most of the activities at Colorado's many lake- and reservoir-based parks, Colorado State Parks has initiated many programs to assist water users to safely enjoy their stay at any of the water-based parks.

Boating

Although boating is fun, even a good thing can be overdone. Boating for hours on end can leave you tired, thereby slowing your reaction time in case of an emergency. Some of the main safety guidelines and regulations for boaters include avoiding any excess intake of alcohol and taking a boating safety class offered by Colorado State Parks or the U.S. Coast Guard Auxiliary. In Colorado, anyone who operates a motorboat or sailboat on any of the public waters of the state is considered to have expressed his or her consent to be tested, when requested by a law enforcement officer, for blood alcohol level or the presence of a controlled substance in his or her bloodstream.

Boaters are advised to know the load limit for their boat, always carry the necessary safety gear of flags and throw lines, and know the rules of operation for the particular lake or reservoir they visit. A new Colorado law requires that each vessel, no matter what length it is or what type of propulsion it has, must carry one wearable personal flotation device (PFD) for each person on board. Each device must be Coast Guard approved, in good condition, the proper size for the intended wearer, and readily available for use.

White-water Boating

Colorado State Parks also manages three areas famous for their whitewater river-rafting opportunities: Picnic Rock State Park on the Cache la Poudre River, Colorado River State Park's three sites, and the many recreation sites of the Arkansas Headwaters Recreation Area. Boaters should always know the section of the river that they are running by using detailed and updated maps and guides. The weather is also crucial. Too high a snowmelt can turn a Class III rapids into a Class V very easily. And certain rivers are cold enough to require wet suits. Find out these types of water conditions before you leave.

Each boat should have all the necessary emergency equipment: extra life jackets, 100-foot throwing rope or throw bag, spare paddles/oars, a complete patch and repair kit, first aid kit, drinking water, and fresh supplies. Like hikers in the backcountry, river rafters can never be sure how long they will be out.

Know your boat's capacity and never go beyond it. Some rafts' capacity is based on flat stretches of water, not necessarily white water. When taking a rafting trip into a wilderness area, let someone know the details of your trip (just as for hiking): where, when, for how long. And when you return, tell them that you are safely back.

Appropriate dress is crucial. Shoes that will protect the feet must be worn, and eyeglasses need to be secured and perhaps an extra pair taken along. A helmet should be worn by both kayakers and canoeists. When the air and water temperature added together total 100 degrees Fahrenheit or less, a wet suit is mandatory. I rafted the Arkansas wearing a wet suit, and appreciated the extra insulation it provided.

Once on the river, always wear your life jacket. Never boat alone . . . three kayaks, two canoes, or two rafts are the minimum party size. Your boating party should stay together, with designated sweep and lead boats. Scout rapids and blind spots from shore before running them. High water can conceal logs or other obstacles. When arriving at a rapids that is too difficult to run, get out and portage your boat. The idea is to have a safe and enjoyable trip . . . not to see how far over your head you can get! Before you ever raft with a group that is not professionally guided, get some classroom skill as to what river rafting is all about. Movies will not teach you the "skills" you need.

In case of an emergency, such as a person overboard, the person in the water should tuck his or her body up with feet downstream to protect from rock blows, and either head for shore or ride out the rapids. In the case of capsizing, avoid loose ropes and gear, get from under the boat, and head for shore, especially if the water is cold.

White-water rafting is an enjoyable and safe sport when people do the right thing. This includes packing out all garbage, refraining from dumping any litter and soap into the river, respecting both the private and public lands you travel through, and respecting the rights of other boaters and fishermen you might encounter on the river.

Hiking

It is advisable to carry the Ten Essentials for a safe hiking experience:

1. Adequate food, so that some is left over after the hike
2. Extra clothing, enough for an extra change if you get wet
3. First aid kit
4. Matches, in a weatherproof container
5. Sunglasses, especially important for snow conditions
6. Knife
7. Fire-starting material, such as chemical fuel
8. Compass
9. Flashlight, with extra batteries
10. Map of your hike and the immediate area

Let someone know where you are going and when you expect to return. Most trails are well signed and in good condition, so stay on the trails and go only as far as you are physically conditioned for.

Altitude sickness can affect hikers, usually above 8,000 feet. The Colorado State Forest is a high-altitude state park with mountains reaching above 12,500 feet. Visitors coming to this park from lower elevations (especially from the plains) need to immediately seek lower elevations if they find themselves getting dizzy, nauseated, or weak.

A late afternoon rainstorm is common in the mountains during summer; hikers need to carry proper rain gear and warm clothing. Often rain can turn to hail or snow. Fifty miles away on the plains it can be 90°F, while a mountain storm front can drop temperatures to below freezing.

A chief safety concern during a hike is the possibility of meeting a mountain lion or bear. Even with this real danger, fewer than a dozen fatalities involving mountain lions have occurred in North America during the past 100 years. If you do chance upon a mountain lion or bear, do not approach it. Stay calm and move slowly back away from it. If you meet a mountain lion, speak calmly, move slowly, and do all you can to appear larger. If attacked, fight back with whatever is available. But remember that most wildlife seek to avoid direct contact with humans. Any sightings or encounters should be reported to the Division of Wildlife (see appendix A).

HOW TO USE THIS BOOK

In this book, Colorado is divided into four regions: the Denver Metro Region, the North Region, the South Region, and the West Region. Accompanying the description of each region is a map showing the state parks in that region, as well as the major highways and cities en route to the parks. The state parks found in that particular region are grouped by geographical proximity.

Each park's in-depth description begins with an informational summary listing hours and season, total area in land and water acres, facilities, attractions, and access information. Then follows an overview of the park, a brief history of it and the surrounding area, a description of the park's amenities and activities, and information on wildlife found in the park. The park description concludes with a sampling of nearby attractions, including, where appropriate, hiking areas near the state park.

In appendix A is a comprehensive list of important agencies, parks, and organizations that have resources that could add to your recreational experience. Free brochures are readily available, and often these resources include maps and other guidebooks that also help. The Colorado State Parks publishes many helpful brochures that outline what is offered at a particular park, and what recreational pursuits can be found. Appendix B gives a detailed account of each of the state park's handicapped-accessible facilities.

A NOTE ABOUT SAFETY

Safety is an important concern in all outdoor activities. No guidebook can alert you to every hazard or anticipate the limitations of every reader. Therefore, the descriptions of roads, trails, routes, and natural features in this book are not representations that a particular place or excursion will be safe for your party. When you follow any of the routes described in this book, you assume responsibility for your own safety. Under normal conditions, such excursions require the usual attention to traffic, road and trail conditions, weather, terrain, the capabilities of your party, and other factors. Keeping informed on current conditions and exercising common sense are the keys to a safe, enjoyable outing.

The Mountaineers

MAP SYMBOLS

highway	═══════	paddling	🛶
road	▬▬▬▬▬▬	fishing	🎣
service road	─ ─ ─ ─ ─ ─	waterskiing	🎿
trail	··········	sailboarding	🏄
interstate highway	(25)	swimming	🏊
US highway	(87)	marina	⚓
Colorado state highway	(86)	entrance station	👤🏠
county road	[14]	visitor center / ranger station	🏠
body of water		handicapped accessible	♿
dam	▬▬▬	picnic area	⅂⅂
marsh	⚘⚘⚘	shelter	⌐
wakeless boating zone		building	■
area closed to public use		group picnic area	
buoy line	●—●—●—●—●	sanitary dump station	
park boundary		trailer camping	
peak	▲	campground	⋀
trailhead	⊤	backcountry campsite	Λ
mountain pass	)(	cabin	⌂
bridge	⊨	wildlife observation	🔭
boat ramp		scenic overlook	📷
boat access		foot trail	🚶
non-motorized boating	⛵	bike trail	🚲
boating at wakeless speed		horse trail	
		4WD road	

29

ROCKY MOUNTAIN NATIONAL PARK

Colorado also boasts of one of the premier "hiking parks" in the national parks system . . . Colorado's Rocky Mountain National Park, which offers hundreds of miles of hiking trails, over 550 camping sites, seventy-six peaks over 12,000 feet high, and many scenic wonders scattered over a 415-square-mile area. Hikers who come to Colorado to hike must visit Rocky Mountain National Park.

An especially good representation of the best hiking Rocky Mountain National Park has to offer is the 10-mile loop hike from Bear Lake Trailhead to Fern Lake and ending at the Cub Lake Trailhead in Moraine Park. The trail makes a gentle 1,000-foot climb toward Odessa Lake. Along the way are spectacular views of the lower elevations and valleys that sweep down from the park and eventually meet the high plains east of Estes Park. As hikers make the turn toward Odessa Lake, they travel a high alpine mountain valley situated between two mountain ranges. Fern Lake and Odessa Lake can be seen in the distance, resting like blue topaz jewels in the bottom of the lake valley. The trail looks out toward soaring peaks surrounding this valley, and with snow still on the mountain tops in mid-summer, the views can be breathtaking. Eventually the trail reaches the lower forest elevations, follows several roaring streams, and offers two trails that lead back to the parking area. The Cub Lake route encompasses one more mountain lake setting, while the route past the Fern Lake Trailhead is a hike along a beautiful creek and past generous stands of quaking aspen. A shuttle bus makes regular pickups from the Fern Lake and Cub Lake trailheads and takes hikers up to the Bear Lake Trailhead, which allows you to make this loop hike mostly downhill, without having to park a vehicle at the upper trailhead.

Another spectacular hike in this national park begins from the Glacier Gorge Junction Trailhead, located near the Bear Lake Trailhead, and leads to a high alpine lake known as Sky Pond. This is a 9-mile hike that leads through a scenic valley pass, by the Loch Lake and the Lake of Glass, and into the higher rocky terrain surrounding Sky Pond. On the way, hikers can take a side route to Andrews Glacier, located just beneath the Continental Divide. The elevation gain for this hike is over 1,600 feet, and for the side trip to Andrews Glacier is 2,450 feet.

The highest peak in Rocky Mountain National Park is the famous Longs Peak (14,255 feet). The trailhead to the top of this imposing mountain begins at the Longs Peak Ranger Station (9,300 feet) and proceeds up a long 16-mile round-trip route that climbs over 4,800 feet in elevation. Most hikers who attempt this peak need to be in top physical condition. It is advised, also, to get a very early start, even well before sunrise. It is not just a matter of returning before dark; summer afternoon thunderstorms near the peak can be quite heavy.

Located in the far southwestern corner of the park are Grand and Granby lakes. From these lakes, the largest naturally occuring lakes in Colorado, hikers can return to the trail systems found inside the park, while boaters can enjoy some of the most scenic boating anywhere in Colorado.

In the far southeast corner of the park, in an area sometimes missed by tourists and visitors unfamiliar with the geographical make-up of the park, is the famous Wild Basin Trailhead. This section of the park is best accessed by driving from Highway 7, coming in from Lyons or from the Peak-to-Peak Highway 72. Many spectacular trails are found along this trailhead.

Aspen grove

One of these, a very popular trail that offers several possible destinations from branch trails coming off of it, is the hike to Thunder Lake via Calypso Cascades and Ouzel Falls. The hike begins in a thick forest area, immediately approaches North St. Vrain Creek, and follows the stream 1.8 miles to the spectacular Calypso Cascades (2 miles from the trailhead). These series of roaring cascades pour down from a steep mountainside, within touching distance of the trail, which crosses a bridge near the cascades. Bring your camera for this one. On a hot summer day, many less adventuresome hikers are content to bask in the cooling mist before returning back to the trailhead. The trail continues another mile to the beautiful Ouzel Falls. These falls are especially dramatic after a wet winter with heavy snowmelt. Many tourists make this 5-mile, 1,000-foot elevation-gain trip, but hikers must realize that even 5 miles and 1,000 feet in elevation gain can be demanding.

For those going on to Thunder Lake, the trail takes a steep turn up the face of a mountain before leveling off. The last 2 miles take hikers past a bowl of soaring mountains and into a flat area where Thunder Lake glistens beneath Mount Alice. Along the way up to this lake, the imposing and dominant Mount Meeker (13,911 feet) fills the horizon to the north. The hike to Thunder Lake is 13.6 miles round trip, with 2,100 feet of elevation gain. If hikers want an added experience of bagging another high alpine lake, the return route intersects with a trail that takes you to Bluebird Lake. The distance to Bluebird Lake from the Wild Basin Trailhead is 13 miles, with a climb of 2,500 feet.

All of these hikes originating from the Wild Basin Trailhead are spectacular in their own right; on busy summer weekends the trailhead can get quite crowded, so it is a good idea to arrive early and avoid the parking space problems that sometimes occur. These trails are not only opportunities for exercise, but traverse beautiful lands that feed our need for aesthetic nourishment. Trails in Rocky Mountain National Park are well signed, groomed, and maintained. Mountain bikers and equestrians also use many of these trails, where permitted, and there is a healthy mutual respect among every group using the trail systems.

Castlewood Canyon as seen from Bridge Canyon Overlook

DENVER METRO REGION

The Denver Metro region is at the heart of the state of Colorado. It extends north from Denver 30 miles to Boulder, east 70 miles into the plains, south 40 miles to Castle Rock, and west 100 miles to Vail. The seven state parks located in this region are within 30 miles of Denver, providing easy access to outdoor recreation for city dwellers and visitors to this metropolis.

Denver is both the last of the great high-plains cities and the first of the great western and mountain metropolises. The prairie that sweeps across the Midwest for a thousand miles and rises dramatically in elevation to become the high plains ends abruptly 12 miles west of Denver. The uplifting effect of the Rocky Mountains is total. No gradual and slowly building mountain system here . . . 14,000-foot peaks lie just a score of miles from the plains and Denver. The "transition zone" between plains and mountains is only a few miles of foothills, changing in elevation from 5,500 feet to over 10,000 feet in a short span of 25 miles. This sudden emergence of Rocky Mountains from flat plains is accompanied by dramatic changes in the topographical features that surround the city and metropolitan region of Denver.

Within 30 miles east of the city is Barr Lake State Park, a wetlands-riparian lake habitat reminiscent of the beautiful Chesapeake Bay along Maryland's south shore. To the southeast of Denver, the plains have been abruptly uplifted an additional 1,000 feet, covered with a dense ponderosa pine woods known as the Black Forest, then carved by Cherry Creek into a canyon gorge that forms Castlewood Canyon State Park, before making its way into Denver to form Cherry Creek State Park. In the distance, massive Pikes Peak looms. Not far away is Chatfield State Park, a boater's paradise located at the confluence of the South Platte River and Plum Creek.

A few miles southwest from downtown Denver is a colorful red-rock setting like Sedona, Arizona: Roxborough State Park is an incredible "sunsets-in-sandstone" wonderland, set against the lush green relief of the first towering, forested mountain peaks of the Front Range. Located just 30 miles to the northwest is a slice of canyon grandeur with sheer 1,500-foot cliffs and rock faces that rise vertically out of the plains. The terrain of Eldorado Canyon State Park challenges the best rock climbers in the world.

Just down the road from Eldorado is the first hint of the high country and alpine terrain found in the central third of the state. Golden Gate Canyon State Park offers

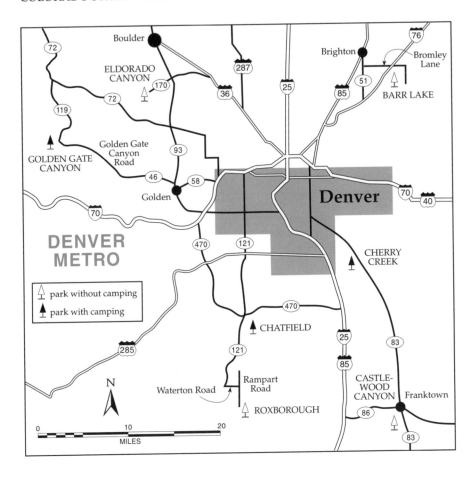

panoramic vistas covering over 80 miles of soaring peaks, many miles of great forest, mountain and meadow hiking trails, and a cool retreat from the hot plains below. The air is crisp and sweet at this park accented by mountain streams, aspen groves, and sweeping grasslands.

The weather in the Denver Metro Region is split between the eastern plains and the western mountains. Summers are cool and temperate in the mountains, while on the plains summers are hot, with temperatures often reaching into the 90s. Late afternoon mountain rainstorms travel eastwards and become evening thunderstorms on the plains. Snow falls in the mountains during late fall, with an occasional surprise snowfall in Denver as early as mid-September. However, once winter begins, the entire region receives generous amounts of snow. Spring can be quite delightful if April and May rain is broken up with balmy dry spells; however, the weather in this region is fast-changing and erratic . . . sometimes seasons follow each other on a daily basis!

In the mountain parks of Golden Gate Canyon and Eldorado Canyon west of Denver, grasslands quickly give way to piñon and juniper woodlands, which in turn become montaine forests of ponderosa pine, aspen, and Douglas fir. Roxborough State Park and Castlewood Canyon are accented by prairie grasses

Quiet fishing along the banks of Chatfield Reservoir

and scatterings of piñon, juniper, and ponderosa forests. Barr Lake, Cherry Creek, and Chatfield State Parks are almost entirely a mixture of grasslands, some trees, and riparian wetlands, highlighted by reeds, cattails, marshes, and cottonwoods.

The varied flora and wetlands of this region support hundreds of species of migrating waterfowl, especially ducks, geese, and egrets. Coyote, fox, prairie dogs, deer, elk, and raccoon are often seen in the mountain and grassland parks—and on rare occasions mountain lions. Some black bear have been spotted in the higher elevations of the mountain parks, but have rarely been a problem for people.

Denver itself offers many cultural opportunities found in any great metropolitan center. It is also home to some highly acclaimed natural attractions. The Denver Zoo can be found almost next to the expansive City Park and the famous Denver Museum of Natural History. This museum contains detailed exhibits about wildlife, Colorado natural history, and geology found throughout the state. The Denver Botanic Gardens and the Colorado History Museum are also must-visits. And for afficionados of the Old West, the city of Denver maintains a standing herd of buffalo in a natural setting 20 miles from the city. These buffalo are direct descendants of the last wild buffalo herd left in the United States. Both in the city and less than 30 miles from the state capitol, hiking and walking trails, such as the Highline Canal, the Platte River Greenway, and along Cherry Creek, invite residents and visitors to enjoy the great outdoors in a pleasant natural setting within the metropolitan area (which includes Boulder, Vail, Louisville, Castle Rock, Evergreen, Englewood , and Aurora).

The major highways in the Denver Metro Region include the east–west Interstate 70, which travels west from Kansas through the heart of the Rocky Mountains on its way to Utah, and the north–south Interstate 25, which runs parallel to and just east of the Front Range. These two interstates intersect in Denver. Highway 93 parallels Interstate 25 and provides access to the mountain parks, while Highway 36 takes visitors north from Denver to Boulder. Denver is circled on the southwest by Interstate 470, which bypasses the city proper and connects to Interstate 25, providing easy access to Chatfield State Park. Interstate 76 exits Denver to the northeast on its way to Nebraska, and passes by Barr Lake State Park just 20 miles east of Denver. The roads in the Denver Metro Region are in good condition, and even the 30-mile commute between Boulder and Denver can often be done in just over 30 minutes.

The seven state parks in the Denver Metro region have been developed for all to enjoy, with most parks including accessibility for the physically challenged. Denverites can enjoy expansive recreational offerings within minutes from their front doors at these state parks. Their natural landscapes offer relief from the concrete and steel, noise, and busy rush of the city. It is even possible in these parks to find yourself feeling as if you have taken a journey of many miles to reach outdoor retreats that calm the urban stresses, when in fact your place of work can be just around the corner.

BARR LAKE STATE PARK

Hours/Season: Day-use; 5:00 A.M. to 10:00 P.M., with night fishermen permitted restricted access during night hours; year-round

Area: 543 acres, plus 120 acres of leased land; 1,918 surface water acres (at high water)

Facilities: 32 picnic sites, 9 miles of bicycle and hiking trail, wildlife observation stations, nature center, rest rooms, drinking water, boat launch ramp

Attractions: Boating, fishing, hiking, bicycling, horseback riding, cross-country skiing, ice fishing, nature center, interpretive programs, wildlife- and bird-watching

Access: From Denver take I-76 northeast 20 miles to Bromley Lane; go east on Bromley Lane to Picadilly Road, turn right, and drive south to the park entrance in 1.5 miles from I-76

Less than 20 miles east of Denver, out in the first reaches of the semi-arid, rolling high plains, is Barr Lake State Park, a premier and stunningly beautiful wildlife and bird sanctuary in tall prairie. This major prairie reservoir is home to over 330 species of birds, making it both nationally and internationally famous. The southern half of Barr Lake is designated a wildlife refuge, and it has drawn birds unequaled in number or variety anywhere else in Colorado.

Over 100 years ago, a buffalo wallow occupied what is now Barr Lake. Buffalo escaped the hot, dry plains to get a cool mud bath in this natural depression where water accumulated, causing lush vegetation and trees to grow, providing food and water for animals. Indians gathered around this same watering hole in search of their main food supply, the buffalo. By 1866 the area was impacted by the Goodnight-Loving cattle trail, which passed near the wallow on its way to Denver and on to Cheyenne, bringing cattle that displaced the buffalo. Homesteading and farming began to flourish, influenced by the gold and silver booms in the nearby Rocky Mountains.

By 1883 the Chicago, Burlington, and Quince Railroad was constructed through the area, with the last spike ceremony held at Platte Summit, later renamed Barr City to honor a civil engineer working for the railroad. Soon after, the early settlers built a dam on the north side of the wallow and dug several canals to the South Platte River, thereby creating the Oasis Reservoir. Farming had asserted its need for water. In 1896, the Oasis Outing Club was created to take advantage of what was even then known as a great fishing and shooting area. Farming interests, however, again asserted themselves and a new dam was constructed in 1909 and organized as the Farmers Reservoir and Irrigation Company (FRICO). This assured the farming community of water, even in drought times.

Unfortunately for the reservoir, the headgate that fed it was downstream from the Denver Stockyard and Denver Metro Sewage Treatment Plant. From 1930 to 1965, raw sewage traveled into the lake and, trapped by the dam, polluted the water

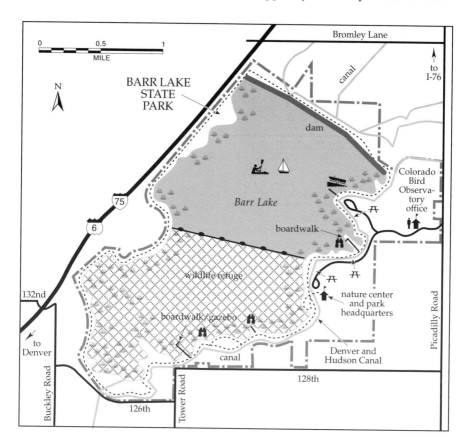

A fisherman with his catch; the snow-capped Front Range in the distance

so much that the hunting club, surrounding home owners, and even the wildlife all left the area. The reservoir was saved when the 1965 Denver flood washed the lake free of contaminants, and the Denver Metro Sewage Treatment Plant was relocated out of the area. The Colorado Division of Parks received a recreational lease from FRICO in 1975, and by 1977 had opened Barr Lake as a state park.

A day-use-only park, Barr Lake State Park has 32 picnic sites, each with picnic table and grill, located in three picnic areas on the lakeshore. The lake is bisected by a buoy line; to the south is the wildlife refuge area. Boating is permitted in the northern half of the lake, limited to sailboats, hand-propelled craft, and boats with electric trolling motors or gasoline motors of 10 horsepower or less. The boat ramp is located 0.25 mile north of the park entrance road, where the road turns south to the nature center.

Fishing is also permitted in the northern half of the lake, with a well-stocked supply of channel catfish, small and large-mouthed bass, rainbow trout, walleye, blue-gill, and wiper. The serenity of the place provides a perfect fisherman's "escape."

Since 1982, visitors to Barr Lake State Park have enjoyed the highly informative Barr Lake Nature Center, constructed by the state Division of Wildlife. The nature center offers a variety of educational programs and experiences. Wildlife exhibits are creatively displayed, including skins of animals that people (especially kids!) can touch. There is even a working beehive encased in glass that allows observers to see bees swarming at a feverish pace, while working to upkeep the hive. A well-stocked book store sponsored by the Rocky Mountain Nature Association offers a variety of books on birds and wildlife, natural history, Colorado geology, and more. The nature center also serves as park headquarters and is open from 9:00 A.M. to 4:00 P.M. daily during the summer and Wednesday through Sunday from Labor Day to Memorial Day.

The park is home also to the Colorado Bird Observatory, whose mission for the conservation of birds is realized through education and research. The CBO's staff operates banding stations and offers public programs relating to bird life. The CBO office is located at the park entrance.

The trail system around Barr Lake is constructed so that vehicles can drive only as far as the nature center. From there it is a 9-mile hike, bike, or horseback ride along the lake's peaceful shores. This is an authentic riparian wetlands ecosystem; the lakeshore is lined with cottonwoods, marshes, aquatic plants, abundant wildlife, and of course birds! A staff naturalist, along with park rangers, offers guided walks around Barr Lake, with special attention given to the several wildlife observation stations from where the many species of birds and wildlife can be seen. These provide shelter even during stormy weather. The silence of the tranquil beauty is only broken by the singing of birds or the disturbance of the lake's stillness when pelicans and other large waterfowl break free of the water's surface and soar high above!

Barr Lake State Park is truly an educational experience about wildlife, responsibility for the environment, and learning up close and firsthand what a beautiful harmony can be created between humans and nature. The hiking/biking/equestrian trail surrounding the lake allows you to truly learn about the plants and wildlife unique to Barr Lake, either on your own or in the company of a park

Waterfowl and nesting bald eagles can be observed from the boardwalk and gazebo at Barr Lake State Park.

ranger. Early morning educational walks, night astronomy sessions, and nature walks are offered free to both groups and schools. Topics covered might include a nature hike for the hearing-impaired, learning to fish, birding through your senses, grass and plant identification, wildlife photography, bee keeping, and animal uses of grasses and plants. Park rangers and naturalists sponsor a "volunteer naturalist program," training local residents to act as nature interpreters.

Barr Lake is one of the best wildlife- and bird-watching areas in the United States. From Canada, hundreds of migrating birds follow the northwest–southeast migration corridor known as the Central Flyway. This migration path passes directly over Barr Lake (and all the other state parks in Colorado's east plains), drawing over 350 species of birds. On my visit I saw several pelicans and a host of smaller birds. Woodpeckers, raptors, herons, deer, fox, ducks, owls, and egrets are also often sighted.

Since 1986 one of the main attractions has been a pair of nesting bald eagles (one of the few pair living along the entire Front Range), easily seen from the boardwalk and gazebo found at the south end of the park. From a viewscope, one sees both eagles in an exposed tree directly in front of the viewing deck. On the day that I was there, several eaglets graced the tree as well.

In the off season, cottonwoods form a brilliant yellow ring around the lake as fall eases into winter. Winter offers cross-country skiing and ice fishing, and allows birders views unobstructed by tree leaves. A walk around Barr Lake might yield a sweet wind from the prairie, and perhaps a fleeting vision of those once-native buffalo staring back at you with the peaceful gaze that the serenity of Barr Lake imparts to any visitor.

Because Barr Lake State Park is so close to Denver, the nearby attractions are to be found in Denver itself, and are therefore of a mostly urban nature. See the description of Denver's highlights in the region's introduction.

CHERRY CREEK STATE PARK

Hours/Season: Overnight, year-round; day-use, 5:00 A.M. to 10:00 P.M. Mar.–Nov., 6:00 A.M. to 7:00 P.M. Nov.–Mar.

Area: 3,835 acres; 880 surface water acres

Facilities: 102 campsites, 3 group campgrounds, 106 picnic sites, 5 group picnic areas, swim beach, 2 snack bars, 2 boat ramps, marina, bathhouse, horse stables

Attractions: Camping, picnicking, interpretive programs, boating, waterskiing, sailboarding, jet skiing, fishing, 12+ miles of trail, hiking, horseback riding, biking, cross-country skiing, ice skating, ice fishing

Access: *East entrance* from Denver drive southeast on CO 83; 1 mile south of I-225, on Parker Road, find the park entrance; *West entrance* from CO 83 at I-225, drive south on Yosemite Street 1 mile, then east on Union Avenue 0.5 mile to the park entrance

▲ Opened in 1959, Cherry Creek State Recreation Area was Colorado's first state park. Since then, its proximity to Denver and the metropolitan area has secured its ranking as the most heavily visited park in the Colorado State Parks system. Urban dwellers flock to Cherry Creek as an "island refuge" in a sea of urban development. Perhaps few major cities in the United States can boast of such a diverse

The marina at Cherry Creek

recreational offering set in such a natural environment. As you leave the city streets and enter the park, the city seems to disappear from view, save for the tops of buildings scattered along various sections of the skyline. Within minutes you are driving through wetlands, marsh areas, and rolling grasslands, past wooded glades, and in the center of it all rests a magnificent 880-acre lake, Cherry Creek Reservoir. Along its shoreline can be found sandy swim beaches, jet skiing areas, a marina, and other water-sports facilities. Cherry Creek additionally offers a dog trials area, a trap and rifle range concession, and even a model airplane field! It is the combination of so many and varied recreational activities, surrounded by so much beautiful open space mixed with wildlife habitat (usually found on land miles away from Denver) that makes Cherry Creek so pleasantly unique.

As far back as the early 1800s, Native Americans warned settlers not to build along the banks of Cherry Creek. Their warnings fell on deaf ears, but by 1933, several devastating floods convinced authorities that something must be done to control the flood threat from Cherry Creek. Finally in 1950 the U.S. Army Corps of Engineers completed a 14,300-foot-long dam and reservoir that eventually became Cherry Creek State Park.

At Cherry Creek, the swim beach is alive with kids and adults venturing out from the tree-lined beach area to frolic in the cool lake waters. Cherry Creek State Park has excellent recreational access for the physically challenged; parking for people with special needs is signed throughout the park. Boaters of all types are everywhere on the water, while nature lovers walk the many hiking trails and bikers flow past you as they cruise the open grasslands and through wooded glens . . . the energy is almost alive and visible!

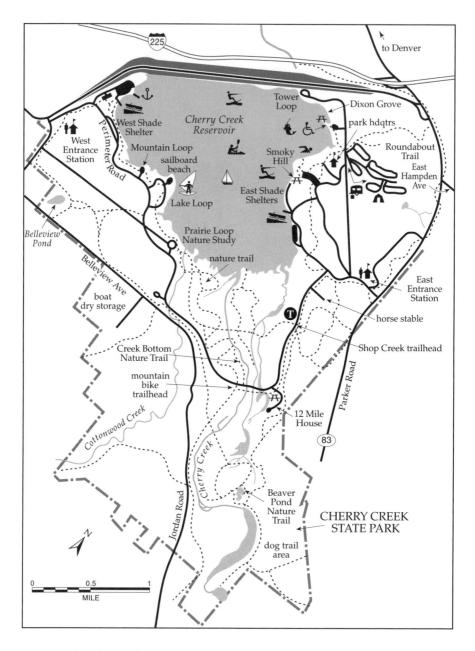

Located in the northeast section of Cherry Creek State Park is a modern 102-site campground, equipped with showers, laundry, and dump station. There are facilities at the campground for the physically challenged. At an amphitheater near the middle of the campground, interesting nature and park programs are provided. Three group campsites are included within the campground. This campground is *very* popular. Call well in advance to make reservations (see appendix A). Stays are limited to 14 days during any 45-day period.

Picnickers can choose a quiet, vegetated spot in the shade of the tall cottonwoods at Dixon Grove picnic area, or go beach-side at the many sheltered tables located throughout the park. Group picnic areas include Hobie Hill, 12 Mile House, and Smoky Hill. Special facilities for the physically challenged are located at the Dixon Grove picnic area and the group picnic sites. The views of the wooded glens, the Rockies, and the lake all combine to satisfy any nature lover.

Boating is a major draw at Cherry Creek. A well-equipped marina offers scuba diving and rowing lessons and a variety of equipment rentals. Jet skiing is also very popular, but because the lake is so huge, boaters are out and away from the shore, where visitors who enjoy quiet can still find it.

Fishing at Cherry Creek is accented by the state record walleye having been caught at the reservoir. Other sought-after species include trout, bass, crappie, pike, catfish, and carp. Fishing access is provided by the Tower Loop trail area near the dam, and at the south end of the reservoir at Lake and Mountain Loop trails. There are also fishing access areas for the physically challenged.

Swimmers at Cherry Creek enjoy a clean, sandy beach, with food concessions, bathhouse, and first-aid station located at the beach area. Special facilities for the physically challenged are located at the swim beach. The views take in the snowcapped peaks of the Front Range along with the expansive lake and Cherry Creek Dam. Shade trees and picnic tables are located just a few yards from the shore, convenient for escaping from too much sun, and for enjoying a tasty picnic lunch.

Hikers, bikers, and horseback riders have over 12 miles of trail, most located

Group picnic area on Cherry Creek's south side

away from the lake, in the more wooded and grassy sections. All trails are open to nonmotorized uses, except the Prairie Loop Nature Trail, which is open to foot traffic only. Nature study can be pursued at the Prairie Loop Nature Study area, which is close to the lake and is known as a good trail for bird-watching, or the 1.5-mile Shop Creek Nature Trail, which passes through a wooded delta and highlights cottonwood and willow trees, bats, grasslands, the growth of wild licorice, and Cherry Creek Dam. Other nature trails include the Beaver Ponds, where active beavers are often spotted, the Roundabout Trail, found near the "B" loop campground, and the Creek Bottom Nature Trail, which passes through a creek bottom that brings visitors in close contact with plant and animal life and is so popular that it has its own environmental guide printed for visitor use. The park rangers conduct campfire programs and lead interpretive walks that are so popular that groups of school children and adults book weeks in advance, with ten summer programs often scheduled per week. Thus inner-city children have a readily available and nearby resource for learning natural history and biology right where they live!

Popular winter activities include ice fishing and ice skating (when the ice is thick enough) as well as cross-country skiing, which is available throughout the park, although there are no groomed trails.

Beaver and raccoon have been spotted in the park near the marsh areas, and deer are occasionally seen. The park also hosts wood ducks, hawks, and, in the fall, Canadian geese and other migratory waterfowl.

Because of its close proximity to Denver, nearby attractions are found in the city itself. Cherry Creek State Park itself is host to many special events throughout the year—bicycling and running events, triathlons, company picnics, weddings, sports festivals, and even sailing regattas. This is a real "peoples' park," offering many recreational opportunities to a large and nearby population. Combined with the beautiful and appealing combination of open spaces, riparian wetlands, abundant wildlife, a generous offering of trees and plants, and rich grasslands, Cherry Creek State Park truly is a natural oasis for the people of Denver.

CASTLEWOOD CANYON STATE PARK

Hours/Season: Day-use; 8:00 A.M. to 9:00 P.M.; year-round
Area: 873 acres
Facilities: 55 picnic sites, group picnic area, rest rooms, visitors/nature center
Attractions: Picnicking, nature center, interpretive programs, 13+ miles of hiking trail, rock climbing, cross-country skiing
Access: *East entrance* from Denver take I-25 south 25 miles to Castle Rock, turn east on CO 86, go 6 miles to Franktown, then turn south on CO 83 and go 5 miles to the park's main entrance; *West entrance* from Castle Rock take CO 86 east 6 miles to Castlewood Canyon Road, turn right, and continue 2 miles to the park entrance

Beginning almost 10 miles south of Denver and extending for many miles south toward Colorado Springs spreads a wide, cool, uplifted area known as the Arkansas Divide. This highland region is a mixture of high prairie grasslands and a scattering of dense woods, composed of ponderosa pine and Douglas fir, known as the Black Forest. This higher tableland comes almost as a surprise to travelers expecting the high-plains grasslands to flow right up to the foothills of the Rockies, as it does in many other places along the Front Range.

Equally surprising is the magnificent canyon just 30 miles south of Denver, carved out of the same bedrock supporting miles of forest and grasslands. The forces of erosion that created Castlewood Canyon were primarily the work of Cherry Creek, which over the eons cut through the bedrock to create a canyon several hundred feet deep.

In 1890, the Castlewood Dam was constructed on Cherry Creek, which flows through Denver. From the outset citizens, especially those directly in the creek's path, thought the dam to be unsafe. Between 1891 and 1933, the dam experienced numerous leaks, which were repaired but which did not allay citizens' concerns. Then, on the stormy night of August 3, 1933, after three days of heavy rain, the dam collapsed, sending a 15-foot-high wall of water all the way to Denver, where it caused extensive damage, but little loss of life. Afterwards, the Cherry Creek Dam and Reservoir were built in Denver, and the concerns over Castlewood Canyon faded into memory. In 1980, the area was opened as a state park and the modern visitors center was added in 1993.

The main entrance into the park, where visitors are immediately greeted by the canyon, is marked (especially in the spring and early summer) by rolling grasslands dotted with many colorful varieties of wildflowers. Extending above the grass, to the southwest, is stunning Pikes Peak, majestically filling the horizon.

The park is open to day-use only, with Castlewood Canyon the main attraction. The area surrounding the west entrance is considered more backcountry, whereas the main (east) entrance is where the main visitors center is located. Favorite activities include hiking in and along the canyon rim, enjoying the beautiful picnic spots scattered along the trails beside it, photographing the unique and fascinating canyon features, enjoying the close encounters

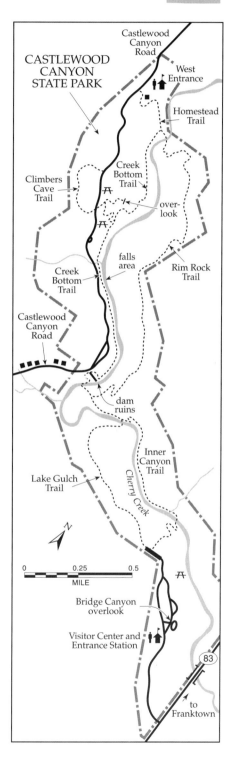

45

with the flora and fauna of the canyon, and, for the more energetic, rock climbing within the canyon proper.

Picnickers can lay claim to their own individual picnic site, arranged as separate units scattered along the canyon rim. No crowding here; each site gives users the feeling that the "canyon is all mine." Many of the sites' tables are located under ponderosa pine trees, which provide needed shade on hot days.

Located at the Lake Gulch Trailhead is a group picnic facility with three shelters. The group picnic area has a wonderful vista looking out upon the entire length of the Front Range. The picnic shelters can be rented (for a $6.75 reservation fee plus $20 per shelter), either singly or all together, for group events. Park management asks that, for weddings, birdseed be thrown at the happy couple rather than rice, to protect the wildlife. A few hundred yards from the visitors center is the Bridge Canyon Overlook, with a magnificent view. A small covered platform built at the canyon's edge, this facility is often reserved for weddings.

The park naturalist hosts a number of interpretive programs throughout the year. Some of the topics include area geology, a photography hike, cactus and

Group picnic shelters at Castlewood Canyon State Park

succulents, spring wildflowers, bird-watching, and a tour of the dam ruins. The visitors center also offers an informative slide show that depicts the story of Castlewood Dam. You can pick up the brochure entitled "Birds of Castlewood Canyon," which inventories the many and varied species of birds seen at the park, how common they are, and what their primary season is.

There are more than 13 miles of hiking trails that allow hikers to explore both above and within the canyon. Beginning near the main entrance is the Canyon View Nature Trail (0.25 mile). From the trail, hikers look down into the canyon and note the grasses and cottonwood and willow trees along the canyon bottom. Starting at the group picnic area are the Lake Gulch Trail (0.9 mile) and the Inner Canyon Trail (1.2 miles). The former remains mostly above the canyon, and drops down at its end to connect to the Inner Canyon Trail. The Inner Canyon Trail is a hike along the canyon bottom all the way to the dam ruins. At the dam ruins, the Dam Trail (0.3 mile) circles west of the dam. The Inner Canyon trail, along with the Creek Bottom Trail (1.7 miles) that joins the Inner Canyon Trail, offers the most intimate exploration of the canyon. The nearby Rim Rock Trail (1.9 miles) is another above-canyon hike that offers views to the surrounding horizons and into the canyon proper. All these trails are short and mostly moderate, but can be combined for a longer hike.

Suggested combined hikes include the Inner Canyon Trail and Lake Gulch Trail, a moderate loop hike of 2 miles in the southern end of the park; and the Dam Trail, Creek Bottom Trail, and Rim Rock Trail, a moderate to steep loop of 3.9 miles in the northern part of the park.

From the west entrance, the short Homestead Trail (0.4 mile) travels downhill to access both the Rim Rock and Creek Bottom Trails. The Climbers Trail (0.25 mile) can be accessed 1 mile south of the west entrance along Castlewood Canyon Road. This trail takes climbers along a section of 40- to 60-foot-high rock wall that is excellent for rock climbing. This same trail merges into the Cave Trail (0.1 mile), where two sheltered caves 15 feet long can be explored. The Overlook Trail (0.1 mile) leads to a view of Castlewood Canyon.

Castlewood Canyon Road runs north–south inside the northwest edge of the park, connecting to Colorado Highway 86 outside the park. This road affords access to the dam ruins and the west entrance, but does not connect to the east entrance and visitors center. The falls area (just south of the caves) is best visited only when spring runoff is highest. Several 20- to 25-foot falls tumble over boulders, but are almost nonexistent as summer heat lowers the height and flow of Cherry Creek.

Canyon visitors may see a variety of wildlife. Prairie falcons, red-tailed hawks, turkey vultures, great blue herons, wrens, finches, raccoons, porcupines, badgers, red fox, mule deer, and even pronghorn antelope have been seen in the park.

Castlewood Canyon is a surprising change from the miles of grasslands stretching east of the park. Cherry Creek has carved a delightful canyon akin to the canyons found in the West Region's Colorado Plateau. The ponderosa pines and juniper accent what grasslands cover the park, while the creek encourages thick growth of reeds, cottonwoods, and vines . . . a river canyon oasis on the high plains. Hikers can travel directly within the canyon itself or view its riparian vegetation from the rim above, while picnickers enjoy the last stretch of the prairie before it collides with the western Front Range.

The town of Castle Rock, 8 miles northwest of Castlewood Canyon State Park, is a good source for picnic supplies. Visitors can also enjoy the 40-mile scenic drive to Colorado Springs by taking Colorado Highway 83 south from the east entrance. Views encompass unspoiled ranchlands, the dense green sprawl of the Black Forest, and magnificent Pikes Peak, towering just outside of Colorado Springs.

CHATFIELD STATE PARK

Hours/Season: Overnight; year-round
Area: 3,768 acres; 1,550 surface water acres
Facilities: 193 campsites, 139 picnic sites, group picnic area, rest rooms, drinking water, visitors center, laundry, bathhouse, snack bar, marina, stables, dump station
Attractions: Camping, picnicking, visitors center, interpretive programs, swimming, boating, waterskiing, sailboarding, jet skiing, fishing, 25+ miles of trail, hiking, biking, horseback riding, cross-country skiing, ice skating, ice fishing
Access: *West entrance* from Denver, head south on CO 121 (Wadsworth Boulevard); at its intersection with CO 470, continue south for 1 mile and then turn east into the Deer Creek entrance; *South entrance* from CO 470, head south on US 85 (Santa Fe Drive) for 4 miles, turn west onto Titan Road for 1 mile, then right onto Roxborough Park Road for 1 mile to the park

Chatfield State Park bears close resemblance to its almost-sister park, Cherry Creek. Both were constructed by the U.S. Army Corps of Engineers to protect Denver from recurring floods. Both are huge parks highly focused toward water sports. Chatfield Lake has a very open feeling, with views of the Front Range to the south and west, the tree-lined shore, and Chatfield Dam. Because Chatfield State Park is located in a basin, with the Chatfield Dam built higher than the surrounding land, there is an almost "hidden-away" feeling, with little evidence that Denver is just a few miles north.

Chatfield State Park is another Denver-area recreational facility whose history is closely tied to the impact of floods upon the metropolitan area. In 1870, Civil War Lieutenant Issac W. Chatfield bought 720 acres of land at the confluence of the South Platte River and Plum Creek. He farmed the land until he moved in 1879, but the area still bears his name.

Serious floods devastated the area in 1933, 1935, 1942, and 1965. Citizens worked with state and federal agencies to have Chatfield Dam built as a flood control measure. In 1974, Colorado State Parks leased the land for recreational purposes and in 1976, the U.S. Army Corps of Engineers completed the dam. Since then, the site has been developed as Chatfield State Park.

A single large campground is located at the south side of the park, directly accessible from the south by Roxborough Park Road. The camping area looks out onto the wide expanse of the Chatfield reservoir, and is surrounded by most of the recreational land area of the park. Facilities include pull-through sites, some electrical hookups, flush toilets, hot showers, laundry, centrally located drinking water, firewood, and a dump station. A group campground is also available. This park is popular with Denver campers, so early reservations are advised (see appendix A). Added attractions for campers (or perhaps not!) are the close proximity to an active prairie dog colony just east of the area, a model airplane field south of the campground, and a hot air balloon launch field.

Picnic sites with grills and tables are located throughout the park. All picnic areas—Massey Draw, Jamison, Catfish Flats, Fox Run, Kingfisher, Lakeview, Riverside, Stevens Grove, Owl Glen, and Cottonwood Grove—offer scenic lake views, as well as views to the surrounding mountains.

Although many of the recreational offerings at Chatfield are self-guided, the park rangers and staff can answer questions concerning the many species of wildlife found within the park, and are available by appointment for interpretive programs.

Near the Deer Creek Canyon Road entrance is the Chatfield Arboretum. The arboretum, operated by the Denver Botanic Gardens, offers a huge selection of trees, shrubs, flowers, native grasses, and display gardens. Just northeast of the dam is a fish-planting base facility, where trout are prepared for stocking lakes and streams.

There is a full-service marina located on the reservoir's south shore just north of the campground, with boat ramps nearby, as well as a boat ramp at the north shore, west of the Chatfield Dam. There are designated water-ski beaches, and boaters must observe lake markers and zoning restrictions. Swimmers are given a separate swim beach, away from most of the noisier boating activities.

Fishing is one of the most popular pursuits at Chatfield. Besides a generous population of trout and walleye, the lake supports channel catfish, yellow perch, crappie, bluegill, sunfish, and carp. Early spring seems to be the best time for trout fishing, along with fall's cooler temperatures, which bring the trout back into the shallows from the deeper waters they prefer during summer. Ice fishing is also good at the lake, with trout, perch, and crappie being the main catch. A fishing pier for the physically challenged is located near the marina on the south side of the lake.

Over 25 miles of trails wind around the park. Many of these trails are continuation trails from other places. The Highline Canal Trail originates in the southwest corner of the park and continues into Denver. The Centennial Trail and Columbine Trail from Denver enter or touch the park at various places and, together with the

A quiet lagoon with a blue heron

trails built within the park proper, give hikers, bikers, and equestrians plenty of space to move around in. This trail system is fully accessible to the physically challenged. Trails are paved and wide and level enough to accommodate wheelchairs. With heavy snowfall, cross-country skiing takes place on the hiking trails and across any grassy areas. Trail maps are available at the park's main entrances.

Equestrians can ride on these same 25 miles of trails winding around the lake.

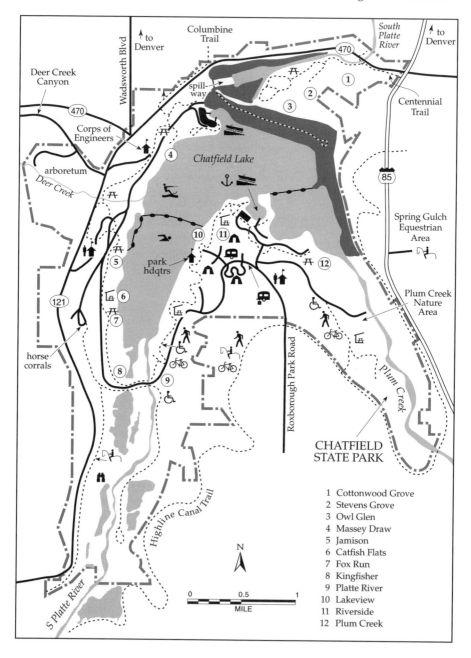

CHATFIELD
STATE PARK

1 Cottonwood Grove
2 Stevens Grove
3 Owl Glen
4 Massey Draw
5 Jamison
6 Catfish Flats
7 Fox Run
8 Kingfisher
9 Platte River
10 Lakeview
11 Riverside
12 Plum Creek

Horse trailer parking, corrals, unloading ramps, and the trailhead are located on the park's west side, accessible from the Deer Creek entrance. Horses may be leased from the Chatfield Livery, located west of the swim beach. Visitors may leave their horses in the corrals overnight if they are camping within the park, but must furnish their own feed; water, however, is available at the corrals. The rules at Chatfield are simple. Riders must stay on designated trails, and horses are not permitted at picnic sites, at the swim beach, or in campgrounds.

They have even thought of dogs and recreation at Chatfield! Located in the north section of the park is a dog training and exercise area. This open field and pond environment allows dogs to be off-leash for training and exercise, and is the only area in the park where dogs are permitted off-leash.

Chatfield State Park definitely favors wetland and riparian habitat. In all, over eleven separate wetland areas are found within the park boundary. A 27-acre heron rookery, located on the southwest arm of the lake, is the breeding grounds for over fifty pairs of great blue herons. They can be easily viewed from a park observation area. Beaver, muskrats, whitetail and mule deer, coyotes, rabbits, and foxes are often seen. Hawks, osprey, kingfisher, and more than 300 other winged species are sighted at Chatfield. Turtles, waterfowl, and other wildlife can be observed along the banks of Deer Creek, near the Chatfield Arboretum. A beaver pond overlook and the Plum Creek turtle pond and nature area provide other opportunities to watch the many species of wildlife on or near the lake.

Fishing from the banks of Chatfield Reservoir

Chatfield State Park, much like Cherry Creek, is a recreational and outdoor wildlife observation opportunity that is rare among urban areas. It is well worth the visit to enjoy an area once feared because of the threat of floods, now loved for the rich outdoor offering it provides.

Because Chatfield State Park is practically in Denver itself, nearby attractions are found in the city, as described in the region's introduction.

ROXBOROUGH STATE PARK

Hours/Season: Day-use only; 8:00 A.M. to dusk; year-round
Area: 1,620 acres
Facilities: Visitors/nature center
Attractions: Interpretive programs, slide show, nature walks, hiking, wildlife- and bird-watching, cross-country skiing
Nearby: Waterton Canyon, Colorado Trail, Pikes Peak Forest
Access: From Denver, take Colorado 470 to the Wadsworth Boulevard (Highway 121) exit; on Wadsworth, go 4.4 miles south to Waterton Road, turn left, and proceed 1.6 miles east to North Rampart Range Road; turn right and proceed south 2.3 miles to Roxborough Park Road, turn left, and go one block to the turnoff onto the park access road; drive south 2.2 miles on the access road to reach the park

Perhaps it is a day in late spring or early summer and you need a restful time away, spiced with something different from life's daily routine. Curiosity motivates you to make the 20-mile drive from Denver southwest to the area known as Roxborough State Park. In the cool early morning, the park entrance road ushers you ever closer to the nearby mountains, past rolling, lush green meadows and prairie, dotted with a colorful array of wildflowers. Soon you pass broken slabs of mountains formed of many compressed, colorful rock layers, tilted upward like hands folded in prayer, draped with deep green forests, shrubs, and flowering plants. Within minutes, a new and almost mystical rock formation begins to surround you, sculpted in shades of red and rust, a thousand colorful sunsets captured in rock, standing like geological statues . . . the spectacular Fountain Formation. These rocky shapes thrust upward at a sixty-degree incline, arranged row after row . . . soldierlike rocks following along the tilt of the higher mountain range above. The scene is strongly accented by the trees, grass, and plant life which, like a gentle sea green ocean, surrounds the stately red and rust rock slabs that powerfully reach upward to pierce the deep azure Colorado sky. The place is almost too incredible to be real.

The accolades bestowed upon Roxborough State Park reflect its unique components, both natural and historical. It is a designated state natural area, a National Natural Landmark, and a National Archaeological District. The park is a composite of 500-million-year-old rock formations, with some rock located less than 2 miles away calculated to be more than 1.5 billion years old! The park was formed and is still being affected by the uplifting forces of the nearby Rocky Mountains. The eastern park boundary consists of a crest of uplifted sandstone rocks known as the Dakota Hogback, followed by more easily erodible layers of shale and limestone, another uplifted area called the Lyons ridges, then finally the spectacular reddish-colored sandstone (a cousin to Sedona, Arizona, and Utah's

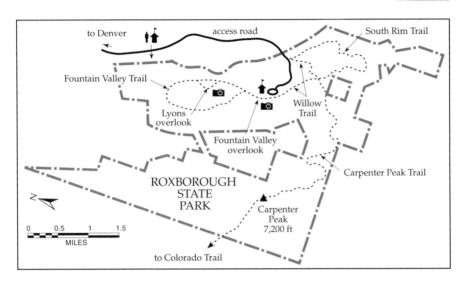

to Denver

access road

South Rim Trail

Fountain Valley Trail

Lyons
overlook

Willow
Trail

Fountain Valley
overlook

Carpenter Peak Trail

ROXBOROUGH
STATE
PARK

N

0   0.5   1   1.5
MILES

Carpenter
Peak
7,200 ft

to Colorado Trail

Zion National Park, etc.) known as the Fountain Formation. These famous ridges and monolithic spires sweep up from an elevation of 5,900 feet to 7,200 feet at the top of Carpenter Peak. Their unique placement has created a scattering of micro-climates throughout the park, which have in turn produced nine different ecotypes, ranging from grasslands to marshes and ponderosa pine forests . . . all within a 3-mile length of space! Unusually cool, moist pockets encourage aspen to grow 1,300 feet below their normal range; these same conditions allow Gambel's oak, a shrub-sized species, to grow up to a height of 40 feet in some places.

The Fountain Formation from Fountain Valley Overlook

Early humans were drawn to this park, verified by the discovery of over forty archaeological sites, including remains of campsites, quarries, and rock shelters. Early inhabitants lived here from 5000 B.C. to 1000 A.D. The first recorded sighting of Roxborough occurred in 1820, when a Dr. James of the Major Stephen Long expedition wrote, "The woodless plain is terminated by a range of naked and almost perpendicular rocks, visible at a distance of several miles, and resembling a vast wall parallel to the base of the mountains . . . with interesting views of singular color and formation, the whole scenery truly picturesque and romantic" (quoted in a state park brochure). From 1910, the property had been sought or considered a prime possible recreational purchase by the city of Denver, but it was not until 1987 that Colorado State Parks opened the property as a state park. Other land purchases, still ongoing, have increased the size of the park from 500 to 2,245 acres.

How did this unique natural wonderland come to be? What other treasures does it hold for those who walk its gentle paths? The visitors center is the educational focal point in the park. There is no camping, biking, horseback riding, fishing, etc., available . . . just the resources of the visitors center and use of the trails. For those who discover Roxborough State Park, these prove more than enough. Even rock climbing is not permitted due to the fragility of the rock.

While no formal picnic facilities exist, anyone is welcome to bring a snack or

The Fountain Formation at Roxborough State Park

Visitors Center at Roxborough State Park

lunch and eat at one of the benches found at locations along the hiking trails.

Begin your visit with a 15-minute slide show at the visitors center. Magnificent photos depict the various seasonal changes seen at the park, the history of the place, the geology of the rock formations, and special rules to follow while walking the trails. A well-stocked book section complements the various wildlife and geological displays that interpret what can be found at the park. Many informative nature publications, such as the trail guide for the Fountain Valley Trail, highlight the flora and fauna found at Roxborough. Brochures on birds, history, and geology are also available.

Volunteer naturalists conduct many interesting programs at the visitors center. Some educational, fun activity is offered almost every other day during the summer. Topics or activities might include full moon hikes, edible and medicinal plants, geology of the park, wildflower hikes, photography hikes, and bird-watching. There are also opportunities to volunteer at the visitors center and to do trail maintenance work.

Hiking is available on five trails. The Willow Trail, a gentle 1.25 miles round trip, offers a view of a riparian, wetlands community. The Fountain Valley Trail (2.25 miles) is a moderately gentle trail that takes hikers through the heart of the Fountain and Lyons Formations, with the Fountain Valley overlook and 0.5-mile Lyons Overlook Trail offering spectacular scenic vistas of the formation's entire length. South Rim Trail is 3 miles of moderate trail, while the Carpenter Peak Trail is a 5.8-mile round-trip hike to the highest point in the park at 7,200 feet. The view from the peak encompasses all the various geological formations with one sweep! From the peak there is a connector trail of 4.4 miles that joins up with the famed 470-mile-long Colorado Trail, which begins just northwest of Roxborough State Park and ends in Durango. Those wishing a longer hike can continue from the Carpenter

Peak Trail on the connector trail to the Colorado Trail, for a total round-trip distance of 14.3 miles.

Because the park is in a transition zone, hikers see yucca and cactus growing almost next to aspen and wild roses, and if they hike all the trails, they will see representatives of all nine different ecotypes. Wildlife common along the trail include mule deer, coyotes, and rock squirrels, while golden eagles, falcons, and hawks soar overhead. Other birds common to the area include the canyon wren, western meadowlark, scrub jay, black-capped chickadee, and dark-eyed junco. Occasional sightings of bobcat, bear, and elk take place.

In each season of the year, Roxborough State Park offers special treasures: snowcapped red rock formations, rivers of wildflowers, orange and gold autumn leaves. This natural cathedral, standing where plains and mountains—the old and the ever new—dynamically meet, quietly renews the spirit and inspires the imagination with its peace and mystical beauty.

Located just a few miles northwest of Roxborough State Park is another recreational area known as Waterton Canyon. The South Platte River runs the length of the canyon and affords good fishing opportunities. A hiking trail or road begins at the mouth of the canyon and leads up to Strontia Springs Dam, offering great river views of the South Platte, and eventually ends where the famed Colorado Trail begins. For more information on Waterton Canyon, call Denver Water, (303) 628-6000. By hiking up the first few miles of the Colorado Trail, you can connect with the trail to Roxborough State Park, via the Carpenter Peak Trail. Information about the Colorado Trail is available from the Colorado Trail Foundation (see appendix A). Hiking is also available in Pikes Peak Forest. For hiking information into the Pikes Peak Forest area, call the U.S. Forest Service (see appendix A).

GOLDEN GATE CANYON STATE PARK

Hours/Season: Overnight; year-round

Area: 14,000 acres; 20 surface water acres

Facilities: 168 campsites, group campground, 288 picnic sites, dump station, laundry, showers

Attractions: Camping, picnicking, visitors/nature center, interpretive programs, fishing, 35+ miles of trail, hiking, biking, horseback riding, cross-country skiing, ice skating, ice fishing

Nearby: Indian Peaks Wilderness Area, Walker Ranch, Boulder Mountain Parks

Access: *South entrance* from Denver, take I-70 west to the Highway 58 exit; go 5 miles west to CO 93; go north on CO 93 for 2 miles to Golden Gate Canyon Road, turn left, then go 15 miles north to the park; *West entrance* take Highway 119—the Peak-to-Peak Highway—to 10 miles south of Nederland, then turn east onto Highway 46 and travel 5 miles to the visitors center; from Black Hawk, travel north on Highway 119 to Highway 46, then turn right and continue 5 miles to the park

▲ Golden Gate Canyon State Park is an outstanding outdoor recreational experience just minutes away from downtown Denver. Over 14,000 acres are configured around 35 miles of scenic hiking trail, making Golden Gate Canyon a true "hikers' destination park." The park is located in the Front Range of the Rocky Mountains, with elevations ranging from 7,400 feet to 10,388 feet at the top of

Tremont Mountain. The park's 14,000 acres are highlighted by steep ridges, rocky outcrops, forests interspersed with beautiful open meadows, and numerous streams, gulches, and Ralston Creek. While there are no lakes in the park, several 1- to 5-acre ponds have been built.

The area is rich in both human and geological history, and reflects the western flavor of this part of Colorado. For centuries the Ute Indians visited the land that is now Golden Gate Canyon State Park, to cut lodgepole pine for tepees, hunt game, and collect plants and herbs for food and medicine. The fur trappers of the early 1800s explored Ralston Creek back into the foothills of the Rockies, but it was the discovery of gold in 1859 near Central City and Black Hawk (a place that would become the "richest square mile on earth") that led to the development of the area. Within a month the Golden Gate Canyon Toll Road was opened ("Golden Gate" signified the gateway to the nearby rich goldfields), and over 5,000 miners poured into the region in search of the mineral treasure. Ironically, no gold was ever discovered within the area that is now the park!

For the many years that followed, economic life in the area settled down into ranching, farming, and logging operations. For a brief period during prohibition, the area became the moonshining and bootlegging hub for Denver and the surrounding area. In the early 1960s, 198 acres were purchased from the Kriley family's Ralston Buttes Ranch to form the nucleus of the new Golden Gate Canyon State Park. The Krileys, who settled in the area in 1880, so loved the land that when they had to sell it they sold to the Colorado State Parks system rather than see it purchased by land developers. Other ranchers followed their lead, until the park reached its present 14,000-acre size.

Remains of homestead cabin at Frazer Meadow

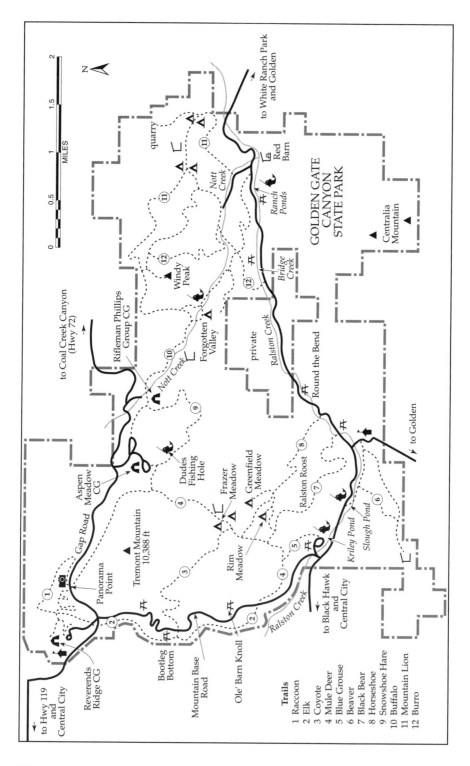

GOLDEN GATE CANYON STATE PARK

Trails

1 Raccoon
2 Elk
3 Coyote
4 Mule Deer
5 Blue Grouse
6 Beaver
7 Black Bear
8 Horseshoe
9 Snowshoe Hare
10 Mountain Lion
11 Buffalo
12 Burro

On the drive to the park, spectacular views to the west act like a magnet, pulling you along the scenic highway dotted with quaint ranches and rolling grassy meadows toward the breathtaking scenery of the soaring mountains of the Continental Divide. Once you arrive at Golden Gate Canyon State Park, your recreational options are numerous.

Many scenic areas scattered throughout the park offer camping. Reverend's Ridge Campground in the northwest corner of the park accommodates recreational vehicles and tents, and offers flush toilets, hot showers, and laundry facilities. Campfire programs are presented during the summer in an outdoor amphitheater. Aspen Meadow Campground, off Gap Road on the park's northern edge, provides thirty-five tent-only campsites. Facilities include vault toilets, fire rings, and water pumps. Rimrock Loop at Aspen Meadow Campground offers camping sites and parking designed for equestrians' horse trucks and trailers. Both areas are near the scenic Mule Deer and Snowshoe Hare hiking trails, with easy access from the campground. Rifleman Phillips Group Campground, located 2 miles east of Panorama Point, is open only in summer and accommodates seventy-five tent campers by reservation only, with tables, grills, vault toilets, and a water pump.

For campers looking for a more primitive experience, four backcountry shelters are scattered throughout the park at Frazer Meadow in the west, at Forgotten Valley in the north, in the quarry area in the northeastern corner, and in the park's far southwestern corner. These shelters are three-sided structures, with a roof and wooden floor, built in the traditional Appalachian trail-hut style, and can sleep up to six people with no tent needed. Besides these shelters, there are twenty-three backcountry tent sites throughout the park, at Rim Meadow (five), Greenfield Meadow (five), and Frazer Meadow (six) in the western area, at Forgotton Valley (three) in the north, and near the quarry in the eastern area (four).

Golden Gate Canyon State Park is a perfect place to escape the summer's heat, with more than 275 scenic picnic sites located along Ralston Creek and at the roadside access points of Ole' Barn Knoll, Bootleg Bottom, Panorama Point, Kriley and Slough ponds, Round the Bend, Bridge Creek, and Ranch Ponds. Picnic sites feature streamside tables, wooded glens, fantastic mountain scenery, and colorful fall displays of aspen. Groups of up to 150 can reserve the Red Barn group picnic area, with barrier-free access to covered picnic tables, grills, vault toilets, and a volleyball court. Of special note is the Panorama Point Scenic Overlook and picnic area. A large wooden deck provides views of the nearby snowcapped Continental Divide. Wedding parties of forty or fewer people can be scheduled at the overlook by contacting the park office.

The visitors center, located inside the south entrance of the park on Golden Gate Canyon Road, offers books, brochures, and information, with some displays depicting plant and animal life found nearby, as well as a topographical scale model of the park. Also featured is the Wilbur and Nellie Larkin Memorial Nature Trail. This trail, accessible to the physically challenged, winds around the park's rainbow trout show pond. Information kiosks are also found at the self-service entrances on the west, north, and east sides of the park, as well as at the Reverend's Ridge Campground office at the park's west entrance via Highway 119, staffed from mid-May through Labor Day.

Interpretive programs are offered by the rangers and staff, for both children and adults. Campfire programs, the "I hiked Golden Gate" program, Junior Rangers, and orienteering and adventure packs all teach about survival skills, animals and plants found in the park, and hiking.

Golden Gate Canyon is not noted for its fishing, although a few streams and ponds do exist. Species caught are almost exclusively trout.

Golden Gate Canyon State Park's more than 35 miles of well-maintained and very scenic hiking trails are designated easy, moderate, or difficult. The trail marking system at the park is unique. Instead of bearing traditional names, each of the twelve trails is named after an animal, many of which are native to the area, and trail signs are the representative footprint of each of the animals.

The hike to Frazer Meadow is especially beautiful, with some spectacular highlights along the way. The trail begins less than 1 mile northeast of the visitors center at Frazer Meadow Trailhead—the Horseshoe Trail—with the designated marking a horseshoe footprint trail sign. The hike first takes you along a creek, up the side of a mountain, with views toward the park's eastern boundary. The trail plateaus in the expansive, lush Frazer Meadow (1.8 miles), surrounded by glorious stands of aspen. In the meadow is the ruins of an old homestead barn, considered quite large for its time. This meadow is incredibly beautiful. The nearby mountain peaks look down at the meadow, and to the east, hikers see rolling vistas of mountains spreading out to meet the horizon. Late spring and early summer finds the meadow a lush green, ripe with wildflowers, while autumn paints the aspens a golden yellow.

At Frazer Meadow, the Horseshoe Trail connects with the Mule Deer Trail, which takes you north through a wooded area before climbing all the way to Panorama Point (3.8 miles from Frazer Meadow). The one-way mileage up to this point is 5.6 miles, with an elevation gain of almost 1,300 feet. At Panorama Point, you look across a valley to the string of mountains making up the Continental Divide, with

The Rocky Mountains and the Continental Divide from Panorama Point

the view filling the entire south–north horizon. To enjoy the added scenic touch of massive snowcover on these peaks, do this hike before midsummer.

Hikers can return the way they came for a less strenuous 11.2-mile round-trip hike, or have the option of adding another 1,000 feet and taking a loop route back. For this option, from Panorama Point take the Raccoon Trail north to Reverend's Ridge Campground (2.5 miles), then take the Elk Trail out of the campground to the Bootleg Bottom picnic area (about 3.5 miles), then take the Coyote Trail to reconnect at Frazer Meadow with the original Horseshoe Trail (5.5 miles). Be advised that this trail system can get very hot during a summer heat wave.

Another interesting option is to shuttle hike, by parking cars at Frazer Meadow Trailhead and at Nott Creek Trailhead along the park's eastern edge. From Frazer Meadow Trailhead, take Horseshoe Trail to Frazer Meadow (1.8 miles), and then Mule Deer Trail for a mile beyond Frazer Meadow to connect with the Snowshoe Hare Trail (2.8 miles) to Rifleman Phillips Campground (about 4.8 miles). There pick up the Buffalo Trail to Forgotten Valley (6 miles). The scenery is gentle as you come down the ridge, with views toward the lower eastern section of the park. At Forgotten Valley, take the Mountain Lion Trail, which swings toward the far eastern park boundary. The land is sloping, and the trail follows several creeks in places. The land here has an eastern woodlands look, with some of the trail traversing low, grassy hills, until finishing at Nott Creek (about 10.5 miles). Total elevation gain is 1,200 feet. This is another trail best done when the weather is cooler, or early in the day.

The other trails in the park also offer beautiful scenery. Black Bear Trail (2.8 miles) goes from Ralston Roost Trailhead to Greenfield Meadow. Blue Grouse Trail (0.7 mile) connects Mule Deer Trail with Kriley Pond. Burro Trail is a 4.5-mile loop from Bridge Creek Trailhead that skirts Windy Peak. Beaver Trail is a 2.5-mile loop from the visitors center, with a spur to Slough Pond. There are many combination hikes you can take by crisscrossing these trails, and joining different segments together for longer and more diverse hikes. However you do it, these trails will not disappoint! All trails are open to foot and horse traffic only; mountain biking is allowed only on the park roads.

Cross-country skiing is permitted anywhere in the park, and ice skating and ice fishing are available at Kriley and Ranch ponds, although both are quite small.

Black bear, mule deer, raccoon, beaver, squirrel, and fox are sometimes observed in the park. Golden eagles, hawks, and migratory birds can also be seen, especially in the spring and fall.

Hiking opportunities outside the park can be found nearby in the Indian Peaks Wilderness Area, which is a 14-mile drive from Golden Gate and offers hundreds of miles of beautiful and challenging trails. (From Golden Gate Canyon State Park, continue west to Highway 119; take a right and drive north to the town of Nederland; at the sign to Eldora Ski Area, Highway 130, turn left and go about 4 miles to the Hessie Trailhead.) From Hessie, you can take the magnificent Devil's Thumb Trail for a 7-plus-mile, 2,500-foot-elevation-gain hike to the Continental Divide, where you actually stand on the Divide, looking for miles toward Winter Park Ski Resort and at the far-western Rocky Mountains. On a clear day, you *can* see forever from here! If snowfall has been heavy during the winter, this trail might not be passable until late July or early August. You can also continue driving past Hessie to reach the Fourth of July Trailhead in 5 miles. From here, take the scenic Arapaho Pass Trail to the Continental Divide for another spectacular vista. This hike is shorter than Devil's Thumb by about 4 miles, with an elevation gain of almost 2,000 feet. Both sections of road into Hessie and Fourth of July can be rough on a car, so check ahead concerning road conditions (see appendix A).

Frazer Meadow trailhead

Other hiking opportunities can be found in the Walker Ranch hiking area and the Boulder Mountain Parks area, both in or near the city of Boulder (see appendix A). To reach Boulder from Golden Gate Canyon State Park, continue west to Highway 119; take a right and drive north to the town of Nederland; turn right in Nederland on Highway 119, and drive the 20 miles along a scenic river canyon route.

ELDORADO CANYON STATE PARK:
INNER CANYON, CRESCENT MEADOWS

Hours/Season: Day-use; sunrise to sunset; year-round
Area: 885 acres
Facilities: 42 picnic sites, group picnic area, visitors/nature center
Attractions: Picnicking, interpretive programs, fishing, hiking, mountain biking, horseback riding, rock climbing
Access: *Inner Canyon* from Boulder, on CO 93 (Broadway Street), drive 4 miles south, then turn right onto CO 170 at the sign for Eldorado Canyon State Park; *Crescent Meadows* from Denver, take CO 93 north to CO 72, go west for 9 miles to the Gross Dam sign, then turn north on Gross Dam Road and follow it for 3 miles to the parking lot

Eldorado . . . the land of riches sought by Spanish explorers. Eldorado Canyon State Park, while not the much-hoped-for golden land, does hold vast recreational wealth in its natural wonders.

The park is divided into two noncontinuous sections. Visitors approaching from the north via Boulder first come to the Inner Canyon, where massive rock walls abruptly rise 1,500 feet above the canyon floor while looking down into the raging South Boulder Creek, which cuts through the length of the canyon. A hiking trail joins this section of the park with the Crescent Meadows section, located almost 2 miles to the west.

The geology of the canyon mirrors the geological history of the surrounding Rocky Mountains. As you first enter the park, the exposed rock is the 240-million-year-old bedrock upon which an earlier Rocky Mountains was formed. The tremendous uplift visible at the Inner Canyon entrance is due to the ongoing uplifting effect of the present-day Rocky Mountains. Just a mile upstream at the visitors center, some of the rock has been calculated to be over 1.5 billion years old! The swarms of rock climbers making their way up the steep canyon walls are often climbing up an exposed sedimentary sandstone formation between 240 million and 300 million years old. At other locations in the park, both metamorphic and igneous rock are found, making Eldorado Canyon a valuable study site for geologists.

At the turn of the century, the Fowler family built a resort at the mouth of the canyon to lure visitors to the warm artesian springs. This area eventually became the town of Eldorado Springs. Deeper into the canyon a luxury hotel, the Crags Hotel, was also constructed. Located on a grassy knoll that enjoyed incredible down-canyon views into the resort of Eldorado Springs and the rolling prairie beyond, this hotel became a favorite weekend escape for well-heeled Denver citizens of the time. In 1912, a fire destroyed the hotel. All that remains is a few fireplaces and pieces of foundation.

Eldorado is a day-use-only park, and only the Inner Canyon area is developed; the Crescent Meadows area is an undeveloped meadow with a hiking trail. At the Inner Canyon, picnicking is a favorite pastime; the picnic area, located near the rushing South Boulder Creek, is surrounded by stunning canyon scenery. A sheltering forest canopy of pine joins with lush green grass to provide a cool place to beat the summer's heat. Canyon temperatures can be 15 degrees cooler than the nearby plains. The creek's relaxing burble becomes an exciting roar during peak spring runoff.

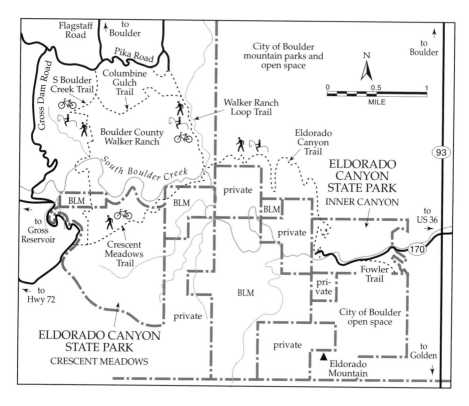

The visitors center offers some very informative booklets and publications on topics ranging from geology to bird-watching. Ask for the "Birds of Eldorado Canyon State Park" brochure, which lists all the species seen in the park, along with those reported fewer than ten times in the state, or those considered unusual in any region of Colorado.

The park naturalist offers exciting, informative interpretive programs, known as the Eldorado Explorers. Anyone is welcome, but kids really enjoy the opportunity to touch animal skins, feel bones and claws, and learn about the animals and wildflowers found in the canyon. Some of the topics might include animal tracks, the history of Eldorado Canyon, identifying wildflowers, and exploring wildlife homes.

South Boulder Creek offers fishermen a real challenge. Spring and summer are the best seasons; because the creek is fed from snowmelt, water levels in the fall and winter can get very low. This backcountry mountain stream is just waiting to offer up its rich catch of rainbow trout . . . only 7 miles from the city of Boulder!

Hikers have many excellent trails to choose from. For those wanting a close-up view of both South Boulder Creek and the many rock climbers scaling the faces of the inner canyon, the Streamside Trail takes you on a 1-mile round-trip walk along the north side of the creek that offers a view into a cave, as well as close contact with the water. Hikers are sure to see groups of rock climbers at the trail's edge, preparing their ropes and gear for their assaults up the steep canyon walls. Picture-taking opportunities abound along this trail.

A more challenging hike is the Rattlesnake Gulch Trail, which begins on the south side of the canyon and winds its way up from 6,000 feet to a rock overlook at

7,200 feet. Along the way there are beautiful views through the canyon and out into the plains. When hikers look south above the trail, they can see the still-working Denver and Rio Grande Railroad. This same railroad once brought passengers to enjoy the Crags Hotel. After almost 1.5 miles, the ruins of that once-glorious hotel are reached. Not much remains, but the views from the rock promontory are still breathtaking. The trail ends in an upper loop that offers one last look down the canyon before turning back to retrace the route.

The longest and most difficult hike in the park is the Eldorado Canyon Trail, which leads from the trailhead on the road just above the visitors center all the way over to the Crescent Meadows section of the park. The total round-trip distance is 11 miles, with close to a 3,000-foot elevation gain. This trail begins with a steep ascent through an area resembling a Pacific Northwest rain forest, then quickly enters a more typical pine forest. In less than 2 miles hikers begin to see the soaring Rocky Mountains and Continental Divide due west. The trail makes its way to the top of a meadow area, from where the views continue to amaze, before plunging a steep 600 feet down to the bottom lands of the Boulder County Walker Ranch, a hiking park with a trail system that connects with the Eldorado Canyon Trail, allowing hikers to either continue to the Crescent Meadows section of Eldorado Canyon State Park, or to make a long loop around Walker Ranch. The total distance from the Inner Canyon to and around Walker Ranch Loop is 14 miles, with a hefty 4,500-foot elevation

Picnic grounds at Eldorado State Park

View of the eastern plains from Eldorado Canyon's Rattlesnake Gulch Trail

gain. This loop includes sections of Columbine Gulch Trail and South Boulder Creek Trail.

Mountain bikes are allowed only on the Walker Ranch and Crescent Meadows portion of this loop and on the Rattlesnake Gulch Trail. However, in the nearby Boulder area, miles of mountain biking trails exist and are easily accessible from Eldorado Canyon State Park.

Horseback riding is also available, offered by a concessionaire near the park. The trail rides offer the same spectacular canyon scenery, while operating mainly on or near the east side of the park.

It is the technical rock climbing at Eldorado that has made it world-famous. Often a multitude of different languages can be heard, all with only one meaning . . . where are the most challenging routes and what is the best way to climb them? The dominating Shirttail Peak (7,500 feet) at the park's northern boundary looks down upon a series of world-class scaling walls and cliffs—the Rotwand, Hawk-Eagle Ridge, Redgarden Wall, the West Ridge, and, along the south side of the creek, the famous "The Bastille" (6,100 feet), considered one of the finest climbs in the world for what the nature of the rock offers. For rock climbers, Eldorado is a place that keeps you on the edge, as it pushes the envelop of your experience and tests every skill and confidence you possess. The park rangers advise that those wishing to learn the sport do so before they come to Eldorado, or take advantage of the park concessionaires that operate climbing schools and guide services just outside the park entrance. It is also important to be familiar with technical rock climbing regulations before attempting the park's soaring cliffs. It is especially important to note that bolts, pitons, and other fixed gear are *not* maintained by the park. Climbers use these anchors at their own risk.

The Crescent Meadows section of the park is reached by hiking on the Eldorado Canyon Trail, out of the Inner Canyon section of the park, and into the Boulder County Walker Ranch Park area. The Crescent Meadows Trail intersects the Eldorado Canyon Trail, then proceeds west along South Boulder Creek for 0.25 mile before climbing onto a ridge. The trail follows the ridge and after 0.75 mile enters the actual Crescent Meadows section of Eldorado Canyon State Park. The views from this ridge include the mountains to the south of Eldorado Canyon, a look through the canyon to Denver nestled on the plains, the Front Range south of Boulder, and, finally, the soaring mountains of the Indian Peaks Wilderness Area to the west. The last 0.5 mile of the hike passes through an expansive meadow which gives the trail its name. Remnants of wooden ranch buildings can be seen south of the trail.

Golden eagles, deer, Albert's and golden mantled ground squirrels, mule deer, trout, and even an occasional black bear and coyote can be seen in the park. Rattlesnakes are quite rare, even though the name of Rattlesnake Gulch Trail might suggest otherwise. A park naturalist gives guided talks on wildlife and habitat.

The beauty of Eldorado instantly captures you. The relief of sheer and colorful canyon walls and soaring mountains offers diversity from the normal fare of nearby prairie and rolling plains. Just minutes from the Denver metropolitan area, it is an Eldorado of the natural world!

Nearby attractions include Golden Gate Canyon State Park to the southwest and the prominent Indian Peaks Wilderness Area to the west. This area offers hundreds of miles of hiking trails and views of the Continental Divide. Boulder, just 7 miles north from the east entrance, offers the many trails of the Boulder Mountain Parks and Open Space.

Homestead Picnic Area at Lory State Park

NORTH REGION

▲The North Region of Colorado stretches from the eastern rolling high plains on
⊥Colorado's eastern border with Kansas, to the heart of the Rocky Mountains in
the west at Vail, on Interstate 70. The North Region stretches from Colorado's
northern border with Wyoming, from approximately 70 miles east of Utah clear to
the Kansas border, and south from Wyoming to the Denver Metro Region. This area
encompasses the complete transition from grassland prairie to 14,000-foot peaks
forming the core of the Continental Divide and the spectacular Rocky Mountain
National Park. Sweet prairie grasses stretching to the horizons, serene mountain
lakes, expansive lush meadows, vast conifer forests, roaring streams, and vistas
filled with soaring snowcapped peaks all accent this diverse natural wonderland.

In the eastern part of the North Region, the centerpiece is its high-plains reservoirs, created by taming the waters of the high-country rivers and creeks like the
Big Thompson and the Saint Vrain. Boaters can laze through a summer's day catch-
ing the cool breezes blowing down from the nearby Rocky Mountains. These are
the prairies drained by the South Platte River that inspired James Michener's *Centennial*. Etching its way across the region is the Cache La Poudre, the only designated Wild and Scenic river in Colorado. Some of the best fishing in the state, some
of the most scenic alpine hiking trails carpeted with colorful wildflower displays,
some of the most glorious high-country boating lakes, some of the most spectacular
camping sites found anywhere, and some of the finest river rafting in the
state . . . all are found in the North Region's state parks.

North Sterling Reservoir and Jackson Lake State Parks, located on the eastern
plains, are water-based recreation areas for the dry surrounding prairie. These
parks are mainly boating and fishing destinations. Barbour Ponds State Park, where
pond fishing is the primary attraction, lies just 15 miles east of the Front Range and
35 miles north of Denver in the grasslands leading up to the Rocky Mountains. Another 20 miles north of Barbour Ponds is the premier water-based state park of the
North Region: Boyd Lake State Park. Boyd Lake offers sailing, boating, and swimming in the last of the eastern plains parks.

Lory State Park rests 15 miles northwest of Boyd Lake State Park, on the transition zone between prairies and mountains. This park offers real mountain hiking
as well as hikes in its lower grassy foothills. Less than 10 miles northwest of Lory
State Park is Picnic Rock State Park, situated in the eastern mountains of the Front
Range along the Cache la Poudre River. Picnic Rock is a major river access point

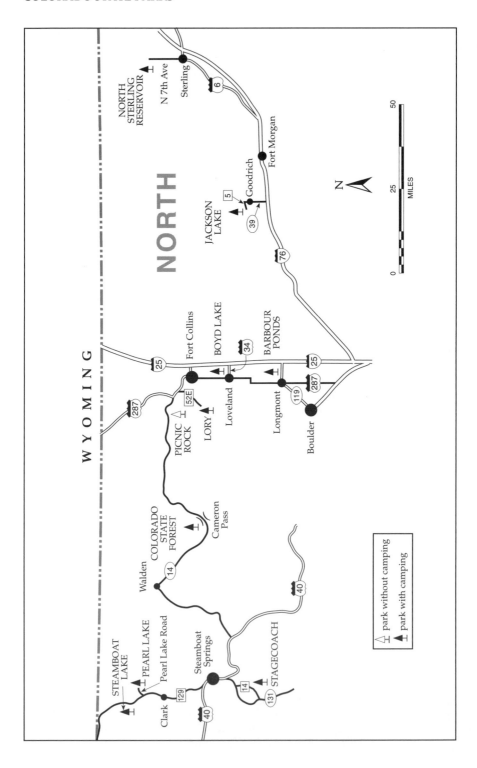

Cache La Poudre River

into the Cache la Poudre. Colorado State Forest lies 60 miles west of Picnic Rock, in the very heart of the Rockies. This massive state park extends 28 miles north from Cameron Pass nearly to Wyoming, and offers alpine hiking and fishing at between 8,000 and 12,500 feet.

Steamboat Lake and Pearl Lake State Parks are another 75 miles west of Colorado State Forest. These parks are true high-country experiences, with surrounding mountains towering to over 12,000 feet. Both these parks, real "away-from-it-all" recreation sites, lie in scenic mountain valleys. Stagecoach Park, another high-country water-based park surrounded by mountains, is 40 miles southeast of Steamboat Lake. Located in a flat valley, Stagecoach is a great fishing destination, with magnificent views of the distant Flat Tops Wilderness Area.

The weather in the North Region's eastern plains is much like Denver's; in the rest of the region, weather is often severe in the winter. The cold season can begin in October and last to May, with snow on the ground sometimes into June. The high-country parks enjoy cool to warm summers, while the parks on the eastern plains are generally hot, with temperatures approaching 100°F.

The high-country parks are located in subalpine forests of Engelmann spruce, fir, lodgepole pine, and limber-bristlecone pine, as well as in the montane forests of aspen, Douglas fir, and ponderosa pine. Extensive meadows, marshes, and mountain shrublands are interspersed between forests. The parks of the eastern plains are dominated by prairie grasslands, some cactus, sagebrush, and riparian ecosystems of reeds, cottonwoods, and marshlands located in and near the waterways feeding each park.

Both from one's vehicle and, more often, along a backcountry trail, elk, deer, and bighorn sheep are frequently observed. The largest moose herd in northern Colorado can be found at Colorado State Forest, between Steamboat Springs and Rocky Mountain National Park. Visitors wishing to see wildlife close up should travel through Rocky Mountain National Park.

The North Region has many outdoor opportunities to complement the state parks. Lake Granby and Grand Lake, which border Rocky Mountain National Park to the west, are the largest natural lakes in Colorado. They provide many miles of boating pleasure, connected to nearby hiking trail systems, with wilderness and outdoor photography opportunities all year-round and some of the best cross-country skiing anywhere.

Some of the most famous ski resorts are found in the North Region's winter wonderland . . . Copper Mountain, Vail, Breckenridge, and Winter Park are just a sampling of the fantastic skiing available. These resorts operate in the summer as home to diverse cultural events and great high-country hiking.

To learn about Colorado mining history, geology, and mining operations, visitors can travel to gold mines that still operate and dig for their own wishful "big strike." Many of the old mining towns offer a trip back through time to the heyday of the "big boom" in mining.

The North Region contains a Scenic Byways paradise for the Sunday driver out to find the most exotic, beautiful roadways. The drive along Highway 14 takes you to Picnic Rock State Park through the Cache la Poudre River Canyon, to Colorado State Forest's Cameron Pass and down into the North Park area. The Peak-to-Peak Scenic and Historic Byway (Highway 119) between Black Hawk and Estes Park or the incredible views found along Highways 131 and 14 as they pass through the Yampa River Valley toward Steamboat Lake and Pearl Lake State Parks are a small sampling of what many travelers consider to be one of America's most scenic areas.

Travelers can stop along the way and partake of some of the unique Colorado experiences found in the North Region. Visitors can ride behind a narrow-gauge steam locomotive and visit an 1870s silver mine on the famous Georgetown Loop Railroad. How about opera in the high country? Central City still operates their restored 1878 Victorian Opera House, funded in that century by some of the richest gold discoveries in the Old West. Need to relax those tired muscles after miles of hiking in the high country? Hot Sulphur Springs offers a rich tradition of hot springs treatments to help you on your way.

The North Region combines the best mix of outdoor recreation, inspiring scenery, Colorado history, and mountain culture, from the Old West to the modern ski resort. This area allows visitors to leave the last vestiges of civilization behind as they hike along the same high-mountain pass trails once frequented by the Utes and Arapaho Indians, who shuttled between cool high-country summer pastures to high-plains winter encampments. From the plains beneath the Rockies, the snowcapped peaks hint of alpine valleys awash in crisp, clean, pine-scented air and invite all to get up into the high mountains.

JACKSON LAKE STATE PARK

Hours/Season: Overnight; year-round; closed to boating Nov. to ice-off (late March)
Area: 440 acres; 2,700 surface water acres
Facilities: 262 campsites, 60 picnic sites, swim beach, marina, boat ramp, dump station, laundry, showers, snack bar
Attractions: Camping, picnicking, boating, swimming, fishing, sailboarding, jet skiing, waterskiing, hiking, interpretive programs, cross-country skiing, ice fishing, ice skating
Nearby: Pawnee National Grasslands
Access: From I-76 68 miles northeast of Denver, at the I-76/US 34 interchange, take CO 39 north 7.25 miles through Goodrich, then go west on CR Y.5 (follow the paved road) for 2.5 miles to the park entrance

The approach to Jackson Lake State Park takes you through the rolling high plains and semi-arid desert of eastern Colorado. This is the land that James Michener made famous in his historic novel *Centennial*. It is the same South Platte River highlighted in that novel that provides the water for Jackson Lake State Park, sometimes referred to as "the oasis of the plains." On a hot summer day, Jackson Lake surprises you with its tree-lined blue waters emerging like a shining jewel from the endless prairie.

For thousands of yearly visitors, Jackson Lake State Park is a welcomed recreational resource. Landlocked Colorado prides itself on having developed a string of eastern plains state parks that answers the needs for water recreation . . . especially boating and fishing. Many Denver water enthusiasts make the trek over the prairie to join vacationers from eastern Colorado and nearby Nebraska to use and enjoy the outstanding water recreational opportunities offered at Jackson Lake State Park.

The reservoir that was to eventually become Jackson Lake State Park was built at the turn of the century. Since then, it has served as a source for badly needed

Entrance sign at Jackson Lake State Park

irrigation water used by local farmers and ranchers. In 1965 it was established as a state park.

The campgrounds at Jackson Lake, 53 with electric hookups, are situated for the most part along the western shore, at Northview, Cove, Lakeside, Sandpiper, Fox Hills, and Pelican campgrounds. The Dunes campground, which takes its name from the surrounding low sandy hills, gives the camper a view directly north across the lake.

Picnic facilities are located north of Pelican campground, east of Cove campground, and just east and west of the Dunes campground; each area affords great views across the lake. Interpretive programs can be arranged with rangers on weekends during the summer.

A boat ramp and marina offer services from the west shore of the lake. The south shore area complements lake boating with an outstanding natural sandy beach and picnic area. This setting gives users the feeling of being on a Pacific beach . . . minus the 6-foot waves and tides! And sailboarding is excellent due to the steady flow of winds blowing down from the nearby Rocky Mountains. Boating is not permitted in the winter, after November 1, due to waterfowl hunting season and icy conditions.

Jackson Lake has become a popular draw for anglers. Trout, walleye, catfish, perch, bass, crappie, and wipers make their home in the warm waters of Jackson Lake. However, fishing is restricted during waterfowl hunting season and is prohibited from the swim beaches year-round.

Swimmers are drawn to the lake's natural sandy bottom free from any hazards and its gradual slope into deeper waters. A beautiful arc of cottonwood trees accent the south shore swimming area.

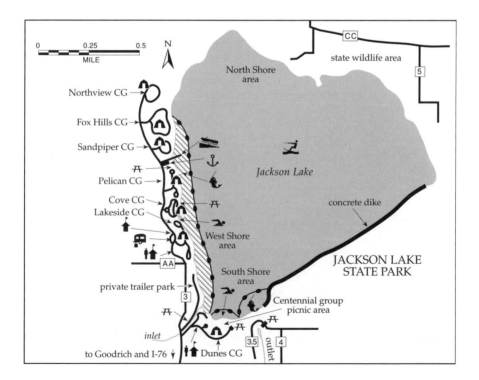

Jackson Lake from the south shore

There are no hiking trails at Jackson Lake, but hikers are permitted to walk cross-country through the surrounding grasslands. Winter sports include ice fishing and ice skating on the lake, while wildlife observation and photography can be enjoyed from anyplace along the surrounding shoreline.

A wide variety of ecosystems can be found at or near Jackson Lake. Short-grass prairie, wetlands, an actual working sand dune, sand hills, and semi-arid desert provide a variety of natural settings for heron, deer, coyote, hawks, eagles, pelicans, numerous shorebirds, and waterfowl. In the quieter autumn and winter months, visitors can enjoy peaceful walks around the lake in hopes of seeing some of the abundant wildlife. Be aware, however, that controlled hunting is permitted at Jackson Lake from the Tuesday after Labor Day through the Friday prior to Memorial Day.

Visitors can travel 22 miles to the historic town of Fort Morgan or venture to Orchard, just 4 miles away. Much of the movie *Centennial* was filmed in and near this small town, while to the north Pawnee Buttes served as perhaps the inspiration for the setting of Rattlesnake Buttes.

The Buttes are located in a very special ecological area known as the Pawnee National Grasslands, located in Weld County in northeastern Colorado. Almost 200,000 acres are designated as national grasslands. This prairie actually sweeps down from the Rocky Mountains to the west, and forms what Americans think of as the Great Plains. The Pawnee National Grasslands represents a special section of the plains, set aside for all time as a living witness to the millions of acres that once flourished along with the buffalo. A network of numbered roads have been established to permit visitors to get within walking distanceof most of this grassland area. The relatively flat surface of these lands has encouraged a great popularity among mountain bikers.

The modern history of the Pawnee National Grasslands goes back to the Great Depression and the severe weather that created the Dust Bowl of the 1930s. The federal government began buying the depleted farms and land from ruined farmers and ranchers between 1933 and 1943. By practicing good soil management techniques, the land has been restored to the original healthy grass cover it once enjoyed. The restored ecosystem is a short-grass prairie, where rainfall measures between 12 and 15 inches per year. Two short sod-forming grasses dominate these plains: blue grama, the Colorado state grass, and buffalo grass.

Scattered throughout the grasslands are prickly pear cactus, chokecherry, and winterfat. As the prairie has returned, so have the animals: pronghorn antelope, mule deer, coyote, swift fox, badger, and of course . . . prairie dogs! A visit to this area is a visit back in time to when the grasses were tall and sweet and stretched to every horizon. Information on this beautiful and very special place can be obtained by calling the Pawnee National Grassland in Greeley, Colorado (see appendix A).

NORTH STERLING RESERVOIR STATE PARK

Hours/Season: Overnight; year-round
Area: 1,000 acres; 3,000 surface water acres
Facilities: 50 campsites, 13 picnic sites, 4 boat ramps, marina, dump station
Attractions: Camping, picnicking, boating, warm-water fishing, sailing, water-skiing, swimming, wildlife observation, interpretive programs
Nearby: Overland Trail Museum
Access: Take I-76 northeast from Denver 125 miles to the Atwood exit, and go north on US 6 (Chestnut Street); continue north on Platte Street, turn right on North Third, and go 4 blocks; turn left on Broadway and go north 4 blocks; turn right on North Seventh Avenue, go north 12 miles, and follow the signs to the reservoir

North Sterling Reservoir State Park sits in the northeastern high plains of Colorado. The park draws visitors from throughout the high plains region. Water is a precious and highly conserved natural resource in Colorado, and North Sterling has become a real mecca for folks wanting to enjoy a water-based park. Far-reaching vistas are accented by a hill region that allows people to peer even further out into the seemingly endless prairies. If you travel to North Sterling Reservoir State Park in the late spring and early summer, expect the sweet scent of rich, green grasslands and wildflowers. In fall, these same lands turn an autumn yellow, but at any time, the visitor is struck by the majestic bluffs and Chimney Canyons surrounding the park to the northwest and always the expansive views of the endless prairie.

Almost 130 years ago, this area played host to the most well-traveled road in the land . . . the Overland Trail. From 1862 to 1869, this pioneer road conducted the greatest westward migration of people that the country had ever seen. Drawn to the gold fields of Colorado and the promise of rich farmlands in the Far West, settlers followed

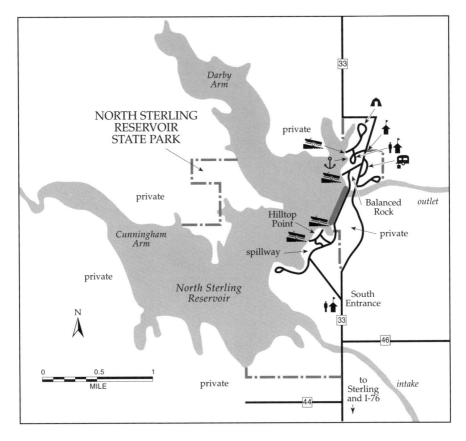

the trail along the South Platte River toward Denver. Today, Interstate 76 has re-placed the Overland Trail, which was located just 12 miles south of where North Ster-ling Reservoir State Park now operates.

The park had its early beginnings as an irrigation facility in 1910. Colorado State Parks acquired th area in 1992, with a perpetual easement with North Sterling Irri-gation District. For a high-plains reservoir, North Sterling is fairly deep (50-plus feet), and is fed by a system of inlet ditches from the South Platte River. During high irrigation use or drought conditions when shallower reservoirs in northeast Colo-rado are closed to boating, the deeper North Sterling Reservoir still offers boating.

The paved road through the park crosses over the dam from the south to access the marina and Elks Campground area, and affords spectacular views across the reservoir to the surrounding bluffs. Currently the facilities at Elks Campground are still being finished, but will include electrical hookups, a picnic pavilion, and other standard campground amenities. South Turnaround is a road-end area where open camping is permitted near a grove of cottonwood trees.

Picnic facilities include 8 sites with tables and electrical outlets located just north of the marina, and 6 sites located at Balanced Rock. Informal picnicking is permit-ted near the beach located south of the spillway, which also serves as an informal day-use area for swimming and boating.

North Sterling Reservoir is known for water sports and is a boater's paradise.

Swimming and boating south of the North Sterling Reservoir spillway

The reservoir provides a wide array of coves and fingers to explore and fish in. Some have even compared it to Lake Powell, because boaters get the feeling of being away from it all, protected by the contour of the land. Boating and waterskiing are the central recreation enjoyed at North Sterling Reservoir. There are no high mountain passes one must pull a boat over to access the park.

A full-service marina is operated by concessionaires from May through September, offering boat rentals, slips, storage, fuel, food, licenses, and camping supplies. North of the marina is the Elks boat ramp. Hilltop Point also has been developed to include a four-lane concrete boat ramp with low-water access. These additions reflect the growing emphasis on boating at North Sterling Reservoir.

To insure a peaceful lake setting, boats are required to maintain a wakeless speed around launch facilities, within 150 feet of shore fishermen, and at other marked areas. Water-skiers must ski in a counterclockwise direction, and have an observer on board in addition to the operator. A 12-inch-by-12-inch red flag must be displayed whenever a skier is down or equipment is in the water.

Since the South Platte River feeds North Sterling Reservoir, water levels can fluctuate during the irrigation season. This requires boaters to be especially alert for submerged hazards. Because of ice conditions and wildlife considerations, boating at the reservoir ends on November 1, through the end of the migratory waterfowl hunting season. During the spring, North Sterling Reservoir sometimes hosts the Leisure Sports Boat Show, and often plays host to many successful fishing tournaments.

The reservoir has become an excellent warm-water fishery featuring walleye, wiper, perch, catfish, bluegill, and bass. Fishing is permitted year-round, with ice fishing allowed even during the migratory waterfowl hunting season, as conditions warrant.

The small cove just south of the spillway offers great swimming. The area is bounded by a sandy beach, which helps keep the kids busy making sand castles.

The reservoir is host to a variety of wildlife, including deer, coyotes, rabbits, pelicans, many species of waterfowl and shorebirds, and, during the winter, over 100 nesting bald eagles.

In the nearby town of Sterling are antique shops and the Sterling Country Club and Golf Course; for information contact Logan County Chamber of Commerce (see appendix A). Sterling also boasts the famous Overland Trail Museum, which presents the history of the Overland Trail. The museum building is located in a replica of an old fort. The grounds are beautified by trees, native prairie grasses, and wildflowers. A Concord Stage is displayed, and pieces of pioneer farm machinery, some dating back to homestead days, are found throughout the grounds. Indoor exhibits highlight artifacts that the pioneers brought with them on their trek across the prairie, as well as Indian *metates* used to grind corn, arrowheads, and buckskin clothing. There is even a one-room school, Stoney Buttes, on the grounds, and summer sessions for children still take place. The museum also includes an authentic Daily Country Store, a blacksmith shop, a barn, and a surprisingly large collection of branding irons. The Overland Trail Museum hours are 9:00 A.M. to 5:00 P.M. Monday through Saturday, 10:00 A.M. to 5:00 P.M. Sunday and holidays (April 1–October 31); 10:00 A.M. to 4:00 P.M. Tuesday through Saturday (November 1–March 31).

BARBOUR PONDS STATE PARK

Hours/Season: Overnight; year-round
Area: 50 acres; 80 surface water acres
Facilities: 60 campsites, 15 picnic sites, dump station
Attractions: Camping, picnicking, fishing, boating, interpretive programs, nature trail, cross-country skiing, ice skating, ice fishing
Nearby: Longmont, Loveland, Big Thompson Canyon
Access: From Boulder, take Highway 119 north to Longmont; 7 miles east of Longmont, turn north on CR 7 for about 2 miles to the park entrance; from I-25 north of Denver, exit onto Highway 119 westbound and in a short distance turn right onto CR 7, continuing 2 miles to the park

Sometimes great value can be found in small packages. Barbour Ponds State Park is one such package. Located just 30 miles north of Denver, Barbour Ponds is a collection of four ponds which together make up a prized old fishing hole and quiet retreat. To the west looms Mount Meeker and Longs Peak, a 14,000-foot massif highlighting the horizon in the direction of Rocky Mountain National Park. Cottonwoods line the ponds, providing beautiful picnic shade and a scenic backdrop for lazy days at the fishing hole. Some of the best warm-water fishing in northern Colorado is found at Barbour Ponds.

The park began, surprisingly enough, as a group of gravel pits dredged for highway construction. Reclamation began in 1962, when the Colorado Game, Fish and Parks Department received the ponds in a swap with the highway department. The fledgling recreation area was named after Roy N. Barbour, a longtime Longmont resident and organizer of the Longmont Izaak Walton League.

Camping is available at sixty campsites located in the park's east and west campgrounds near the water, and near the north end of the park at a group site that can accommodate twelve units. The campgrounds are located on flat terrain, and offer only the basic amenities.

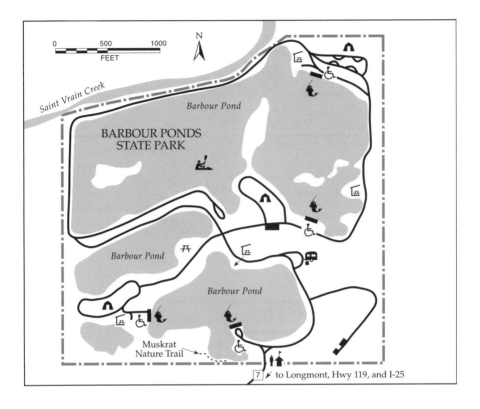

Barbour Pond

BARBOUR PONDS
STATE PARK

Barbour Pond

Barbour Pond

Muskrat
Nature Trail

7 ⚡ to Longmont, Hwy 119, and I-25

Picnicking is a quiet pastime enjoyed at the ponds. The emphasis is on quiet at this prairie retreat. When I visited the park, I found people very relaxed and speaking in almost hushed tones in honor of the nature of the place. This park is very accessible to the physically challenged because the land around the ponds is relatively flat. Concrete ramps to the rest rooms are provided.

The park permits only small vessels operated at wakeless speeds to use the ponds. Because the water area is small, visitors often feel that "this fishing hole is all mine!" Barbour Ponds are stocked with generous amounts of rainbow trout and bass, along with bluegill, channel catfish, and crappie.

The Muskrat Nature Trail near the park entrance leads visitors on a short 0.1-mile walk along the ponds, where aspects of wildlife are pointed out. A walk around any of the ponds provides many opportunities for viewing wildlife and nature study. Anyone who requires assistance will find a ready and willing staff person to help them or to point out some of the more interesting aspects of the wildlife and habitat.

The ponds provide habitat for frogs and turtles, a variety of waterfowl, and wading birds, along with many interesting aquatic plants. Songbirds can be found in the many willows, cottonwood trees, and cattails. During the winter, large numbers of waterfowl make their home at the ponds, with even bald eagles often spotted.

During the winter, the ponds support ice skating and ice fishing. Cross-country skiing is limited to the grasslands around the park.

There are plenty of nearby attractions to interest visitors to Barbour Ponds State Park. Just 7 miles west, in the city of Longmont, is the Longmont Pioneer Museum.

View north across the ponds, Barbour Ponds State Park

This museum depicts the history of the city from the pioneers to modern Longmont.

Northwest of Barbour Ponds lies the historic city of Loveland, the gateway to Rocky Mountain National Park, just 30 miles west. Few cities along the Front Range can boast of such a unique concentration of artists as Loveland. Over forty artists and sculptors contribute in making the city home to many art collections, art festivals, studios, and foundries, the latter because sculpturing is the focal point of art in Loveland. Benson Park hosts an outdoor sculpture garden and, in August, features the largest juried exhibition of sculpture in the United States—the famed "Sculpture in the Park Show and Sale." Visitors to the show can see demonstrations by artists, tour the foundries where sculpture is cast, and enjoy the hundreds of displays by some of the nation's finest sculptors. For information, contact the Loveland High Plains Arts Council (see appendix A).

Just 20 miles west of Barbour Ponds is Big Thompson Canyon, through which flows the Big Thompson River. Scenic vertical cliffs and sheer rock walls accent this canyon, and hiking trails can be found along the entire length of the canyon.

BOYD LAKE STATE PARK

Hours/Season: Overnight; year-round
Area: 197 acres; 1,800 surface water acres
Facilities: 148 campsites, 95 picnic sites, group picnic pavilion, visitors/nature center, dump station, bathhouse, snack bar, marina, boat ramps, nature trail, bicycle trail, swim beach with lifeguards
Attractions: Camping, picnicking, interpretive programs, boating, swimming, waterskiing, sailing, jet skiing, fishing, bicycling, cross-country skiing, ice fishing, ice skating
Nearby: Larimer County Parks, Rocky Mountain National Park
Access: From I-25 near Loveland, take US 34 west for 4 miles, turn north on Madison Avenue, and follow the signs 1.25 miles to the park

Boyd Lake State Park is perhaps the premier water-sports park in northern Colorado. It is a scenic wonderland at the westernmost edge of the plains at the foot of the Rockies and the Continental Divide. Spectacular sunrises and sunsets can be enjoyed whenever clouds have gathered over the nearby mountains or drape the eastern horizon.

The lake served the city of Greeley as a source of drinking water and the local Colorado farms as irrigation water before becoming a state park in 1972. It continues to provide water for Greeley and area farms.

The beauty and manicured upkeep of the lake area and surrounding facilities are

Marina and docks at Boyd Lake

impressive. Trees generously spaced along the shoreline create a boulevard-like setting, while still allowing visitors magnificent views across the water to both mountains and prairie. A beautiful 3-mile walking and biking path graces the west shore and offers access to the many campgrounds, picnic spots, and swim beach found in that section of the park. The eastern side of Boyd Lake has been left undeveloped. This ensures unobstructed views toward the eastern horizon.

The camping at Boyd Lake is first-class. The park offers 148 paved pull-through campsites located on grassy knolls dotted with trees. These sites are readily accessible and all are near the lake. They offer picnic tables and grills, and accommodate tents and recreational vehicles. Three modern rest rooms with showers, playground equipment for the kids, and even horseshoe pits (bring your own horseshoes) are available throughout the campgrounds. A dump station is also offered. Not only are the campgrounds beautiful, but a friendly, almost villagelike atmosphere prevails.

Picnicking is a real favorite at Boyd Lake State Park. Picnic sites are found at the swim beach, along the west side of the lake, and at the north end of the park. A magnificent group picnic shelter accommodating as many as 200 sits atop a small ridge overlooking the lake and park area. The pavilion includes fire grills, electrical outlets, fireplace and sink, tables, and even a volleyball court nearby. The area is surrounded by lawn, and a trail leads to the lakeshore, where boats can be beached during a picnic.

BOYD LAKE STATE PARK

The nature center at the park entrance has a display of birds and wildlife commonly found at the park. Rangers answer questions and offer interpretive programs. To complement the wildlife education programs at Boyd Lake, park rangers conduct outdoor survival courses for interested school children. During "Eco-week," rangers from Boyd Lake travel to the YMCA of the Rockies Camp in Rocky Mountain National Park. For 2½ days, young people are shown survival and hiking skills; proper use of equipment; and the basics of food, water, and shelter. They then take an 8- to 15-mile hike to apply the skills just learned. Outdoor education programs are available year-round and topics covered include boating basics, outdoor survival, water safety, and Boyd Lake wildlife.

A large, modern marina located on the west side of the lake offers dock slips and mooring; ski, fishing, sailing, jet, and pontoon boat rentals; and hot and cold food and supplies. Boats can be launched nearby using the lake's six two-lane ramps. The entire lake is open to boating and sailing, with the south end open to waterskiing. The park hosts numerous regattas and other special events throughout the year.

The underwater ridges and inlet areas in the lake are prime areas for fishing when the water is flowing in. On my visit I came across dozens of contented anglers dotting the shores, quietly waiting for the "big one" to bite. Bass, catfish, perch, rainbow trout, and walleye are all found at Boyd Lake. Ice fishing is a popular winter activity for anglers who are year-round enthusiasts.

Swimming is another popular water sport at the lake. A sandy swim beach is staffed by lifeguards and has a swim pavilion with showers, rest rooms, first-aid station, and food concessions. Boyd Lake is an ideal getaway on a hot Colorado summer day.

The best way to see Boyd Lake is on foot. Whether it is one of the first warm days of spring when the prairie is at its deepest green, or on a bright summer day with the west winds gently blowing down from the Rockies, or in the quiet fall season when autumn yellows and browns have replaced the green of summer, Boyd Lake offers serene beauty and open vistas. The walking and biking paths meander along the beaches, take you to the water's edge, or allow you to brush under the majestic cottonwood trees. These trails join with the city of Loveland's regional trail system found at the north and south end of the park. During winter, these same trails serve as cross-country ski routes.

Wildlife viewing is excellent at Boyd Lake, due to the close proximity of the Rocky Mountains. Fox, beaver, coyote, and small mammals can be frequently seen. A large bird population includes great blue heron, egrets, great horned owls, hawks, eagles, and white pelicans.

Boyd Lake is located in Larimer County, where there are over 650 miles of hiking trail. The combined agencies of Larimer County Parks, Colorado State Parks, U.S. Forest Service, Rocky Mountain National Park, and Fort Collins administer over 300,000 acres of land devoted to diverse outdoor recreation. The famous Cache la Poudre and Big Thompson Rivers are just two of the many scenic rivers with fishing and rafting available. For a complete listing of what is available in the area, call

Swim pavilion at Boyd Lake

Larimer County Parks (see appendix A) and ask for their Outdoor Recreation Guide, or pick up a copy while you are at Boyd Lake State Park. For visitors planning a trip into Rocky Mountain State Park, Boyd Lake offers a less-crowded, watersports base for excursions to the many vacation opportunities found in this part of northern Colorado.

LORY STATE PARK

Hours/Season: Overnight (backcountry only); day-use 8:00 A.M. to 10:00 P.M. (summer), 8:00 A.M. to dusk (all other seasons)
Area: 2,500 acres
Facilities: 6 backcountry campsites, 17 picnic sites, 25 miles of hiking trail, 15 miles of bicycling trail, 20 miles of horseback trail, equestrian jumping course
Attractions: Camping, picnicking, interpretive programs, hiking, horseback riding, mountain biking, rock climbing, cross-country skiing
Nearby: Horsetooth Reservoir, Horsetooth Mountain Park, Rocky Mountain National Park
Access: From Fort Collins (62 miles north of Denver, just west of I-25), take Highway 287 north through Laporte; at the Bellvue exit (CR 52E) turn left, drive 1 mile to CR 23N, turn left, and go 1.4 miles to CR 25G; turn right and proceed to the park entrance

▲ The beautiful drive to Lory State Park, through the northern Colorado farmland and by pastured horse ranches, brings the visitor out of the prairie and into the foothills of the Rockies, into direct contact with the Front Range. The park is in the transition zone from 5,500 feet to 7,000 feet, and features both prairie and mountain ecosystems and the varied flora and fauna representative of each. Lory State Park is a hiking park that also offers trails to bicyclists and equestrians. Lory State Park is at its best when the snow is still blocking entrance into Colorado's high country, when the first blush of spring has encouraged the wildflowers to make their appearance, when the lazy days of a green summer recede into the quiet yellow and amber of fall. Lory State Park encourages a simpler, backcountry nature experience.

For many years the area that is now the park was ranchland, until the state of Colorado purchased it in 1967. It was named and dedicated in honor of Dr. Charles A. Lory (1872–1969), president of Colorado State University from 1909 until 1940.

Enter the park by driving along the only road on the property, which takes you 3 miles to the park's south end. Only backcountry camping is allowed in the park, at designated sites and by permit only. No open fires are permitted; backpack stoves are recommended. Vehicular camping is not allowed, nor are tents at lower elevations.

As visitors travel the road through the park, they find the picnic areas and hiking trailheads situated along either side of the road. A sheltered group picnic area 0.5 mile south of the entrance station can accommodate groups of up to 150. The facilities include tables, barbecue grills, a fire ring, rest rooms, a volleyball court, and a horseshoe pit. Water is not available on site but can be obtained near the park entrance.

Outdoor education is provided through a series of informative nature programs. These slide and lecture presentations cover topics such as the history and geology of the park, animals, artifacts and ecosystems found at Lory (with a most graphic

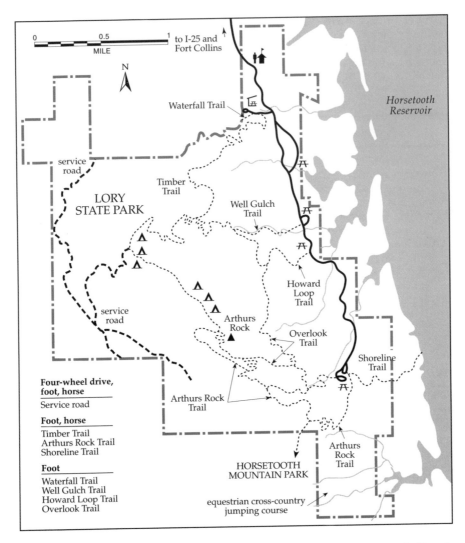

0   0.5   1   to I-25 and
MILE   Fort Collins

N

Horsetooth
Reservoir

Waterfall Trail

service
road

Timber
Trail

LORY
STATE PARK

Well Gulch
Trail

service
road

Arthurs
Rock

Howard
Loop
Trail

Overlook
Trail

Shoreline
Trail

**Four-wheel drive,
foot, horse**

Service road

Foot, horse

Timber Trail
Arthurs Rock Trail
Shoreline Trail

Foot

Waterfall Trail
Well Gulch Trail
Howard Loop Trail
Overlook Trail

Arthurs Rock
Trail

Arthurs
Rock
Trail

HORSETOOTH
MOUNTAIN PARK

equestrian cross-country
jumping course

display of antlers, skulls of deer, a fox pelt, a rattlesnake skin, and red-tailed hawk feathers), and the Colorado State Parks system. The rangers are also available for guided general ecology hikes, including a mule deer interpretive hike.

To the left of the road is Horsetooth Reservoir, with its fantastic coves and inlets. This reservoir is accessible from the park via many hiking trails, but it is not within the park proper. Boaters and other water-sports enthusiasts can contact the Larimer County Parks Department (see appendix A) for information about that facility and proper access points.

Just inside the park entrance is the 0.1-mile-long Waterfall Trail. Though it is short, it still affords a pleasant walk to a series of waterfalls in the spring and summer. Wetland vegetation and spring wildflowers grace the trail as well.

Also near the park entrance is the trailhead for the longest trail in the park, the 3.5-mile Timber Trail, open to both hikers and horses. A moderate to difficult trail, it intersects the Well Gulch Trail in 1.25 miles and once the trail reaches the

Horses waiting to ride into the high country above Lory State Park

ridgetop, six backcountry campsites are found. Near the highest elevations of the Timber Trail, it connects with a four-wheel-drive park service road that seconds as a hiking and equestrian trail; this road accesses the westernmost and northernmost reaches of the park. The Timber Trail ends at its junction with Arthur's Rock Trail.

Continuing along the park road from the two trailheads near the entrance, within another mile are the Well Gulch and Howard Loop trailheads. Well Gulch is an easy foot trail that heads west up a drainage, meeting the Howard Loop Trail in 0.5 mile and ending at the Timber Trail in another 0.5 mile. By combining the first half of the Well Gulch Trail with the Howard Loop Trail, one can enjoy the 1.3-mile Well Gulch Self-Guided Nature Trail. Along the way are markers that highlight twenty points of interest described in the trail guide brochures found at the trailhead. Some of the topics covered include grassland community, mountain slopes, lichens, rock uplift, mule deer, and water patterns. The Howard Loop trail is an easy to moderate foot trail that reaches the site of the old Howard family homestead, which is now a picnic area.

At the south end of the park, at road's end, are two trailheads for Arthur's Rock Trail. The foot trail is a 1.7-mile moderate to difficult hike; the 2-mile equestrian trail begins in the cross-country jumping area and provides access to trails in Horsetooth Mountain Park. Both Arthur's Rock trails lead to a massive granite rock named after an early inhabitant of the area. From the top are marvelous and expansive views of the reservoir, the plains sweeping down into Fort Collins, and the Front Range extending toward Denver to the south and Wyoming to the north.

Near Arthur's Rock equestrian trailhead is the easy 1-mile Shoreline Trail, providing the park's best access to the edge of Horsetooth Reservoir. Deer are often seen feeding along this trail, which also brings you close to the uptilted red sandstone hogback rock formations that border the reservoir. Shoreline Trail is open to

Mountain bikers about to enjoy the many trails at Lory State Park

both foot and equestrian traffic. During winter, cross-country skiing takes place on the roads, rolling hills, and trails where the grade permits.

The 1.9-mile Overlook Trail (foot traffic only) connects the Howard Loop Trail and the Arthur's Rock Trail, running along the ridge beneath Arthur's Rock through a variety of vegetative habitats offering the chance to see birds and wildlife. The moderate to difficult Overlook Trail ends at a spur trail that offers a short, steep ascent to the base of Arthur's Rock.

The Double Diamond Stables are found on the left of the roadway less than 0.5 mile from the park entrance. This concessionaire offers trail, mountain, breakfast, and dinner rides, along with riding lessons and special parties. Many equestrians trailer their own horses to the park, and are quite enthusiastic about the quality of the trails and the spectacular beauty they offer. At the south end of the park is a premier equestrian cross-country jumping course. The course sits in a grassy valley and looks out over the rolling plains and down the length of the Front Range. Users of this course might have difficulty concentrating on what they are doing, because it would be so easy to get lost in the surrounding beauty!

Any trail in the park offers opportunities to view the spectacular flower display and wildlife. Squirrels, fox, coyote, weasels, mule deer, wild turkey, blue grouse, rabbit, and even black bear are all found within the park. Colorful birds such as goldfinch, tanagers, and warblers also make their home in the park.

About an hour's drive southwest of Lory State Park is Rocky Mountain National Park. The national park offers over 350 miles of hiking trail, many interpretive nature trails, and some of the most beautiful high-country scenery found in Colorado. Because glaciers account for much of the landscape relief in Rocky Mountain

National Park, many of the geological points of interest, such as Glacier Gorge and Moraine Park, are glacier-related. If Lory State Park whets your appetite for hiking, then the national park is the main course. Other nearby attractions include Horsetooth Reservoir, where water sports can be enjoyed, and Horsetooth Mountain Park, a premier equestrian park.

PICNIC ROCK STATE PARK

Hours/Season: Day-use; year-round
Area: 13 acres
Facilities: 20 picnic sites, boat ramp
Attractions: Picnicking, river rafting, fishing
Nearby: Poudre Canyon
Access: From Fort Collins, north of Denver just west of I-25, go north on US 287 to CO 14, then continue west for 3 miles

Picnic Rock State Park is located at the entrance to Poudre Canyon, through which runs the only river in Colorado designated a Wild and Scenic River. Under this designation, 75 miles of the Cache la Poudre River, from Poudre Park to Rocky Mountain National Park, have been preserved from development for future generations. Picnic Rock is one of many access and take-out points along the Poudre. However, there is only one stretch of beginning white-water anywhere along the river. This stretch runs from above Picnic Rock down to the Lower Picnic Rock River Access Area, which makes Picnic Rock significant for river runners.

The river gets its name, which means "hiding place of powder," from when French fur trappers in the 1820s stored large amounts of gunpowder (*poudre*)—used in their hunting rifles—in a hiding place (*cache*) along the river.

Besides the fee entrance station, there are eight picnic tables, several fire grates, and restrooms. This is simply a river access area for river rafters, anglers, and those who enjoy rustic picnics along a beautiful river.

Trout fishing on the Poudre is taken to an art form. Brown, brook, and rainbow trout are the main species swimming the river. Over 53,000 catchable trout per year are stocked in non-wild trout areas by the Division of Wildlife. There are also two river sections totaling almost 9 miles that are designated as Wild Trout Water. These challenging waters are not stocked, and only fishing with flies and lures is permitted. The bag limits for these areas are two fish 16 inches or longer.

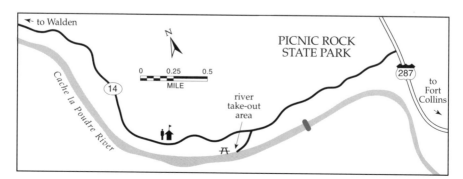

River rafters entering the wild and raging Poudre River

The entire 101-mile length of the Poudre Canyon has been named the Cache La Poudre–North Park Scenic Byway. It follows the river along much of its incredible 7,000-foot drop from its headwaters to its confluence with the South Platte River. The Poudre is truly a wild river, especially at peak runoff following a wet winter. During these times, there are many places along the river that are not attemptable by anyone, using any kind of boat. For this reason, boaters are strongly advised to be completely familiar with the various stretches of river they plan to run, and to honestly assess their abilities. All craft entering the river are required to have a personal floatation device (PFD) for each person on board, and have permanently affixed to the vessel the name and address of the owner. This river means business, and is not to be taken lightly.

Whether you drive, hike, or raft along the Poudre River, you are sure to see wildlife of some kind. The river corridor is home to bighorn sheep, mule deer, moose, elk, black bear, mountain lion, golden eagles, and falcons. One of my hiking buddies and her family had camped not too far from Poudre Canyon; she was greeted one morning by a bull moose standing directly in front of her tent. She was amazed that after all the backcountry hiking she and her husband had done in Canada, it took a visit to the Poudre Canyon area to finally see a moose up close.

Because the river canyon rises to such a high elevation, there are many recreational opportunities nearby for hiking, fishing, wildlife observation, and camping. Some of the more well-known trails include Grey Rock, Hewlett Gulch, Dadd Gulch, Roaring Creek, and Big South. Mountain bikers can also use some of these trails. For information on these trails and other Poudre Canyon recreational opportunities, call the U.S. Forest Service Visitor Center or the North Park Chamber of Commerce (see appendix A).

COLORADO STATE FOREST

Hours/Season: Overnight; year-round
Area: 71,000 acres; 130 surface water acres
Facilities: 104 campsites, 16 picnic sites, 2 boat ramps, stables/horse rentals, rustic cabins
Attractions: Camping, picnicking, interpretive programs, boating, fishing, hiking, mountain biking, horseback riding, cross-country skiing, ice fishing
Nearby: Jackson County, North Park, Arapaho National Wildlife Refuge
Access: From Fort Collins, north of Denver just west of I-25, drive 75 miles west on CO 14, over Cameron Pass

▲ Colorado State Forest is considered one of the premier Colorado wilderness areas for rugged recreational adventure. The State Forest is truly high country, with its 71,000 acres ranging in elevation from 8,500 to 12,500 feet. The park is 28 miles long north to south, and from 1 to 8 miles wide east to west. It is bounded on the east by the Medicine Bow Mountains and on the south by the Never Summer Range. It is this range, at the northern fringe of Rocky Mountain National Park, that overlooks the Kawuneeche Valley where the Colorado River originates as a narrow

Nokhu Crags from across Ranger Lake

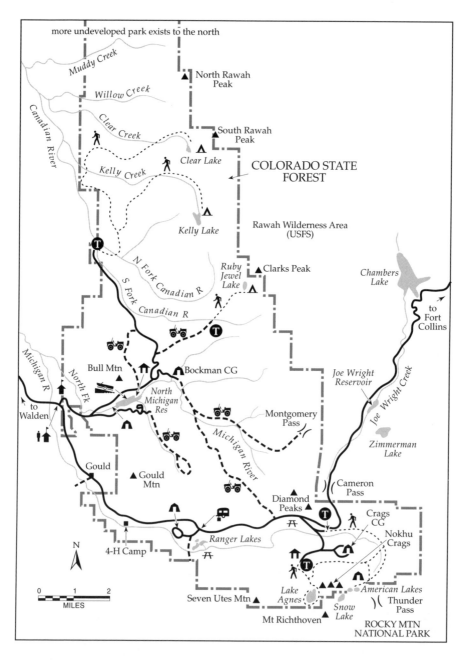

more undeveloped park exists to the north

Muddy Creek

Willow Creek

Clear Creek

Canadian River

Kelly Creek

Clear Lake

North Rawah Peak

South Rawah Peak

COLORADO STATE FOREST

Kelly Lake

Rawah Wilderness Area (USFS)

Ruby Jewel Lake

Clarks Peak

Chambers Lake

to Fort Collins

N Fork Canadian R

S Fork Canadian R

Michigan R

North Fk

Bull Mtn

Bockman CG

Joe Wright Reservoir

Joe Wright Creek

to Walden

North Michigan Res

Montgomery Pass

Zimmerman Lake

Michigan River

Gould

Gould Mtn

Cameron Pass

Diamond Peaks

Crags CG

Nokhu Crags

N

4-H Camp

Ranger Lakes

Seven Utes Mtn

Lake Agnes

Snow Lake

American Lakes

Thunder Pass

Mt Richthoven

ROCKY MTN NATIONAL PARK

0   1   2
MILES

creek. Colorado State Forest is located in Jackson County, one of the least populated areas of Colorado, at one person per square mile. The feeling at Colorado State Forest is one of expansive solitude. This *is* the backcountry! Because of the high elevation, visitors may need time to acclimate. They also need to guard against sunburn in the high, thin, cool air.

Colorado State Forest, despite its somewhat misleading name, is a state park—in fact it is the largest park in the Colorado State Park system. Colorado State Forest was first owned by the federal government as undeveloped forest, and in 1938 the federal government exchanged the land with the state of Colorado for land the state owned. The state continued a recreational lease on the land until 1972, when Colorado State Parks was established and developed the park.

Camping is available at over 104 campsites found at Ranger Lakes and The Crags in the southern part of the forest, and at North Michigan Reservoir and Bochman campground in the western area of the forest. Backcountry camping is allowed throughout Colorado State Forest at Ruby Jewel, Kelly, and Clear Lakes in the north and at American Lakes in the south. The views from Ranger Lakes are especially stunning. The lake looks out at Nokhu Crags (12,400 feet) to the southeast. When capped with snow, Nokhu Crags presents the traditional image of a scenic mountain vista mirrored in a quiet mountain lake.

Besides traditional camping, rustic, primitive cabins are available on a rental basis at North Michigan Reservoir and at the Lake Agnes trailhead in the southern part of the forest. The charming cabins are equipped with a wood-burning stove, a wooden table, benches, and bunk beds with mattresses. Outside are fire grills and picnic tables; no electricity, propane, running water, blankets, or bedding are on site. For reservations and to receive the informative brochure "Cabins . . . Colorado State Forest," contact Colorado State Forest or Colorado State Parks (see appendix A).

If you are really looking for something different, try a yurt shelter for your camping needs. These are circular, tentlike canvas-and-wood structures built high on a wood deck, resembling those used in the Mongolian culture. They are equipped with a wood-burning stove, propane cookstove, lantern, padded bunks, and complete kitchen. Colorado State Forest can provide more information on these shelters, which are located at strategic points throughout the park.

Picnic sites can be found near Ranger Lakes, in the woods just away from the parking lot, and offer a cool respite during the hottest summer days.

Because there is so much wildlife and interesting vegetation to be seen at State Forest, the rangers offer weekend nature interpretive talks on backcountry camping skills, fishing, plant identification, environmental issues, and winter survival. With Colorado State Forest elevations reaching over 12,000 feet in places, the winter survival skills program is especially popular and necessary. Indeed, the Boy Scouts and Girl Scouts stage a winter camp at Colorado State Forest, appropriately know as "Camp Klondike."

The only boating allowed in Colorado State Forest is at North Michigan Reservoir. Power boats are permitted, but must be operated only at wakeless speeds. All other water in the park is closed to boating.

If you enjoy fishing in pristine mountain lakes, you will find plenty of choices at Colorado State Forest. Brook, native, rainbow, brown, and golden trout are the most frequently caught fish. In North Michigan Reservoir and at the alpine lakes, only artificial fly and lure fishing is permitted. The fishing throughout Colorado State Forest is quiet, enjoyable, and rewarding. The scenery more than makes up for any low catch days.

The hiking trails are numerous, with more on the drawing board to be built. In the north, some of the more popular trails are Ruby Jewel Lake, Kelly Lake, and Clear Lake. The Ruby Jewel Lake trail, 3 miles round trip, gains 800 feet in elevation; the lake is nestled below 12,951-foot Clarks Peak (which is not located in Colorado State Forest). The trail to Kelly Lake is 8 miles round trip, with 1,200 feet elevation gain; the trail to Clear Lake is 10 miles round trip, also with 1,200 feet elevation gain. Clear Lake is due west of 12,644-foot South Rawah Peak (also not

The high mountains at Cameron Pass

located in Colorado State Forest). In the south, trails include American Lakes and Lake Agnes. American Lakes Trail is 10 miles round trip, with 1,400 feet elevation gain. Lake Agnes Trail is 2 miles round trip, with 400 feet elevation gain. The views are breathtaking, as the high-alpine Medicine Bow Mountains form the backdrop for almost all these hikes.

Four-wheel-drive roads are located in the southern part of the forest, and all start at North Michigan Reservoir. Roads lead southeast from Bockman campground to Montgomery Pass (12 miles round trip) and Highway 14 near Diamond Peaks. From the south shore of the reservoir, a road leads to Gould Mountain (7 miles round trip). Heading north from the reservoir, the road past Bull Mountain is 3 miles round trip; it connects with the road to hiking trailheads—Ruby Jewel Lake trailhead, 4 miles from North Michigan Reservoir; Kelly Lake trailhead, 8 miles; Clear Lake trailhead, 10.75 miles. Horse stables formerly located at Colorado State Forest are no longer in use.

A feature unique to Colorado State Forest is the large herd of moose. Rangers joke that the size of the moose and the ease of viewing them at Colorado State Forest makes it the "moose capital of Colorado." The herd of 12 was introduced in 1979 almost as an experiment, but now the number of moose has grown to over 600. For a glimpse of these stately creatures, try looking for them in the willow bottoms in the early morning or toward late afternoon. If not moose, you are sure to see elk or deer. Also noteworthy is the only confirmed sighting of a river otter (an endangered species), in the North Park area of Colorado.

As strange as it sounds, Colorado State Forest is home to the only two "cold-climate sand dunes" in Colorado. Over 400 acres of sand dune can be found in the forest. One is used for off-road four-wheel-drive recreation, while the other is strictly for nature interpretation. These are both located in the northern undeveloped reaches of the park (not shown on the map in this book).

The vegetation in Colorado State Forest includes a variety of colorful flora not found in the lower-elevation parks. Lodgepole pine, spruce, fir, and aspen abound. Tundra and alpine meadows are found above 11,000 feet, with the state flower, the Colorado columbine, mixed with a vast array of wildflowers.

Colorado State Forest is near many other public lands, such as Routt and Roosevelt national forests, and the Rawah Wilderness Area to the east. Many other recreational experiences and outdoor events can be found in the nearby area, known as Jackson County and North Park. North Park extends 40-plus miles northwest from Colorado State Forest. This alpine playground hosts lively events in winter, such as the Gould Snowmobile Days, Ski Scramble, and Sled Dog Races; summer events include the Old Timers Festival, the Never Summer Rodeo, and Christmas in July Jamboree; and in fall, the North Park Fair is held. Information for these events can be obtained by calling Walden Town Hall (see appendix A).

For a special wildlife observation experience, you can travel west to the Arapaho National Wildlife Refuge, located several miles south of Walden, along Colorado Highway 14. A self-guided 6-mile wildlife auto tour route starts 3 miles south of Walden, on the west side of Colorado Highway 125. Waterfowl and many species of animals abound. Often sighted are mallard and gadwall ducks, sandpipers, willet, American avocet, great blue heron, hawks, eagles, and falcons, along with badger, coyote, pronghorn antelope, beaver, and muskrat.

STAGECOACH STATE PARK

Hours/Season: Overnight; year-round
Area: 866 acres; 780 surface water acres
Facilities: 100 campsites, 50 picnic sites, 2 boat ramps, marina, 5 miles of hiking/ biking trails, dump station, showers, swim beach
Attractions: Camping, group camping, picnicking, interpretive programs, boating, fishing, swimming, waterskiing, sailboarding, jet skiing, hiking, biking, cross-country skiing, ice skating, ice fishing
Nearby: Silver Creek and Service Creek Wilderness Area
Access: From I-70 67 miles west of Denver at Silverthorne, go north 38 miles on Highway 9 to US 40; on US 40, go west 6 miles to Highway 134, then go west 27 miles on Highway 134 to Highway 131, and on Highway 131 go north 17 miles to CR 14; turn right and follow the signs

Stagecoach State Park is located in the lower elevation of the Yampa River Valley, set amid rolling native grasslands, shrubs, sagebrush, and flowering plants, with aspen and lodgepole forests sweeping down from the mountain ridges above. Visitors enjoy unobstructed scenic views of the Flat Top Mountains to the southwest, the Service and Morrison Mountains to the east, and the cliff face of Blacktail Mountain to the north. The beautiful drive to the park over

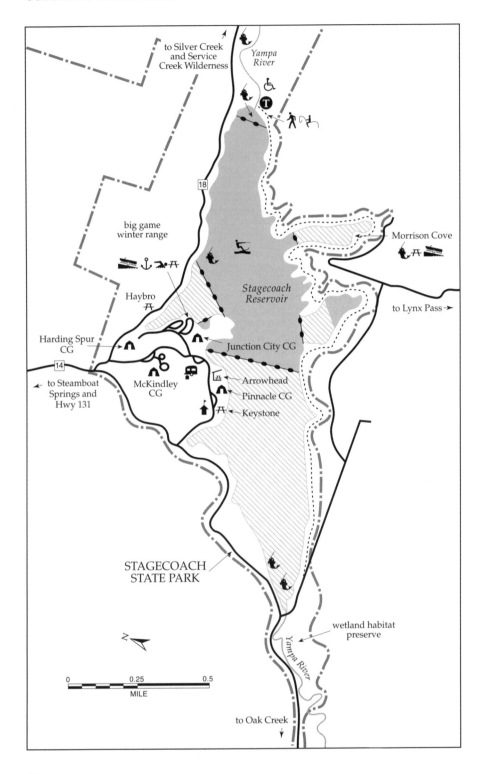

County Road 14 sets the stage for the spectacular Stagecoach Reservoir, seen as you come over the last rise. These rich natural surroundings, including the Yampa River, which passes directly through the lake, complement the Old West history from which Stagecoach State Park derives its name.

Early explorers and settlers were drawn to this part of northwest Colorado by the promise of rich agricultural and coal mining potential. Settlement in the Stagecoach area began in earnest by the late nineteenth century. The park itself is part of what locals called Egeria Park, a large open area bounded by Oak Ridge to the west and Green Ridge to the east. The name Egeria is a Ute word meaning "crooked woman," suggesting the winding course of the Yampa River through the valley.

As the area prospered, boosted by the growing wealth of the farms, ranches, and mines, stagecoaches began traveling over Yellow Jacket Pass (so named for the wasps in the area, although legend has it that an outlaw wearing a yellow jacket once roamed these parts), and delivered goods and passengers to Oak Creek and Steamboat Springs. This stage route passed right through where the present reservoir and dam are located, with a stage stop near where the main park entrance now operates.

Agriculture and coal mining still contribute to the local economy, although the latter has slowed considerably from a high of ten operational mines down to a current four. Recreation now is the center of the local economy, with parks like Stagecoach playing a growing role in the ever-increasing recreational needs of Colorado.

Camping in the expansive scenery is a year-round activity at Stagecoach. The Junction City, Pinnacle, Harding Spur, and McKindley campgrounds are all located on the northwest side of the park. They can accommodate tents or recreational vehicles. One campsite is available for the physically challenged and can be found at Pinnicle Campground. Junction City and Pinnacle campgrounds have pull-through sites and electrical hookups.

Picnicking facilities at Stagecoach are located at Morrison Cove, also the site of the South Shore boat ramp, as well as at Arrowhead, Keystone, and Haybro picnic areas. Each site comes with a picnic table and standing grill. The Arrowhead group picnic area can accommodate up to 100 people on a reservations-only basis.

The interpretive programs at Stagecoach State Park have an educational focus that goes beyond a nature walk. School children from the surrounding area visit the park for a winter environmental outdoors day; presentations on water sampling, hunting, fishing, plant life, and wildlife; and in the spring a huge Earth Day celebration. A unique attraction during the summer is a performance by the Wocus Bay Singers, a Native American drumming and singing group.

Boaters enjoy both the scenic vistas and the several coves where they can find a quieter setting. Access to the lake is provided at the marina near Pinnacle Campground and at the Morrison Cove South Shore area. Waterskiing is permitted only in designated areas of the reservoir, and boats towing skiers must keep 150 feet from shore, have an observer on board besides the operator, and tow skiers in a counterclockwise pattern.

The fishing is good at Stagecoach, famous for its hard-fighting rainbows, with brown, brook, and Snake River cutthroat trout also to be caught, along with northern pike and kokanee salmon. The reservoir has several coves that provide a quiet shelter from the lake's busier activities. There is ample room, however, for both fishing and other water sports, as the lake is more than 3 miles long.

Although only 5 miles of horseback and hiking trails exist in the park, these offer good opportunities to view the abundant wildlife in the area, and are found along the south shore of the reservoir. Ice fishing and ice skating take place on the lake's

Stagecoach Lake from McKindley Campground

surface during sufficiently cold winter months. Cross-country skiing is allowed anywhere in the park when snow levels permit.

At the southwest corner of the lake is a wetland habitat preserve, through which the Yampa River flows. The scenic vistas provide a stunning backdrop for hiking in this park, with late spring offering the best opportunities for still seeing snow on the surrounding mountains. These features combine to offer the interested wildlife enthusiast the chance to see mule deer, elk, beaver, muskrat, blue grouse, sage grouse, duck, Canadian geese, hawks, prairie falcons, osprey, hawks, kestrels, great horned owls, and turkey vultures. Even a nesting pair of golden eagles has been observed.

As nature observers make their way along the trail, they also see a unique representation of prairie and wetland vegetation. Sagebrush, blue grass, bitterbrush, dryland sedge, chokecherry, gambel oak, and green rabbitbrush are found, along with the riparian sandbar vegetation, Geyer willow, alders, bog birch, and several species of rush, grass, and sedge.

If you continue driving on County Road 18 northeast, you can access the many hiking trails found in the Silver Creek and Service Creek Wilderness Area. The U.S. Forest Service at Yampa can provide needed maps and information (see appendix A).

PEARL LAKE STATE PARK

Hours/Season: Overnight; year-round. Closed to camping in winter; foot and snowmobile access only
Area: 350 acres; 167 surface water acres
Facilities: 41 campsites, 8 picnic sites, boat ramp
Attractions: Camping, picnicking, interpretive programs, boating, sailboarding, fishing, cross-country skiing, ice fishing
Nearby: Mount Zirkel Wilderness Area, Steamboat Lake State Park
Access: From Steamboat Springs on US 40, go west 2 miles on US 40 to CR 129; turn north and go 23 miles, through Clark, to Pearl Lake Road; go east 2 miles to the park entrance

▲The drive to Pearl Lake through the Yampa Valley, along the Elk River, is an exceptionally scenic byway that features (in the spring and early summer) lush, rolling green meadows and pasture lands that enfold quaint farms and horse and cattle ranches. Framing the horizons are a string of mountain ranges located within the Routt National Forest and Mount Zirkel Wilderness Area that include parts of the Park, Sierra Madre, and Sawtooth Ranges. Just northwest of Pearl Lake, which itself lies just west of the Continental Divide, is the rugged and somewhat isolated Hahns Peak, which dominates the horizon. And between Pearl Lake and Hahns Peak is Steamboat Lake State Park, just 8 miles from Pearl Lake State Park. The spectacular vistas never seem to end.

Pearl Lake was completed in 1962. It is named in honor of Mrs. Pearl Hartt, a local resident who was instrumental in securing the state's land acquisition for construction of the lake.

The turnoff to Pearl Lake escorts you through a beautiful approach to the lake, with mountains reaching out to touch you. Once at the lake, park and walk down short forested paths until the full splendor of Pearl Lake's sylvan setting reveals itself. The peace and tranquillity of the place are immediate. At over 8,000 feet, Pearl Lake is truly a mountain lake, and reflects on its silent waters the majestic peaks surrounding it.

Camping facilities include forty-one sites located north of the boat ramp. The amenities at Pearl Lake are as simple as possible, uncluttered and relaxed. The woods hug the shoreline in places, giving the look of an undisturbed high-mountain lake.

Adjacent to the campsites are picnic sites that allow good views of serene Pearl Lake. Interpretive programs are available through the park office at Steamboat Lake State Park.

A boat ramp is at the end of Pearl Lake Road. The entire lake is a designated wakeless boating area. Quiet and unhurried is the emphasis at Pearl Lake.

Pearl Lake has, of course, its fishing, featuring mainly brook trout, Snake River cutthroat, brown trout, and grayling. And it is the fishing that visitors mostly come for. Some very special

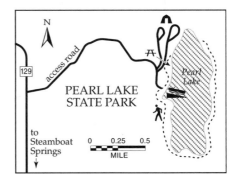

fishing regulations are in effect at Pearl Lake to improve the survival of the fish and insure a trophy-sized catch. All fish under 18 inches long must be released alive. Bag limit is two fish over 18 inches long, and only fishing with flies and lures is permitted.

Some hiking is available at the lake. But the unique gift that Pearl Lake offers visitors is its beautiful simplicity. You can gather yourself together here, picnic in the forests above the lake, sit quietly for hours waiting for a bite on your line, or walk slowly beside the lake and let it work its magic on you.

Birdlife often seen on or near the lake includes ducks and shorebirds, hawks, golden and bald eagles, sandhill cranes, and nearly 200 other bird species. Mammals that might come into view are mule deer, elk, red fox, marmot, beaver, porcupine, and a variety of squirrels. The photography opportunities are many. The combination lake and mountain setting challenges even the best photographer to capture the serene beauty of the place and moment.

Many more hiking trails can be found at the Mount Zirkel Wilderness Area just east of Pearl Lake. Colorado Highway 129 has several forest roads branching off from it and leading to the Mount Zirkel trailheads. Driving from Steamboat Springs on Colorado 129 to Pearl Lake takes you first to the Mad Creek and Red Dirt trailheads, 5 to 6 miles north of Steamboat. Near the town of Clark are Forest Roads 440 and 400, the righthand forks leading to the Roaring Fork and Hinman, South Fork, and Three Islands Lake trailheads. About 4 miles north of Steamboat Lake State Park, just out of Columbine, you can take Forest Roads 550 and 500 to the Manzanares trailhead. For more detailed information, contact the Routt National Forest office or the Hahns Peak district office (see appendix A) and ask for the Mount Zirkel Wilderness Area map.

View of Pearl Lake

STEAMBOAT LAKE STATE PARK

Hours/Season: Overnight; year-round
Area: 1,203 acres; 1,058 surface water acres
Facilities: 185 campsites, 35 picnic sites, 3 boat ramps, marina, swim beach, visitors center, amphitheater, dump station, snack bar
Attractions: Camping, picnicking, nature programs, boating, fishing, swimming, waterskiing, jet skiing, sailing, hiking, horseback riding, cross-country skiing, ice skating, ice fishing, snowmobiling
Access: From Steamboat Springs on US 40, go west 2 miles on US 40 to CR 129; turn north and go 26 miles, through Clark, to the park entrance near Hahns Peak Village

The majestic mountain valley setting of Steamboat Lake State Park is one of the most scenic locations for vacationing in all of Colorado. Indeed, a survey of Colorado State Parks rangers showed that Steamboat Lake was their favorite vacation spot. Adding to the beauty of the lake is stately Hahns Peak, a 10,839-foot volcanic mountain once famous for its gold and silver mines, located just a few miles from the park's north entrance. The nearby soaring peaks of the Continental Divide on the eastern skyline and the towering mountains to the south complete the mountain accents around the lake. Located just 26 miles north of the famous ski and summer resort of Steamboat Springs, the lake and its recreational offerings are a focal point for the area's outdoor enthusiasts.

The park was completed in 1968 when the Steamboat Lake Dam was constructed to capture the waters of Mill, Larsen, Floyd, and Dutch Creeks. The lake serves as a water storage area, but was built primarily as a recreational resource for this part of northern Colorado.

The Sunrise Vista and Dutch Hill campgrounds are located in the northwest section of the park, near the marina. The name Sunrise Vista was well chosen, as the campground has an eastern view across the lake to the soaring mountains of the Continental Divide. The camping sites accommodate tents and recreational vehicles, with some pull-through sites in each campground. Only one camping unit (tent or recreational vehicle) per site is allowed, with a maximum of six people per site. Camping supplies are readily available at the marina store and at Hahns Peak Village, located just east of the park's north entrance.

With so many scenic vistas surrounding the park, picnicking is a good way to enjoy a day at the lake.

As at so many other state parks, the rangers and staff at Steamboat Lake offer outstanding interpretive programs. Some of these are conducted at the park's amphitheater located at Sunrise Vista Campground, along the nature trail, or at key locations throughout the park. The topics covered might include fishing secrets, wilderness ethics, hummingbirds, birds of prey, exploring the nighttime sky, and the mining history of the Hahns Peak area.

Boating is a popular pastime with visitors to Steamboat. However, to help ensure the tranquil atmosphere on the lake, almost half the surface area is zoned for wakeless boating only. The Steamboat Lake marina, located near the campgrounds on the northeast shore of the lake, offers fishing and personal watercraft rentals, pontoon boats with sleepers, groceries, propane, and other supplies to boaters and campers.

Fishing is also very popular at Steamboat Lake. Although it is very large, the

101

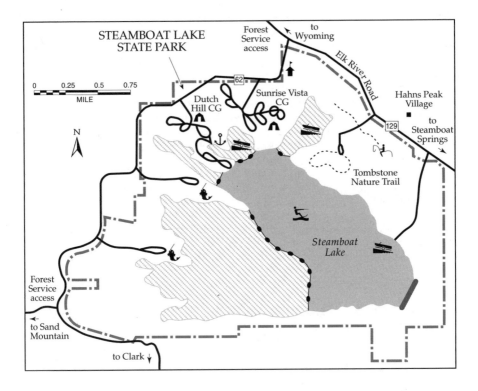

lake has a number of coves that give one the feel of a smaller mountain lake and provide excellent habitat for good-sized rainbow trout. Brook, Snake River cut-throat, and brown are other trout species commonly caught from the lake. Sage Flats, Rainbow Ridge, and Meadow Point are fishing access areas; Sage Flats also has a boat ramp.

Hikers can take advantage of scenic walks around the lake, or visit the Tombstone Nature Trail located at Placer Cove. This 0.75-mile walk is a self-guided tour with an accompanying brochure. Along the trail you learn about the nature and origins of Hahns Peak, the village, Steamboat Lake Dam, and the lake itself.

Horseback riding is offered by a park concessionaire. The trails circle part of the lake, offering plenty of photographic opportunities or just the sheer joy of riding through the backcountry.

Winter is a special time at Steamboat Lake that offers outstanding recreational opportunities. There are miles of trails for snowmobiling and many more miles for scenic cross-country skiing, although none of the trails are groomed—so you must break your own. In addition, there are the challenges of ice fishing. The quiet winter setting might be just what someone needs, after the more crowded and busy down-hill skiing at major ski resorts.

Steamboat Lake State Park is near many other outdoor recreation and cultural/ urban opportunities found throughout the Yampa River Valley. There are many miles of hiking in all the surrounding mountains and in Routt National Forest. Information on hiking is available by calling the Routt National Forest Office (see appendix A). You can also ask the rangers at Steamboat Lake for brochures and information they provide at the park. Other outdoor activities in the area include

Trail guide making the tour around Steamboat Lake

river rafting, boating, mountain biking, llama treks, hot-air ballooning, kayaking, rock climbing, pack trips, tennis, volleyball, and wilderness/wildlife tours.

Cultural events include chamber music concerts, pop concerts, wine festivals, soccer tournaments, jazz festivals, and rodeos. The Steamboat Springs Chamber Resort Association publishes an activity guide and events brochure (see appendix A).

The Arkansas River at Royal Gorge

SOUTH REGION

Colorado's South Region stretches across the prairie from almost the Kansas state line in the east, south from the Denver Metro Region to the New Mexico border, and west across the mountains of the Continental Divide to where the West Slope of the Rockies begins. From the Arkansas River system, which resembles the wetlands of an eastern seashore and stretches in a 148-mile arc across the middle of the state from below Leadville southeast to Pueblo, to the low plateau-and-mesa canyons bordering Lake Pueblo 112 miles south of Denver, to some of the most famous mountain ranges in America—the Collegiate Peaks in southcentral Colorado and the Sangre de Cristo Mountains in southern Colorado—the South Region has it all for outdoor recreation adventures.

Natural wonders abound in the South Region. At Manitou Springs near Colorado Springs is the Cave of the Winds, an underground and colorful cave of inspiring beauty. West of Mueller State Park is the Florissant Fossil Beds National Monument. This outdoor wonder is home to over 80,000 fossil specimens of not animal, but plant and insect, life buried almost 40 million years ago.

Hikers have an assortment of high-country trails to travel, found in the scenic Rio Grande, San Isabel, and Pike National Forests. These lands claim twenty-six of Colorado's fifty-five peaks known as "fourteeners" because of their elevations above 14,000 feet. Mountains famous in the history of both Colorado and the opening of the West are included in this impressive list . . . Pikes Peak, Mount Elbert (Colorado's highest), Spanish Peaks (just a shade under the fourteener designation but famous for the part they played in the days of Kit Carson), and the Collegiate Peaks of Harvard, Columbia, Princeton, and Yale. Much of the 470-mile-long Colorado Trail, stretching from Denver to Durango, can be accessed from lands that it crosses as it passes through this South Region of the state.

The milder climate of this region allows for more year-round use of state parks. During hot summer days on the plains, the temperatures reach 90°F in the lowlands. Whereas in winter, skiers at Wolf Creek Ski Area (18 miles south of South Fork) find slopes that receive the greatest annual snowfall (440 inches!) in the state. All through this region, cross-country skiers enjoy some of the most scenic and spectacular trails in Colorado.

The western half of the South Region is dominated by ponderosa pine, aspen,

COLORADO STATE PARKS

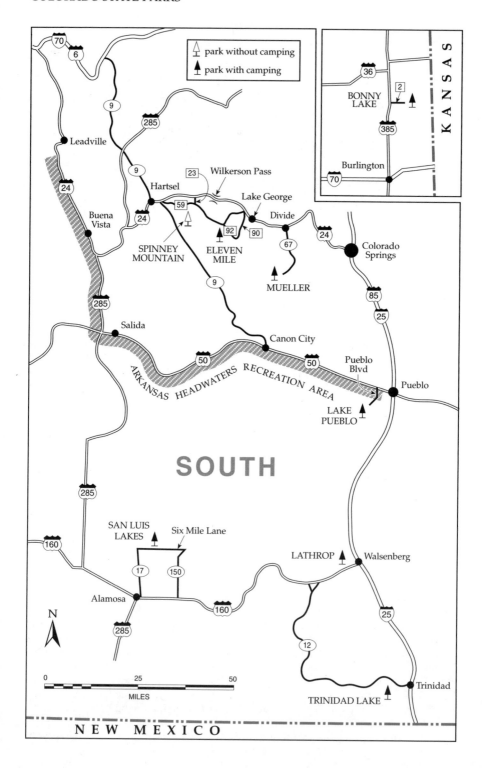

park without camping

park with camping

KANSAS

36

2

BONNY
LAKE

385

Burlington

70

70

6

9

285

Leadville

9

24

Hartsel

23   Wilkerson Pass

59   Lake George

Buena
Vista   24   92   Divide   24

90

SPINNEY
MOUNTAIN   ELEVEN
MILE   67   Colorado
Springs

9   MUELLER   85

25

Salida   Canon City

ARKANSAS HEADWATERS RECREATION AREA   50   50   Pueblo
Blvd   Pueblo

285   LAKE
PUEBLO

SOUTH

SAN LUIS
LAKES   Six Mile Lane

160   LATHROP   Walsenberg

17   150

Alamosa   160   25

N   285   12

0   25   50

MILES   TRINIDAD LAKE   Trinidad

NEW MEXICO

Douglas fir, and lodgepole pine forests, at between 6,000 feet and 10,000 feet, along with the Colorado columbine, the state flower. Above these elevations are found forests of Engelmann spruce and subalpine fir. This western half lies in the southern portion of the Rocky Mountains, from elevations of between 5,000 feet to 14,000 feet. In stark contrast, the entire eastern section of the South Region is prairie of between 3,000 feet to 4,500 feet . . . grasslands, sage, and shrub, with some low-growing cactus. Where water cuts a streambed through the plains, cottonwoods and alder line the banks.

In the mountains of the South Region are found elk, coyote, black bear, mule deer, marmot, snowshoe hare, weasels, and wolverine. Birds of the South Region's mountains include mountain chickadee, blue grouse, Cooper's hawk, Steller's jay, owl, raven, and wrens. The plains are populated by the golden eagle, prairie falcon, meadowlark, sparrow, and kestrel, along with the western rattlesnake, prairie dogs, coyote, gopher, and pronghorn.

Many of the cities found in the South Region played a key role in the history of Colorado. Just below Mueller State Park is the town of Cripple Creek, once home to where almost half of all the gold in the state was found. The riches from Cripple Creek flowed east to build the resort town of Colorado Springs, home to the U.S. Air Force Academy and Olympic Training facilities. Within a few miles of Colorado Springs is found the National Natural Landmark of mysterious, giant red

Columbine flowers alongside a mountain path

sandstone formations known as the "Garden of the Gods." This area closely resembles its cousin, Roxborough State Park, which is just outside of Denver.

The major highways of the South Region include Interstate 25, running north–
south and just a few miles east of the Front Range on its way past Trinidad and into
New Mexico; US Highway 50, running east–west through Pueblo and providing
access to the Arkansas River; and Highway 24, heading west from Colorado
Springs and providing access to Mueller, Eleven Mile, and Spinney Mountain State
Parks. Further south, Highway 160 reaches west past Lathrop and San Luis Lakes
State Parks. In the easternmost portion of the South Region, Interstate 70 passes
south of Bonny Lake State Park just before crossing into western Kansas.

South Region boasts of some of the best trophy fishing waters in the state. Eleven
Mile State Park, Spinney Mountain State Park, and Arkansas Headwaters Recreation Area offer fishermen both river and lake fishing. Boaters enjoy the wide-open
spaces on Lake Pueblo, which offers scenic coves, plateau and mountain vistas, and
expansive, clean, warm waters that allow for enjoyment from spring through fall.
Lake Pueblo State Park rarely knows a true ice-bound condition.

The famous Arkansas Headwaters Recreation Area offers almost 150 miles of
rafting, fishing, camping, and picnicking along its scenic route from Leadville to
Pueblo. White-water adventure at its best awaits rafters at Brown's Canyon and
through the 1,000-foot-high cliffs of Royal Gorge. Calmer waters are found at many
spots along this spectacular river, especially from Canon City to Pueblo . . . but
most visitors opt for something with a little more "bite" to it, like Sunshine, Pin-
ball, and Lose-Your-Lunch Rapids!

A quiet cove on Eleven Mile Reservoir

A trip down south above New Mexico to Trinidad Lake State Park yields a high-country setting near where the historic Santa Fe Trail once crossed between states. Toward the middle of the state, San Luis Lakes State Park lies nestled in the scenic San Luis Valley, just west of majestic Mount Blanca and at the foot of the spectacular Great Sand Dunes National Monument. These 700-foot-high sand dunes are the highest in North America, and rival their distant cousins in Saudi Arabia.

Because there are no state parks found in the southeastern section of Colorado, Lake Pueblo, Lathrop, Trinidad Lake, and Mueller State Parks draw visitors all the way from Kansas, Oklahoma, and New Mexico. Mueller State Park's alpine trails, camping, and picnicking offer cool relief from hot summers on the plains. Bonny Lake State Park serves the people of western Kansas as well as Colorado, offering a tree-lined riparian wetland habitat that has been affectionately dubbed the "oasis on the plains." Visitors all along the Front Range seek out these beautiful parks as natural retreats from the demands of city life . . . places whose diversity offers alpine forests, southwest high-desert lakes, and mountain rivers.

The South Region gives visitors a diverse offering of state parks scattered throughout the high country of the southern Rocky Mountains. From Trinidad to Mueller, from Spinney Mountain to San Luis Lakes, the state parks look out upon the magnificent vistas of soaring peaks and expansive valleys. Some of the best fishing in Colorado is found in the South Region, along with a wealth of historical sites. The Arkansas River draws rafting enthusiasts from around the world, making the South Region a complete vacation destination.

BONNY LAKE STATE PARK

Hours/Season: Overnight; year-round
Area: 5,000 acres; 1,900 surface water acres
Facilities: 200 campsites, 98 picnic sites, group picnic facility, 5 boat ramps, swimming area, fish-cleaning station, marina, showers, laundry, dump station
Attractions: Camping, picnicking, group picnicking, nature trail, boating, fishing, swimming, waterskiing, jet skiing, sailing, wildlife observation, cross-country skiing, winter camping, ice fishing
Nearby: Flagler State Wildlife Area, Hugo State Wildlife Area, Karval Reservoir and State Wildlife Area, Ramah Reservoir; Old Cheyenne County Jail Museum, Kit Carson Museum, Lincoln County Museum, Schoolhouse Museum
Access: From Burlington, on I-70 nearly at the eastern border with Kansas, drive 23 miles north on US 385, then east 1.5 miles on CR 2 to reach the main entrance on the south shore, or CR 3 to reach the north shore area (these two roads circle the lake)

You can drive for endless miles over the rolling grasslands and semi-arid plains of far eastern Colorado. Desert yucca and scrub cactus suggest a sparse rainfall and underscore the high value placed on water. If traveling on US Highway 385, you eventually see a sign indicating Bonny Lake State Park. As you turn toward the east to enter the park, the terrain suddenly changes. Within minutes one sees a wetland and marsh scene reminiscent of Maryland's Chesapeake Bay. Soon a massive lake can be seen from behind sweeping stands of willow trees, large cottonwoods, and expanses of riparian open space, revealing an oasis-on-the-plains.

Bonny Lake State Park serves both the many recreational needs of the region and

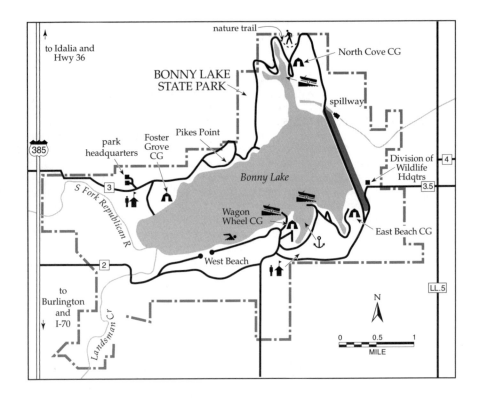

as a retreat, offering a diverse and scenic change from the high plains. This recreational wonderland sits in the broad valley of the South Fork of the Republican River, near the Kansas border.

The history of Bonny Lake reflects the struggles that have shaped this part of Colorado. The small town of Bonny once occupied land 5 miles southeast of the present state park. The town fought for its existence, along with the homesteaders who struggled to raise crops during the frequent droughts that plagued the Great Plains between 1889 and 1904. The town grew slowly, but faced another disaster in the spring of 1935. During the first two weeks of May that year, it rained almost constantly, culminating in the incredible flood storm of May 31. Then, two storms together dumped more than 24 inches of rainfall on the area in less than a day! The resulting flood caused widespread death and destruction. It took until 1951 before a suitable dam was constructed, at a height of 158 feet above the streambed. In 1966, the lake was designated as a state recreation area, and later became a state park in 1982.

All the campgrounds offer beautiful lake views. Wagon Wheel campground, located just southwest of the marina, is equipped with 26 sites having electrical hookups, located in Loop G. North Cove campground is a must for those wanting both a magnificent view of Bonny Lake and the added amenity of being situated along a quiet, long, narrow, tree-lined cove that offers even more of a "getting-away-from-it-all" experience. There are also campsites at East Beach campground, just south of the dam, and at Foster Grove campground on the north shore near the South Fork of the Republican River. Campers are limited to one camping unit and a maximum of six persons per campsite. Throughout the park, facilities and campsites are available for visitors with disabilities; call the park (see appendix A) for information (also see appendix B).

Picnicking is available near the North Cove, East Beach, Wagonwheel, and Foster Grove campgrounds. Visitors are free to picnic anywhere along the roads that allow parking.

The Test Site Point, located south of the dam, was used to test the various composites of soil and dam material that might be used in the dam's construction. Southeast of the dam is the Division of Wildlife Headquarters; this agency owns some property around the lake and helps manage the park.

Like the other eastern high-plains state parks, Bonny Lake is the area's main draw for boating and fishing enthusiasts. Water level fluctuations at Bonny Lake are usually minor, allowing boaters easy access year-round. Water-skiers must ski counterclockwise. Lake zoning information is available at the boat ramps for areas where wakeless boating is required and where waterskiing is permitted.

Considered one of the state's finest warm-water fisheries, Bonny reservoir is well-stocked with walleye, northern pike, freshwater drum, white bass, wiper, crappie, bluegill, and channel catfish. A fish-cleaning station is available near Wagon Wheel Campground, located near the main entrance on the south shore.

Marshlands along Bonny Lake

Picnic area at Bonny Lake

Pikes Point, along the northwest shore, is a local name given to a favorite spot for casting into the deeper waters off the point.

Two swim areas, one below the marina store and the other a larger and deeper area located at West Beach, west of Wagon Wheel campground, allow generous use of the lake's warm water. Please be advised, however, that no lifeguards are provided.

There is a short 0.2-mile nature trail north of the North Cove Campground; this trail crosses over the Bonny Prairie Nature Area while highlighting the short-grass prairie that once dominated the plains in eastern Colorado. Visitors see little blue-stem grass, prairie cone flowers, and prickly pear cactus. When cold enough, ice skating takes place near the Foster Cove Campground. No groomed trails exist for cross-country skiing. All through the fall and winter, bird-watching is popular, especially for snow geese, pelicans, and wood ducks.

Wildlife abounds at Bonny Lake. This is due in part to its being the largest body of freshwater in this section of eastern Colorado or western Kansas. Wildlife found at the lake includes mule and whitetail deer, rabbits, coyotes, badgers, muskrats, bobcats, and beavers (only buffalo seem to be missing in this impressive prairie wildlife list!). An 8-mile road winds around the lake and acts as a hiking trail. On a low-use midweek day, nature lovers and wildlife observers can enjoy a pleasant meander around Bonny Lake and perhaps see a significant number of the resident wildlife . . . and please remember to bring your camera! Because of the ring of cotton-wood trees surrounding the lake, autumn colors can be observed in the late fall, and is a season when wildlife observation is especially rewarded. Be aware, however, that hunting is permitted; check with park staff about seasons.

Like its western cousin, Barr Lake, Bonny Lake is located on the Central Flyway for birds migrating south from Canada. The famous birding area of Sandhill, in Nebraska, lies just to the northeast. Over 70,000 birds representing 250 species rest at Bonny Lake State Park during migrations. Some 30,000 to 50,000 birds actually winter on the lake. These include both snow and Canadian geese, pelicans, wood ducks, osprey, prairie falcons, and golden and bald eagles.

Other outdoor recreation can be found at the Flagler State Wildlife Area, the Hugo State Wildlife Area at Kinney Lake, the Karval Reservoir and State Wildlife Area, and Ramah Reservoir.

The prairie surrounding Bonny Lake State Park has its own rich historical setting. The counties of Yuma, Elbert, Lincoln, Cheyenne, and Carson have come to be known as "Colorado's Outback." Attractions with a historical flavor abound. Antique shops in the area offer pioneer collectibles. Other attractions that these counties offer throughout the year include fairs, rodeos, horse shows, western dances, folk festivals, carnivals, and (of course) cattle drives! Please call the Prairie Development Corporation (see appendix A) for information.

The romance of the rails is alive and well in this part of the prairie. You can enjoy an exciting ride from Falcon to Limon aboard the Cadillac and Lake City Railway. Be prepared for their unusual fare, including murder mysteries, melodramas, county fairs, and even private charters.

The town of Burlington transports visitors back to a turn-of-the-century community know as Old Town. You can shop at the mercantile, visit with the blacksmith, or relax with a glass of lemonade in the saloon. This town also has a State Welcome Center that offers brochures and maps to local area attractions. Pioneer and Old West history museums include the Old Cheyenne County Jail Museum at Cheyenne Wells, the Kit Carson Museum in Kit Carson, the Lincoln County Museum in Hugo, and the Schoolhouse Museum in Limon.

MUELLER STATE PARK AND WILDLIFE AREA

Hours/Season: Overnight; year-round
Area: 12,103 acres; 15 surface water acres
Facilities: 90 campsites, group campground, 41 picnic sites, dump station, laundry, showers, amphitheater
Attractions: Camping, picnicking, interpretive programs, hiking, wildlife observation, fishing, biking, horseback riding, cross-country skiing, ice fishing, winter camping, ice skating (limited)
Nearby: Colorado Trail, South Park, Pikes Peak, Florissant Fossil Beds National Monument
Access: From Colorado Springs, south of Denver on I-25, drive 25 miles west on US 24 to Divide, then go 3.5 miles south on CO 67 to the park entrance

Mueller State Park and Wildlife Area is as rich an outdoor natural treasure as the once fabulous gold mines of Cripple Creek, located 15 miles south of the park. Mueller rests in the very shadow of Pikes Peak, a massive fourteener that fills the park's eastern horizon. To the south, the park looks out to the distant Sangre de Cristo Mountains, and to the west views the equally distant Collegiate Peaks and the Continental Divide. Mueller stands on a high alpine ridge atop an extended plateau that reaches to the very base of the distant mountain ranges. Mueller, then, is

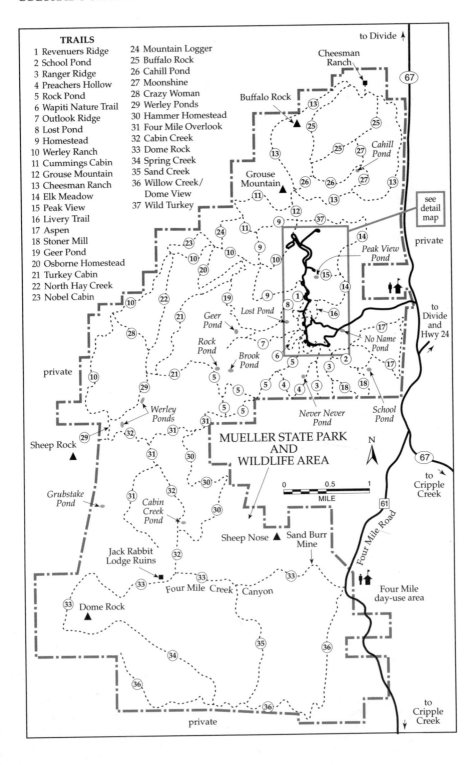

TRAILS

1 Revenuers Ridge
2 School Pond
3 Ranger Ridge
4 Preachers Hollow
5 Rock Pond
6 Wapiti Nature Trail
7 Outlook Ridge
8 Lost Pond
9 Homestead
10 Werley Ranch
11 Cummings Cabin
12 Grouse Mountain
13 Cheesman Ranch
14 Elk Meadow
15 Peak View
16 Livery Trail
17 Aspen
18 Stoner Mill
19 Geer Pond
20 Osborne Homestead
21 Turkey Cabin
22 North Hay Creek
23 Nobel Cabin

24 Mountain Logger
25 Buffalo Rock
26 Cahill Pond
27 Moonshine
28 Crazy Woman
29 Werley Ponds
30 Hammer Homestead
31 Four Mile Overlook
32 Cabin Creek
33 Dome Rock
34 Spring Creek
35 Sand Creek
36 Willow Creek/
   Dome View
37 Wild Turkey

to Divide

Cheesman Ranch

67

Buffalo Rock

Grouse Mountain

Cahill Pond

see detail map

private

Peak View Pond

to Divide and Hwy 24

Lost Pond

Geer Pond

Rock Pond

Brook Pond

No Name Pond

private

Werley Ponds

Never Never Pond

School Pond

Sheep Rock

MUELLER STATE PARK AND WILDLIFE AREA

N

67

to Cripple Creek

Grubstake Pond

Cabin Creek Pond

0   0.5   1
MILE

61

Four Mile Road

Jack Rabbit Lodge Ruins

Sheep Nose   Sand Burr Mine

Four Mile day-use area

Dome Rock

Four Mile Creek Canyon

to Cripple Creek

private

the perfect place for hiking where expansive views are favored.

Since the late 1800s, the area now designated as Mueller State Park was given over to homesteading, small ranches, and farming, following the stampede of prospectors who sought riches during the Cripple Creek gold boom. But beginning in the 1950s, W. E. Mueller bought up ten of the ranches and homesteads to create the Mueller Ranch. Later the Mueller family designated their cattle ranch as a game preserve. In 1980, through donation and purchase from the Mueller family, Colorado State Parks and the Colorado Division of Wildlife acquired over 12,000 acres, from which the state park was built.

As you enter the park you are greeted by massive stands of Douglas fir and aspen that sweep right up to the road that travels the length of the park. Shortly after you begin the short drive west toward the park's interior, the natural setting of Mueller quickly reveals itself. Spaced almost every 0.25 mile or so along the park road are scenic picnic tables and trailheads. By walking to any of these sites, you can look out across miles of rolling valleys and forests below the park, which form a green carpet stretching to all horizons. You know at once that here is a scenic wonderland where hiking is a major pastime.

Camping at Mueller State Park is enhanced by the spectacular scenery

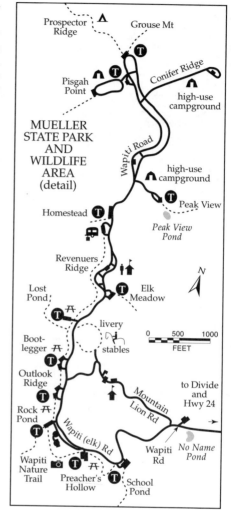

and fresh, crisp natural surroundings. There are four sections to the 90-site campground, located at the north end of the park drive in a lush forest setting of pine, spruce, fir, and aspen. Campers enjoy the magnificent mountain views that have made Mueller famous. The campground can accommodate recreational vehicles and tents, with 12 walk-in tent sites and a reservable group campground also available. Modern rest rooms, hot showers, and laundry facilities are conveniently located in the campground. All sites, except the walk-in tent sites, have electrical hookups, with drinking water nearby. Besides the normal campground rules, the park requests that campers park their vehicles only on the paved campsite pads, refrain from cutting any timber for firewood, and use stakes or poles instead of tying ropes or lines to nearby trees.

Mueller is a picnic park, if ever there was one. Each site offers privacy and the scented shade of pine and aspen, and most afford scenic views to the distant

Livery from across Lost Pond picnic area

mountains. The air is fresh, sweet, and inviting. Facilities include barbecue grills, tables, drinking water, and rest rooms. Most picnic spots are at or near trail-heads . . . so after a hearty lunch, picnickers can meander down the trail or seek the cool comfort of the surrounding shade. It is also desirable to plan for a pleasant hike to end with a picnic lunch or supper! Visitors find Mueller incredibly clean and well-cared for . . . pristine picnicking, undisturbed by the campgrounds located further up the road.

The rangers lead hikes during the summer and interpret the rich ecological and geological heritage the park offers. Group tours and presentations at the park's amphitheater can be scheduled by request.

Mueller offers over 85 miles of hiking trails on forty-five marked and established trails throughout the park (pets are not permitted on trails). The southernmost trails are more easily accessed by driving south on Teller County Road 61, until reaching the Four Mile day-use area entrance. One of the more popular trails in this vicinity is the Dome Rock Trail (9.6 miles round trip), which circles the 9,044-foot peak of that name and takes you past the remains of Jack Rabbit Lodge, constructed in the early 1900s, to the base of Dome Rock. The "rock" rises 800 feet above the valley floor, with the 640 acres surrounding its base designated a Colorado natural area. Spring Creek and Sand Creek trails connect the Dome Rock Trail to the Willow

Creek Trail to the south, for several loop hike options. Heading north from the Dome Rock Trail is Cabin Creek Trail, which connects with Four Mile Overlook, Hammer Homestead, and Werley Ranch trails. These trails are deep in the park's western interior. Werley Ranch Trail winds northward all the way to the campground at the north end of the park road.

One of the more demanding hikes in the park is the Four Mile Overlook Trail. This 9.2-mile trail begins at the Rock Pond trailhead near the main entrance and travels through stands of limber pine, Douglas fir, and ponderosa pine. One of the outstanding features of Mueller State Park is found everywhere . . . the most wonderful high-alpine scents of fir, pine, aspen, and wildflowers together with musty forest floors and thick carpets of grasses! Once at the Four Mile Overlook, hikers can look down into Four Mile Canyon and Creek, view the top of Dome Rock, and see the backside of the Sheep Nose formation. In the far distance are the Mosquito Range, the Sangre de Cristos, the Collegiate Peaks, and Wright's Reservoir.

From the main entrance road, the first trail encountered is School Pond, a gentle 1.5-mile trail that takes you down to a small, quiet pond, excellent for viewing wildlife in the early morning or at dusk. The trail features open meadows rich with wildflowers in late spring and early summer, views south from a ridge, and a trip back through conifer forests. Also in this area are Aspen, Ranger Ridge, and Stoner Mill trails. Ranger Ridge Trail loops west to connect with Preacher's Hollow Trail, which connects with Rock Pond Trail. Located a short distance from the School Pond Trail is the Wapiti Self-Guided Nature Trail. A trail brochure highlights this short but delightful 0.8-mile walk through a variety of ecosystems where many plants and animals can be observed. A Watchable Wildlife kiosk and overlook completes the trail.

A more difficult but spectacular hike is the Outlook Ridge Trail. This almost 2-mile trail follows a ridge line to a series of beautiful views from the Raven Ridge, Red Tail, and Lone Eagle overlooks. The spectacular Collegiate Peaks (so called because the peaks are named after famous colleges—Harvard, Princeton, etc.) of the Sawatch Range to the west are the dominating feature on the western horizon.

As you continue north along the park road, numerous trailheads are found on both sides of the road. Geer Pond and Homestead trails head west; Elk Meadow and Peak View trails head east. From the campground at the north end of the park road, other longer hikes include the Cheesman Ranch Trail, which makes a long loop in the northern reaches of the park and takes the hiker past the remains of the old Cheesman homestead (a red barn and log cabin). Other trails in this area include Grouse Mountain, Wild Turkey, Cahill Pond, Buffalo Rock, Dynamite Cabin, and Cummings Cabin trails. For information on these and other trails, ask at the entrance stations or park headquarters for the Recreational Trails Map.

Fishing is limited at Mueller. Only Four Mile Creek and a few ponds stocked with trout are available for anglers. There is also horse trailer parking located across Lost Pond picnic area. Of the park's 85 miles of trail, 55 are rideable.

The winter sports offered at Mueller include cross-country skiing, sledding, and snowtubing. The many hiking trails are natural cross-country ski trails, while the park has set aside three hills for snowtubing. A brochure on winter recreational information is available on request.

The excellent wildlife observing opportunity at Mueller State Park is in part the result of it being a former private game preserve. Today bighorn sheep and elk flourish, with both these herds sharing residence between the Pikes Peak area and Mueller State Park. Deer, eagles, hawks, and many other species common to the park's altitude of 9,500 feet are abundant.

Looking south from the School Pond trailhead

While Mueller State Park offers more than enough to both draw and keep visitors, there are other recreational opportunities nearby worth noting. Pike National Forest is located due east, north, and west of Mueller, extending over 60 miles in length. For hardy hikers and mountain climbers, there are hundreds of miles of trail and five fourteeners (Pikes Peak nearby, and in the Fairplay area to the west are Mounts Democrat, Lincoln, Bross, and Sherman). The Colorado Trail passes between Georgia Pass and Kenosha Pass, offering spectacular views across the South Park area. More than 50 miles of this trail are within an easy drive of Mueller State Park. A comprehensive recreational and hiking trail map of Pike National Forest can be obtained by calling the Pikes Peak Ranger District in Colorado Springs or the South Park Ranger District in Fairplay (see appendix A).

Just 12 miles west of the park is the famous Florissant Fossil Beds National Monument, featuring volcanic fossils of giant redwoods, insects, and plants. A series of trails through the monument offer glimpses into the distant past of plant life, rather than the fossilized animal remains offered at places like Dinosaur National Park.

ELEVEN MILE STATE PARK

Hours/Season: Overnight; year-round
Area: 4,075 acres; 3,405 surface water acres
Facilities: 350 campsites, 14 picnic sites, dump station, laundry, showers, 3 boat ramps
Attractions: Camping, picnicking, interpretive programs, boating, fishing, sailboarding, jet skiing, hiking, biking, cross-country skiing, ice skating, ice fishing, snowtubing
Access: From Colorado Springs, south of Denver on I-25, take US 24 west for 38 miles to Lake George; 1 mile west of Lake George, turn left on CR 90, then onto CR 92, and follow it south for 10 miles

Eleven Mile State Park lies in the southeastern corner of a vast and scenic 900-square-mile high-altitude upland valley known as "South Park," in the South Region. This grassland area is bordered by Pike National Forest. The surrounding mountains include the Tarryall Range, Pikes Peak, and the snowcapped mountains of the Continental Divide. Eleven Mile Canyon Reservoir is almost 7 miles long, with an average depth of 50 feet, and is fed by the South Platte River. A bedrock formation found throughout the area known as Pikes Peak Granite crops out or underlies nearly all of the north side of the reservoir and much of the southeast shoreline. This rock formation accents the scenic setting of Eleven Mile State Park and provides fishermen solid ground from which to cast or picnickers a unique place to enjoy the view. The reservoir was added to the state park system in 1960 under an agreement with the Denver Water Board.

At 8,600 feet, this is a high-altitude park. Weather conditions can change dramatically, especially when winds sweep down from the nearby mountains. Dress accordingly and protect from sunburn, which can come easily at this altitude.

Eleven Mile State Park offers over 300 campsites that can accommodate tents and recreational vehicles. Campers find little shelter at the campgrounds. An open look across the vast reservoir to the surrounding distant mountains is predominant at Eleven Mile. Rocky Ridge and North Shore campgrounds are located near the main park entrance on the northeast side of the lake. The North Shore campground is rather large, sits close to the shoreline, and hosts the park's amphitheater. The Rocky Ridge campground sits above the North Shore campground and affords a more downward view to the lake. Two boat ramps are found in this area. For the more adventurous campers, 25 primitive walk-in or boat-in campsites are located in the backcountry area of the park, near the east end of the reservoir south of the main entrance. Stoll Mountain campground is a mile or so north of the main entrance on County Road 92; at the junction with County Road 59, turn left to head south down the other side of the lake. Cross Creek campground and Sucker Cove fishing access are located at the far northwestern corner of the lake. Farther south are Lazy Boy, Rodgers Mountain, and Rocking Chair campgrounds. At 0.5 mile farther south is Howbert Point campground. Another mile or so south brings you to the southernmost end of the park and Witcher's Cove campground, with a boat ramp. (The two county roads do not circle the lake.)

Only one camping unit with a single family or a maximum of six people is permitted per site. Electrical hookups are available in the Rocky Ridge campground only. Because of the open area of the lake, sound travels easily. Quiet hours are therefore enforced in all campgrounds from 10:00 P.M. to 6:00 A.M. Waste can be

119

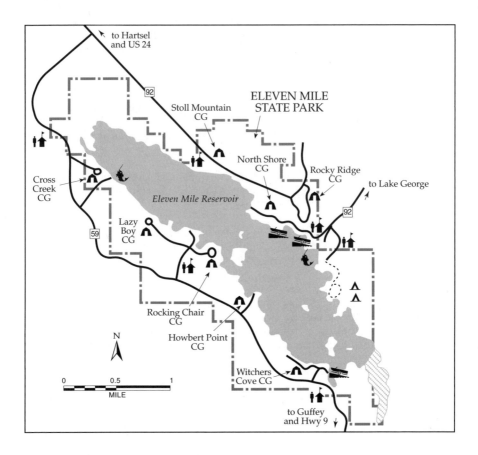

dumped in the dump stations located near the North Shore/Rocky Ridge (southeast) and Witcher's Cove (southwest) entrances.

Boating is spectacular at Eleven Mile, with expansive scenic backdrops provided by the distant mountains and the rocky outcroppings which emerge directly from the water's edge. The almost 7-mile-long reservoir provides plenty of space to fish or just head for a quiet cove to call your own on a bright summer's afternoon. Boating is permitted only from one half hour before sunrise to one half hour after sunset. There is a scattering of islands around the lake, but these are all closed to public use. Sailors find themselves challenged by the tricky crosswinds and the occasional fast-rising storm that blows in from the western mountains. All boaters are also cautioned that because of the rocky conditions, some underwater hazards may not be marked; special care should be taken within 150 feet of any shoreline. Boaters who have not registered their craft can do so at the park's entrance station office.

Fishing captures the most recreational attention at Eleven Mile State Park; some of the state's largest fish have been caught at this reservoir. The generous stock of fish at Eleven Mile include rainbow, brown, and cutthroat trout; mackinaw; kokanee salmon; carp; and northern pike. According to park rangers, the northern pike are abundant and bite quite well. Fishing and boating are prohibited in the

Seagulls gathered on Pikes Peak Granite, north shore of Eleven Mile Reservoir

restricted area near the dam; bow fishing for carp is allowed year-round. During the winter, ice fishing takes place anywhere on the lake, except near the restricted area in front of the dam. Some especially good ice fishing spots are found in front of the North Shore boat ramps and on the waters off the Rocking Chair campground.

There are no hiking trails at Eleven Mile State Park, but visitors are welcome to hike through the surrounding open spaces without restriction.

The wildlife at Eleven Mile State Park inhabit the riparian, short-grass prairie, ponderosa pine, and dry upland vegetation found at or around the lake. The western meadowlark, mountain bluebird, horned lark, mountain chickadee, western grebe, swallows, and many gulls are commonly seen sitting atop the rock formations. Numerous species of shorebirds and waterfowl, in particular Canadian geese, find a seasonal home and nesting area at Eleven Mile Reservoir. Larger animals can be seen in the upland pine forests south of the lake. These include antelope, elk, deer, bear, coyote, and bobcat. Be aware when observing wildlife that hunting is permitted in the park during established legal seasons except in those areas posted as closed.

Eleven Mile State Park offers many water-based recreational opportunities in an uncrowded setting. The views are spaciously scenic, the fishing is award-winning, and the slow, tranquil pace is just right for visitors needing a great getaway spot. Campers find Eleven Mile State Park the perfect base for exploring the many recreational offerings found in the South Park area.

Pike National Forest, found north and south of the park, offers many miles of hiking trails. Near Fairplay, 40 miles from Eleven Mile State Park, hikers can also access the many fourteeners, including Mount Democrat, Mount Sherman, and Mount Lincoln.

SPINNEY MOUNTAIN STATE PARK

Hours/Season: Day-use only; half hour before sunrise to one hour after sunset; approximately May 1–Nov. 15
Area: 3,400 acres; 2,520 surface water acres
Facilities: 20 picnic sites, 2 boat ramps
Attractions: Picnicking, fishing, boating, sailboarding, jet skiing, mountain biking
Nearby: Lost Creek Wilderness Area
Access: From Colorado Springs, on I-25 south of Denver, take US 24 west for 55 miles over Wilkerson Pass; turn left on CR 23, go 2.8 miles, then turn right on CR 59 and go 1.1 miles to the park entrance

Spinney Mountain State Park rests in the southeast corner of South Park, at the base of Spinney Mountain to the north and 39-Mile Mountain to the south. The park looks west to the famous Collegiate Mountain Range. The same South Platte River that supplies water to Eleven Mile State Park is also the source of water for Spinney Mountain Reservoir. This park offers an isolated retreat for those wishing to get away from it all. The facility is a day-use only area, offers no camping (although camping is available just a few miles east at Eleven Mile State Park), and has limited-year use between May and November.

The land upon which Spinney Mountain Reservoir sits was used for homesteading and cattle ranching during the late 1800s. The area is flat and unremarkable, surrounded in the distance by the soaring peaks of the Collegiate Range. The city of Aurora, next to Denver, developed the reservoir as a storage facility for drinking water that eventually makes its way to Denver via the South Platte River. In 1987, Aurora turned over the property for lease by Colorado State Parks as a recreational area.

As you enter the park's main entrance, on the lake's north shore, you gradually drive south along the east shore, past the outlet of the South Platte River (closed to public use), to the south shore facilities. The land is flat, with a gentle slope into the reservoir to the west of the road. Shrub and grasslands gently merge into the lake waters all along the shore. There is also an entrance on the northwest side of the park, near the inlet of the South Platte River.

There are 20 picnic sites around the south and east shores of the lake, with tables and fire rings. However, picnicking is allowed anywhere in the park. The views of the surrounding mountains and the pristine waters of the lake provide a scenic backdrop for a picnic lunch or supper. Rangers from nearby Eleven Mile State Park provide interpretive material upon request.

Boating is offered at the lake, with boat ramps located on both the north and

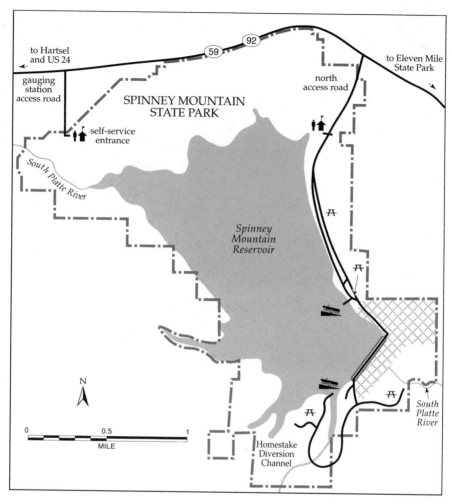

south side of the reservoir. Wind gusts of 30 to 40 miles per hour can readily occur, creating 5-foot waves that mean the larger the boat the safer. Sailing and windsurfing are allowed, but boaters should be aware of the possible stiff wind conditions.

There are several regulations in force at Spinney Mountain State Park that relate primarily to boaters. No boating is allowed from a half hour after sunset until a half hour before sunrise. It is unlawful to enter the waterfowl nesting islands in the northwest section of the lake, and waterskiing and swimming are not permitted. The area below the dam and inside the chain-link fence is closed to all public use.

Although Spinney Mountain State Park is a more rustic recreational experience, fishermen will enjoy the quiet and more primitive setting of its waters..One gets the feeling of being in a high mountain lake, with few distractions to disturb the day's pleasure. Spinney Mountain is considered a trophy fishery and has been designated a gold medal water by the state of Colorado. The waters are home to northern pike

123

Fishermen wading out into Spinney Lake

and brown trout and are stocked with cutthroat and rainbow trout. Anglers may keep only one trout, which must be 20 inches or longer. The bag and possession limit for northern pike is ten fish, with no more than one of these greater than 34 inches long. Only artificial flies and lures are permitted; bait fishing and snagging are prohibited. No fishing is allowed from a half hour after sunset until a half hour before sunrise. Fishermen are advised that the area within the fence below the dam and the Homestake Diversion Channel at the south end of the lake are closed to fishing.

There are no trails for either hiking or mountain biking. However, mountain biking may be done on any of the roads leading into and through the park.

Wildlife-watching gives an additional high-country accent to Spinney Mountain. Coyote, pronghorn antelope, mule deer, badgers, weasels, and muskrats join shorebirds, Canadian geese, and swallows in living and nesting on or near the lake. Even endangered species—the bald eagle and peregrine falcon—have been observed at or near the park.

To the west and north of Spinney Mountain lies the main land area of Park County, with more territory above 9,000 feet than any other county in Colorado. Hiking opportunities are many. Some of the best trails are found in the Lost Creek Wilderness Area, the Guanella Pass Trails, the Jefferson Loop Trail near Jefferson, and the Weston Pass area. The Park County Tourism Office publishes a very complete "Outdoor Adventure Guide" to Park County and the South Region. Hiking trails, mountain biking opportunities, camping, fishing, cross-country ski trails, etc., are all highlighted, with maps provided. You can also ask for "The Pride of Colorado Tour" on Pikes Peak, and the Central Rockies brochure for additional recreational information. To receive information call the Park County Tourism Office (see appendix A).

ARKANSAS HEADWATERS RECREATION AREA:
RAILROAD BRIDGE, FISHERMAN'S BRIDGE, RUBY MOUNTAIN, HECLA JUNCTION, RINCON, VALLIE BRIDGE, LONE PINE, PINNACLE ROCK, FIVE POINTS, SPIKEBUCK, BOOTLEGGER, PARKDALE, PARKDALE SOUTH

Hours/Season: *Railroad Bridge, Ruby Mountain, Hecla Junction, Rincon, Five Points* overnight, year-round; *Fisherman's Bridge, Vallie Bridge, Lone Pine, Pinnacle Rock, Spikebuck, Bootlegger, Parkdale, Parkdale South* day-use, daylight hours only, year-round
Area: 5,697 acres; 148 river miles
Facilities: *Railroad Bridge* river access; *Fisherman's Bridge* river access; *Ruby Mountain* 22 campsites, 6 picnic sites, river access; *Hecla Junction* 21 campsites, 5 picnic sites, river access; *Rincon* 15 campsites, 5 picnic sites, river access; *Vallie Bridge* river access; *Lone Pine* 12 picnic sites, river access; *Pinnacle Rock* 5 picnic sites, river access; *Five Points* 21 campsites, 8 picnic sites; *Spikebuck* 5 picnic sites, river access; *Bootlegger* river access; *Parkdale* 20 picnic sites, river access; *Parkdale South* river access
Attractions: *Railroad Bridge* camping, boating, fishing, wildlife-watching; *Fisherman's Bridge* boating, fishing, wildlife-watching; *Ruby Mountain* camping, picnicking, hiking, boating, fishing, wildlife-watching; *Hecla Junction* camping, picnicking, hiking, boating, fishing, wildlife-watching; *Rincon* picnicking, boating, fishing, wildlife-watching; *Vallie Bridge* boating, fishing, wildlife-watching; *Lone Pine* picnicking, boating, fishing, wildlife-watching; *Pinnacle Rock* picnicking, boating, fishing, wildlife-watching; *Five Points* camping, picnicking, scenic overlook, boating, hiking, fishing, wildlife-watching; *Spikebuck* picnicking, boating, fishing, wildlife-watching; *Bootlegger* boating, fishing, wildlife-watching; *Parkdale* picnicking, boating, fishing; *Parkdale South* fishing, hiking, wildlife-watching
Access: *Railroad Bridge* US 24 south from Leadville to Buena Vista; *Fisherman's Bridge, Ruby Mountain, Hecla Junction* US 285 south from Buena Vista to Salida; *Rincon, Vallie Bridge, Lone Pine, Pinnacle Rock, Five Points, Spikebuck, Bootlegger, Parkdale, Parkdale South* US 50 east from Salida to Pueblo

The Arkansas Headwaters Recreation Area—AHRA, as it is called—consists primarily of the Arkansas River running 148 miles from Leadville, high in the Rocky Mountains, to Lake Pueblo, 112 miles south of Denver. For the first 125 miles, the Arkansas River drops 5,000 vertical feet . . . which makes for a very fast and spectacular river-rafting experience! The river passes through open valleys, past the granite boulders of Browns Canyon, between the awesome 1,000-foot walls of the Royal Gorge, while flowing by the valley cities of Buena Vista, Salida, and Canon City on its way to Pueblo. The stretch of land that the river flows through is known as the Arkansas Valley, considered a high-desert region that enjoys over 300 sunny days a year. Because of the low rainfall, the Arkansas River forms a "living green belt" along its course . . . home to wildlife, fisheries, and plant habitat. Cottonwoods, alder, willow, shrubs, and grasses accent its banks, while spectacular mountain scenery forms the backdrop which delights visitors all along its 150-mile journey.

The early history of the area included a visit in the early 1800s by Zebulon Pike, after whom Pikes Peak is named. Trappers followed the explorer, but it was the discovery of gold in the Arkansas Valley in 1859 that first brought miners to the area. The silver boom in Leadville during the 1870s insured the economic development of the valley, encouraging the Denver & Rio Grande Railway to build its line, with tracks that to this day still follow the river. The Arkansas Headwaters Recreation Area was created in 1989 as a joint management venture between the Colorado State Parks and the Bureau of Land Management; despite the name of recreation area, it is designated a state park. Now, recreation is the mainstay of the area.

The Arkansas River is the most highly used white-water river in the United States, hosting more white-water boating than all the other Colorado rivers put together! Boating, especially white-water rafting and kayaking, has experienced a

View of the Arkansas River from Parkdale Bridge

126

phenomenal growth rate of over 18 percent per year since 1982. Chances are, then, that if you visit the Arkansas River you'll probably at some time be seeing the river from the inside of a boat!

There are scores of commercial outfitters along the Arkansas River that can offer visitors a safe, exciting ride on the river. Trips vary from the famous "wet and wild" kind to more gentle family outings and float fishing. I have run the river in fast conditions with high water, and found the experience exciting and memorable. There are also many private boaters who run the river; they should get specific information about the section of river they intend to run, preferably from the AHRA main office (see appendix A). All boaters should wear a life jacket while on the river. All white-water boats are required to have the owner's name and address legibly written somewhere on the boat.

A trip down the Arkansas River begins just south of the famed mining town of Leadville. At first, the river is fairly calm, passing through open lands and banks accented with Douglas fir and spruce. At Pine Creek Canyon, below the town of Granite, the first serious rapids (Class V–VI) occur, followed shortly thereafter by The Numbers (Class III–V). Private rafters running The Numbers rapids above Buena Vista must launch their boats between 8:30 A.M. and 11:00 A.M. From The Numbers, the river remains technically challenging (Class III–V) down to the town of Buena Vista. Railroad Bridge Recreation Site, a boating and fishing access point (no rest rooms), is a little more than halfway to Buena Vista. The town's name translates into "good view," so named because of the magnificent Collegiate Peaks of Oxford, Harvard, Columbia, Yale, and Princeton located just west of the town.

From Buena Vista, the river passes Fisherman's Bridge Recreation Site, with boating and fishing access, and then Ruby Mountain Recreation Site, with camping, picnicking, and hiking as well as boating and fishing access. Below Ruby Mountain, boaters enjoy the wild rapids and pink granite rock of Browns Canyon (Class III–IV). After this adventurous section of river, the waters calm down. Those interested in going ashore can hike, camp, and observe wildlife at the 6,600-acre BLM Browns Canyon Wilderness Study Area. Fishing is considered quite good in these calmer waters. Just south of the study area is Hecla Junction Recreation Site, with camping, picnicking, and hiking as well as boating and fishing access.

From Hecla Junction to Salida, the waters continue to remain calm, while the terrain begins changing into a more desertlike environment marked by the appearance of cholla cactus. South of Salida is Rincon Recreation Site, with camping, picnicking, boating, and fishing; then one encounters Vallie Bridge Recreation Site, with restrooms and boating and fishing access. Below Salida, the river enters the Lower Arkansas River Canyon (also known as the "Grand Canyon of the Arkansas"). Massive red-orange cliffs tower above boaters as they test their skills through raging rapids with names like Lose-Your-Lunch and Shark's Tooth. The land is scenic and as wild-looking as the river, with plenty of take-out points at Lone Pine (rest rooms), Pinnacle Rock (picnicking), Five Points (camping, picnicking, scenic overlook), Spikebuck (restrooms, picnicking), and Bootlegger Recreation Sites before the river reaches Parkdale Recreation Site (rest rooms, picnicking) . . . the last stop before the "Big One." Parkdale South Recreation Site has no boating access, though it does have fishing access and hiking (no rest rooms).

Just south of the Parkdale take-out, the river dramatically plunges into the Royal Gorge, a 1,000-foot-high walled canyon with the rapids rated Class IV and V. This is another section of river I recommend to any "thrill seeker!" At times the river looks as if it is about to send you crashing directly into the canyon walls,

Arkansas River rafters approaching the Parkdale take-out

while high above you hundreds of people look down from the world's highest suspension bridge and contemplate your fate! But just when the fun seems like it will never end (8 miles of river gorge *does* seem like it lasts forever), the calmer waters above Canon City appear.

From here all the way to Pueblo, the Arkansas becomes a tranquil, meandering river of the Great Plains. Fishing is great, the sun is hot, and anyone who has just survived the Royal Gorge can turn to their fellow rafters and retell the adventure with whatever embellishments seem appropriate! At the Pueblo Reservoir, one will find hiking, picnicking, and a scenic overlook as well as boating and fishing access (see Lake Pueblo State Park).

Much of the land along the river is privately held. Boaters should respect the rights of landowners, as well as the rights of the many fishermen encountered along the river. Keep a sharp eye out for other boaters and livestock, and for hazards in the river such as logs and tree stumps that have broken free. State park staff encourages river runners to observe a quieter demeanor when passing near homes, fishing areas, or wildlife . . . noise is also a form of pollution.

Especially during high water and spring runoff, the Arkansas is a powerful river not to be taken lightly. Certain sections of the river are closed to boating during unsafe water conditions. Be sure to act safely in any boat you may be traveling in, and when shooting the more demanding rapids, stay focused on what you are doing. It may be fun, but it is not "play time."

Fishing is growing in popularity along the river. The Arkansas offers world-class brown trout fishing and good rainbow trout, with catches measuring 10 to 12 inches. Certain sections of the river have been designated as wild trout waters and support self-sustaining brown trout populations. Since most boating takes place at midday and fishing is best early or late in the day, both fishermen and boaters can accommodate each other's needs.

The Arkansas River offers an inviting habitat to many varieties of wildlife. Along the riverbanks one might spot deer, blue heron, beaver, raccoon, and even the Rocky Mountain bighorn sheep, often found from Wellsville to Parkdale in early morning and late afternoon.

The Arkansas Headwaters Recreation Area Office (see appendix A) offers many useful maps and brochures on the river and adjoining land and recreational areas. Ask for the large map titled "Outdoor Adventures in the Upper Arkansas Valley." Maps indicate take-out and entry points, camping sites, and noteworthy land features.

LAKE PUEBLO STATE PARK

Hours/Season: Overnight; year-round
Area: 9,045 acres; 4,646 surface water acres
Facilities: 401 campsites, group campground, 348 picnic sites, dump station, laundry, bathhouse, snack bar, boat ramps, marina, fish-cleaning station, swim beach
Attractions: Camping, picnicking, visitors/nature center, interpretive programs, swimming, fishing, boating, waterskiing, sailboarding, jet skiing, hiking, biking, horseback riding, cross-country skiing
Nearby: Pueblo State Wildlife Area
Access: From Pueblo, south of Colorado Springs on I-25, take US 50 west for 4 miles; turn south on Pueblo Boulevard and go 4 miles to Thatcher Avenue; turn west and go 6 miles

Lake Pueblo State Park is a people's park, serving the recreational needs of both southeast Colorado and visitors along the length of the Front Range. The park is situated at a place where high plains, desert, and scenic mountains all meet, so the topography of the park is both diverse and interesting. The Arkansas River feeds into 11-mile-long Lake Pueblo, formed by the large, imposing Pueblo Dam (10,500 feet long by 200 feet high). The lower elevation of the park (4,900 feet) favors a more year-round use of the facility, complemented by a mild climate. The city of Pueblo is only 5 miles to the east, making Lake Pueblo a recreational resource almost within the city.

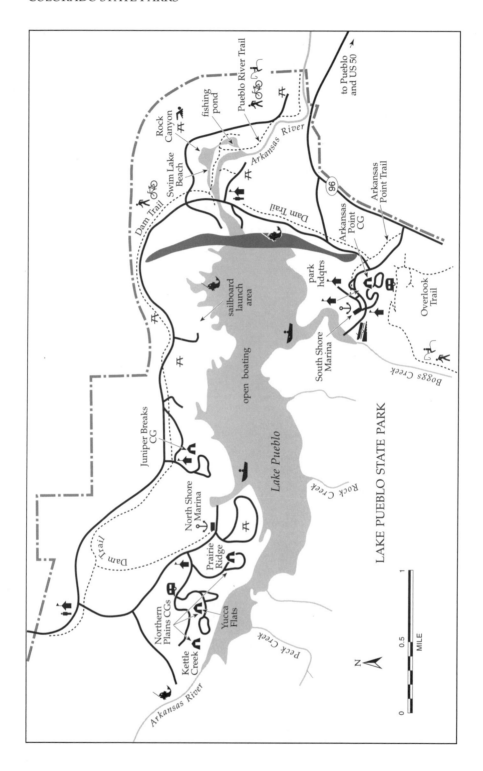

LAKE PUEBLO STATE PARK

View across Lake Pueblo from the north shore

The drive along the north shore of Lake Pueblo quickly highlights the immensity of the place, reminding one of a downsized Lake Powell without the colorful rock displays. The look is definitely Southwest, as a contour of light purple, gray, and beige-colored buttes and limestone cliffs surround the lake's irregular 60-mile shoreline. These features are less dramatic than their high-mesa cousins that rim the north of Grand Junction, thus allowing the spectacular Lake Pueblo to hold its own and occupy the main center of attraction.

The park presents sharp, clean lines, with picnic sites, boating accesses, and trails near the water all neatly laid out in an obviously uncrowded fashion. Traveling around the park reinforces the crispness of the scenery, with vistas across the blue lake waters directing one's view to the distant mesas of the far shore, or to the majestic mountains beyond.

Pueblo, situated at the confluence of the Arkansas River and Fountain Creek, became a natural gathering site for Spanish conquistadors, mountain men, traders, and Indians. Pueblo was the base from which Zebulon Pike began his famous expedition to the nearby mountain that now bears his name. By the 1840s Fort Pueblo was a major trading post. The Colorado gold rush brought a massive influx of settlers into the area, but by the 1890s the valley became economically balanced between farmers, ranchers, and miners, encouraged by the presence of four railroads into the city. Lake Pueblo was built in the early 1970s as a part of the massive Frying Pan–Arkansas Water Storage Project for the primary purpose of providing supplemental irrigation water for 280,000 acres of farmland in the lower Arkansas Valley. This project also provides flood control, water for municipal and industrial use, and recreational opportunities, as developed by Colorado State Parks.

Lake Pueblo can easily be considered a "camping destination" for vacationers wanting to home-base at the lake while visiting the nearby mountains or Arkansas River. Most campground locations offer scenic views across the lake, and to the east at the imposing Pueblo Dam. There are three campgrounds, mostly located along scenic areas of the North Shore. Arkansas Point campground is located just inside the main entrance, on the southeast shore near the South Shore Marina. As you continue north around the lake, you reach Juniper Breaks campground. At the far northwestern edge of the park is the Northern Plains campground, with three camping areas: Kettle Creek, Yucca Flats, and Prairie Ridge. The Arkansas Point, Prairie Ridge, and Yucca Flats campgrounds offer modern toilets, showers, laundry facilities, and electricity. Juniper Breaks and Kettle Creek feature primitive facilities offering vault toilets and no running water. Group camping is also available. Campgrounds are patrolled for safety and assistance to assure the 10:00 P.M. quiet

Swim Lake Beach at Pueblo State Park

time. Dump stations are located in designated campgrounds. The park's amphitheater is located in the Northern Plains campground. Basic supplies can be purchased at the North Shore Marina, located just east of the Northern Plains campground, and of course in the city of Pueblo.

For those who enjoy picnicking, 348 sites are found along the length of the shoreline. The picnic sites offer superb views of the lake and mountains, and are generously scattered throughout the park. Group picnicking is available at two sites near the North Shore Marina, at one near the South Shore Marina, and at one at Rock Canyon in the park's eastern end past the dam. These shelters each accommodate up to 110 people and may be reserved by calling the park headquarters (see appendix A).

The park sponsors a summer interpretive series that touches on subjects like the nature of rivers, wildlife, reptiles, and birds of prey. Information on any interpretive program can be received by calling the visitors center.

Boaters find Lake Pueblo a warm-water paradise. The reservoir is large enough to provide uncrowded boating conditions. Much of the shoreline is accented by quiet coves that provide privacy and great views across the lake. A very large and modern North Shore Marina offers 125 electrical slips and 375 nonelectrical slips, with groceries, marine supplies, a breakfast and lunch grill, floating rest rooms, and fishing boat rentals. Water-skiers enjoy the quiet setting and scenic backdrop, as well as the warm water temperatures that prevail into early fall. Steady winds make for ideal sailing and sailboarding, with boat ramps and marinas buoyed for wakeless speeds.

Boaters are permitted to stay on the water at night if their craft is equipped with proper running lights and anchor. All on-board facilities are required to be self-contained and sealed, and no camping is allowed on the shoreline. Because Lake Pueblo is fed by the Arkansas River, there are low-water times when underwater hazards in shallow areas must be avoided. There are also standing underwater trees west of the marina that boaters need to watch for. Visitors to Lake Pueblo who do not want to rent a boat but wish to see the park from the water can take a tour of the lake on a restored touring boat.

Lake Pueblo is well stocked with a variety of trout, channel catfish, sunfish, crappie, walleye, black bass (none smaller than 15 inches can be taken), wipers, and other species common to warm water. The North Shore Marina stocks fishing supplies, rents fishing boats, and sells fishing licenses.

Swimmers enjoy their own private swim lake and beach at the Rock Canyon swim area. The beach offers a very sheltered, secluded atmosphere. Large cottonwood and other shade trees ring the entire beach area, highlighted by a wide, expansive sand beach looking out at a 9-surface-acre swim lake. Large, grassy areas shaded by cottonwoods provide great picnic spots. A food concession offers hot and cold foods and drinks, while picnic tables, lockers, showers, a covered deck, water slide, bumper boats, volleyball, play equipment, and lifeguards complete this delightful beach scene. Many families, children, adults, and groups enjoy their summer's day at this beautiful and well-provided for setting.

Hikers can enjoy several beautiful trails in and near Lake Pueblo. The Arkansas Point Trail, less than a mile long, offers interpretive signs and benches while leading hikers to the bluffs that overlook the south side of the park. The Dam Trail is almost 17 miles of paved biking and hiking trail, and connects Rock Canyon, South Shore, and North Shore Marina with the campgrounds. The real plus for hikers and walkers, however, is the Pueblo River Trail, which connects Lake Pueblo with the city. Hikers, bikers, and equestrians can enjoy this 12-plus-mile path that follows along the route of the Arkansas River and connects to other trail systems in the city of Pueblo. A map outlining the entire area covered by this trail system is available at the park headquarters. In winter, cross-country skiing takes place anywhere in the park, though no trails are groomed and snowfall is limited.

Mule deer are sometimes spotted along the lake, as well as bighorn sheep and pronghorn in the southern areas of the park. Beaver and raccoon are sometimes spotted along the shore. Hawks, bald eagles during winter, golden eagles, osprey, and blue heron are often seen. Geese and wood ducks are also common.

Lake Pueblo State Park is a very friendly recreational destination that combines a Southwest desert lake setting with the amenities of an urban park without the noise, crowds, or city presence . . . a fun park with all the outdoor natural beauty that is the unique blend of southeastern Colorado.

Colorado State Parks also publishes a very informative map on the hiking, biking, and equestrian trails found in nearby Colorado Springs, Canon City, Trinidad, and the Colorado Springs Wildlife Area. This publication is called the "South Front Range," and is one of several very helpful trail guides published in the "Urban Trails in Colorado" series. To receive this map, call Lake Pueblo State Park or the Colorado State Park main office (see appendix A).

LATHROP STATE PARK

Hours/Season: Overnight; year-round
Area: 1,434 acres; 320 surface water acres
Facilities: 98 campsites, group campground, 40 picnic sites, visitors/nature center, dump station, laundry, bathhouse, 3 boat ramps
Attractions: Camping, picnicking, visitors/nature center, interpretive programs, swimming, boating, fishing, waterskiing, sailboarding, jet skiing, hiking, biking, horseback riding, cross-country skiing, ice skating, ice fishing
Nearby: Spanish Peaks
Access: From Walsenburg, on I-25 near the southern border with New Mexico, drive 3 miles west on Highway 160; the park is located on the north side of the road

Lathrop State Park rests on a high-plains grassland accented with piñon, juniper, yucca, and low-lying cactus. The park offers expansive and unrestricted views to all horizons. The southern skyline is dominated by the twin Spanish Peaks, 13,610 and 12,669 feet in elevation. The Indians named the Spanish Peaks *Wahatoya*, which means "breasts of the earth." Lathrop State Park, opened in 1962, is built around two lakes. Horseshoe Lake is the west lake in the park, while Martin Lake occupies the east area.

Above the northern end of Martin Lake and situated back from an elevated bluff is the Piñon campground. This facility offers 79 sites with pull-through paved sites, electrical hookups, flush toilets, laundry, bathhouse, a playground, and access to the amphitheater. The setting is quiet, private and relaxed . . . a virtual mountain retreat accented by juniper and pine. The Walsenburg Golf Club is a public, nine-hole course adjacent to the park and within walking distance of the Piñon campground (for information, see appendix A). The Yucca campground is found southeast of Martin Lake.

View south towards Spanish Peaks from the north shore of Martin Lake

This campground has seventeen sites plus two group-camping areas, offering primitive camping with gravel pull-in spaces and vault toilets.

Along the north shore of Martin Lake is a scattering of picnic areas, all quietly secluded and offering magnificent views of both the lake and the Spanish Peaks. Driving down the west side of Martin Lake, you find more picnic and shade shelters from which to appreciate the scenic views. This area of the lake is accented with riparian wetlands, cottonwoods, and willows, giving a greener look. Located at the south end of the lake is another picnic area. As you continue along the east side of the lake, now heading north, you cross the dam, with more picnic sites.

A drive around the park should begin at the visitors center, where nature displays highlight the plant and animals found in and near the park. However, the real drawing card at the visitors center are twelve large murals by Paul Busch, painted around the interior walls and depicting the colorful history of Colorado. As good as you will see in any art gallery, these murals capture the feel and flow of the events that shaped Colorado, from the Mesa Verde cliff dwellers and the Spanish conquistadors, past the exploits of Zebulon Pike, Lieutenant John C. Fremont, Kit Carson, and Jim Bridger, to the events of the twentieth century. All are tastefully rendered in vibrant reds, azure, greens, and purples that reflect the colors found throughout the mountains, forests, mesas, and skies of Colorado!

Lathrop State Park provides weekend guest speakers to complement their own staff. These interpretive programs cover the history of the area, focus on specific wildlife found at the park, and even touch on the historical legends which have added their color to southeastern Colorado. A brochure titled "Birds of Lathrop State Park" helps visitors identify what species are commonly seen at the park, and offers good follow-up material to the programs on birdlife presented at the center. Leaving the center, you can drive east past the animal exercise area (and if you are traveling with pets, you'll appreciate why they built this feature!).

Buoys divide Martin Lake into use zones which are posted at the boat ramp on the south shore. Waterskiing and power and sailboating are permitted. A beautiful swim beach is also located on the south shore. Horseshoe Lake offers fewer amenities. A boat ramp is found at the south end of the lake, with sailing, boating at wakeless speeds, and wind surfing permitted. On both lakes, boaters must observe all Colorado regulations, available at the park office; additionally, water-ski boats must have an observer on board with the driver. A red 12-inch-by-12-inch flag must be displayed when a skier is down in the water.

Fishing is popular at both lakes. At Martin Lake, the south shore has a fishing area, and on your left just past the dam is a children's fishing pond for kids under fifteen—which means that no fishing license is required! Along the north shore are quietly secluded fishing spots. In places, rock formations jut out into the lake and make excellent fishing platforms. At Horseshoe Lake, on the east side along the

Fishing on Martin Lake in the shadow of Spanish Peaks

spillway, several fishing piers are available as well as at the boat ramp on the south shore. The lakes are generously stocked with rainbow trout, channel catfish, tiger muskie (the largest fish ever caught in Colorado, at over forty pounds, was a tiger muskie!) bass, walleye, bluegill, and crappie.

Hikers who visit Lathrop can take Hogback Trail, a short 2-mile trail, out of Piñon campground to climb the Hogback Ridge bordering the park to the north. The trail offers good views of the lakes and the Spanish Peaks to the south. The trail also has a trailhead on the park road west of Piñon campground.

Hidden among the trees and desert plants, visitors might see squirrels, mule deer, rabbits, and coyotes. Ducks, Canadian geese, hawks, and an occasional golden eagle may be spotted.

Those wishing to actually hike the Spanish Peaks area can drive west on Highway 160, turn south onto Highway 12, then turn left at Cordova Pass Road and continue for 4 or 5 miles until coming to several trailheads at or near Cordova Pass. The West Spanish Peaks Trail takes hikers onto the Spanish Peaks on a 5-mile round-trip hike. The Apishapa Trail and the Chaparral Trail are also nearby, and offer hikes of 6 and 13 miles round-trip, respectively. Information on hiking these trails can be obtained by calling the San Isabel National Forest office in La Veta (see appendix A).

SAN LUIS LAKES STATE PARK

Hours/Season: Overnight; year-round
Area: 2,054 acres; 890 surface water acres
Facilities: 51 campsites, 27 picnic sites, boat ramp, fish-cleaning station, dump station, laundry, showers
Attractions: Camping, picnicking, interpretive programs, boating, waterskiing, sailboarding, jet skiing, fishing, hiking, cross-country skiing, ice skating, ice fishing, swimming
Nearby: Mount Blanca, Great Sand Dunes National Monument
Access: From Walsenburg, on I-25 near the southern border with New Mexico, take Highway 160 west for 60 miles; drive north on CO 150 for 13.5 miles, then west on Six Mile Lane for 8 miles, then north 0.13 mile to the park entrance

▲ The drive to San Luis Lakes State Park from Walsenburg takes visitors along the same route that Kit Carson traveled, over spectacular North La Veta Pass, through the historic town of Fort Garland, just south of the stunning Blanca Peak (14,345 feet elevation), and into the San Luis Valley, visited in the early 1800s by Lieutenant Zebulon Pike. The park also lies near the headwaters of the Rio Grande River. Just north of the lakes is the massive Great Sand Dunes National Monument, resting in the shadow of the soaring Sangre de Cristo Mountains. A visit to San Luis Lakes is a trip to the historical past of Colorado juxtaposed with the ancient natural forces that created both the Great Sand Dunes and the mountains surrounding it.

The history of the Old West surrounds visitors to San Luis Lakes State Park. Famed Spanish explorer Coronado passed by the San Luis Lakes area in his search for the Seven Cities of Cibola. Much later, fur trappers were present in the San Luis Valley from 1810 to 1840, while Kit Carson took command of nearby Fort Garland by 1866. Farming and small ranching received a big boost when the Guadalupe Main Ditch was constructed in the 1870s to tap the waters of San Antonito and La Jara Creeks. After World War II, the Closed Basin Project began returning water to New Mexico by a system of canals and wells via the Rio Grande River. By 1993, the U.S. Bureau of Reclamation had helped construct San Luis Lakes, which were turned over to Colorado State Parks for recreational use.

The northern half of San Luis Lake is not in the park boundary, but is part of San Luis Lakes Wildlife Area. North of the lake is a wetlands area and north of the wetlands is small Head Lake.

San Luis Lakes offers campers a real destination camping opportunity for exploring the points of interest in and near the San Luis Valley. The Mosca campground is located in the low sand dunes west of the lake. The campsites allow a view of the lake, the San Juan and Sangre de Cristo mountains, and the Great Sand Dunes. The campgrounds are equipped with electrical hookups, sheltered tables and fire grates, drinking water, and a bathhouse with modern rest rooms, hot showers, and laundry facilities. The campground can accommodate recreational vehicles

Entrance to San Luis Lakes State Park with Crestone Peak to the north

and tents. Group camping is available by calling the park office for information. Firewood can be purchased at the entrance station or park office, but no wood gathering or tree cutting is allowed anywhere in the park or wildlife area.

The lake is a quiet getaway spot, uncrowded, with scenic views in all directions. Picnickers enjoy this winning combination. Just within the south entrance is the Needles picnic area, with additional sites dotting the western shore. The tables are sheltered, with a relaxed atmosphere and great views to the surrounding mountains.

Waterskiing, motor boating, sailing, and windsurfing are popular pastimes at the lake. The lake has a sandy bottom with gentle sloping sides and few hazards, allowing good access to the shoreline for swimming. A wide boat ramp assists in easy loading and unloading of boats. All Colorado boating regulations and statutes are in effect, and required safety equipment information is available at the park office. Boaters are cautioned to observe the strict off-limits zone created by the buoy line at the north end of the lake. The large wildlife area north of the buoys should never be entered by any craft, in order to protect the waterfowl nesting habitat located there.

Fishing is a year-round pursuit at the park. Rainbow trout is considered excellent

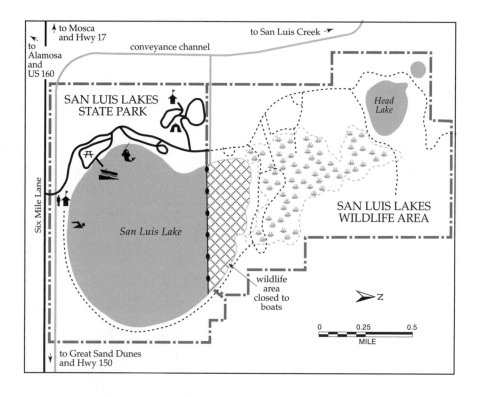

and rangers should be consulted as to the current possession limits. Although ice fishing is available during the coldest winter months, the temperatures in the San Luis Valley are relatively mild, making for thin ice conditions. Caution is advised.

Hikers and walkers can enjoy the wildlife area from a number of easy trails that lead into and around the area. Because these trails are wide and level, the physically challenged can also access these wildlife viewing areas. From the swimming beach on the south shore near the picnic area, a trail follows the east shore of San Luis Lake, crosses through the wetlands area on the north shore, and continues around the lake to the road end near the campground. Another trail goes north from the road end to the west shore of Head Lake, with side trails exploring the wetlands and the south shore of Head Lake.

San Luis Lakes supports a large and diverse wildlife population. The huge wetlands area north of the lake, the San Luis Lakes Wildlife Area, begins on the northern section of the lake, marked by a buoy line. North of this line many migratory birds like sandhill cranes, whooping cranes, bald eagles, and waterfowl, along with raptors and songbirds, nest or winter on the lake or in the wetlands. The park office offers a "Birds of San Luis Lakes" brochure for identifying the species common to the park. The riparian ecosystem also supports many small mammals, amphibians, reptiles, and predators, along with the larger mule deer, pronghorn antelope, and elk. San Luis Lakes is also surrounded by the second-largest bison ranch in the United States. Viewing these magnificent animals is allowed only from your vehicle, at a distance, while driving carefully on the main roads through the ranch. Several private roads surrounding the park post no trespassing signs, and visitors need to honor this warning.

Picnic area at San Luis Lakes State Park

Hikers wishing more strenuous and longer trail systems can look east across the lake toward towering Mount Blanca. This mountain and its sister peaks lie in Rio Grande National Forest (for information, see appendix A) and can be accessed by driving north on Colorado Highway 150 to Forest Road 975. This four-wheel-drive road takes you up to the Lake Como area and Blue Lake, where hikers can pick up Trail 886. If the road is especially rough or washed out, the hike to Mount Blanca is over 9 miles round trip, or 5 miles if the road is completely passable.

Hiking around the Great Sand Dunes National Monument is allowed and several trails cross the monument. Contact the monument for more information (see appendix A). A short but scenic hike that can be accessed off Colorado Highway 150, starting near the 10-mile marker and veering east, is the Zapata Falls and Zapata Trail. Information on these trails can be obtained from the BLM office (see appendix A).

North of the Great Sand Dunes National Monument are several fourteeners, notably Crestone Peak and Crestone Needle. A primitive forest road leading north out of the monument leads to an area that allows access to Mount Herard (over 13,000 feet), while the Mosca Pass Trail heads east from the San Luis Lakes State Park visitors center. Information on these trails and access into Rio Grande National Forest can be obtained by calling the Rio Grande National Forest Office (see appendix A).

TRINIDAD LAKE STATE PARK

Hours/Season: Overnight; year-round
Area: 1,600 acres; 700 surface water acres
Facilities: 62 campsites, 46 picnic sites, visitors/nature center, boat ramp, dump station, laundry, showers
Attractions: Camping, picnicking, visitors/nature center, interpretive programs, boating, waterskiing, sailboarding, jet skiing, hiking, biking, horseback riding, cross-country skiing, ice skating, ice fishing
Nearby: Highway of Legends Scenic and Historic Byway; Louden-Henritze Archeology Museum, Aultman Museum, Baca and Bloom House and Pioneer Museum
Access: From Trinidad, on I-25 very near the southern border with New Mexico, drive 3 miles west on CO 12

Trinidad Lake State Park lies in the foothills of the Sangre de Cristo Mountains in southern Colorado. The piñon and juniper forests that surround the park provide a lush backdrop for the 700-surface-acre Trinidad Lake, which fills the basin behind Trinidad Dam. Facilities are adequately spaced around the lake to avoid congestion, while giving visitors the feeling of having the lake all to themselves. From any vantage point along the shore, there are views across the lake to the surrounding mountains. The spacious atmosphere provided by the park complements the many recreational opportunities available at Trinidad Lake.

This area of Colorado is steeped in history. For centuries, Native Americans inhabited the area where the park now stands. The Spanish conquistadors first came to the area in the 1500s, followed by French fur trappers. It was these trappers who named the Purgatorie River that was eventually dammed to become Trinidad Reservoir. The park is bordered by the famous Santa Fe National Historic Trail and by the Scenic Highway of Legends. Ranching and small farming were the main economic activity during the late 1800s. However, a sizable coal deposit was discovered and mining began in 1886 at the Sophris coal mining camp. Coal mining was dominant until 1940. When Trinidad Dam was built during the late 1970s, the high water covered much of what was once the mining camp. The rich cultural history of southern Colorado is reflected in five museum complexes located in the city of Trinidad, just east of the park.

The drive around the east shore of the lake on County Road 18.3 offers excellent views of the large dam built by the U.S. Army Corps of Engineers in the 1970s, located at the far eastern edge of the park. In 1980, the park was opened. South of the dam, an access road leads to the South Side Park Entrance.

The sixty-two-site Carpios Ridge campground is located on the higher ground northwest of the dam at the park's main entrance from Colorado Highway 12. This campground can accommodate recreational vehicles or tents. Modern amenities include centrally located water hydrants, a coin-operated laundry, electrical hookups, showers, and modern rest rooms. A dump station is located near the campground entrance, for all waste, sewage, and dishwater. The campground and picnic area have reserved parking spaces and campsites adapted for the physically challenged. Rest rooms, showers, picnic tables, and drinking fountains are also accessible.

Located near the campground is an archaeological site that features actual Indian tepee rings and a display board with topics relating to Trinidad Lake and the surrounding area. Interpretive programs are presented each weekend and holiday

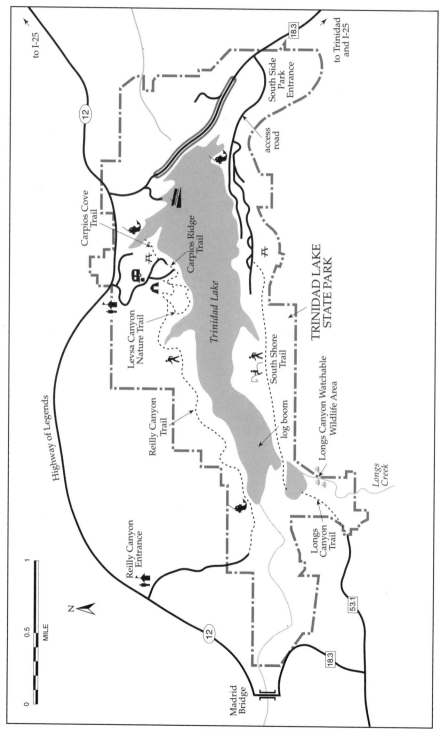

Picnic area near Carpios Cove at Trinidad Lake State Park

evening from Memorial Day through Labor Day at the park's amphitheater. For the program schedule, ask any park employee.

Boating and other water-sports are permitted at Trinidad Lake State Park, but swimming is prohibited. Boaters are asked to observe the Colorado boating statutes and regulations (the park is just a few miles north of New Mexico), which are presented in pamphlet form at the park office and entrances. All boats must observe wakeless speeds around the boat launch area, within 150 feet of shore fishermen, and as indicated by buoys. Boats are not allowed within 200 feet of the dam or the intake structure or behind the log boom at the lake's west end. Water-skiers are required to ski counterclockwise. All boaters are warned that the water level at Trinidad Lake can fluctuate; boaters should be especially watchful for submerged hazards.

Fishing is allowed everywhere on the lake except in the boat launching and docking area. The lake is stocked with rainbow and brown trout, largemouth bass, channel catfish, walleye, crappie, bluegill, and wipers. The lake's scenic mountain backdrop and the tranquil setting adds to the fishing experience at Trinidad.

Several hiking trails can be found at a trailhead located in the campground and picnic area. The short Carpios Cove Trail begins in the campground and winds its way down to Carpios Cove (0.5 mile). The 0.5-mile Carpios Ridge Trail offers views of the reservoir and Fishers Peak, a 9,655-foot mountain that sits just east of the famous Raton Pass, a crossing point for the Mountain Branch of the Santa Fe Trail. Also found in the campground is the longer Levsa Canyon Nature Trail, a self-guided walk that loops back to the campground and contains fifteen interpretive stations. Some of the information found along the trail includes descriptions of piñon pine, juniper, and cholla cactus and explanations of the significant nearby mountain ranges and rivers. More adventurous hikers can connect this trail to the Reilly Canyon Trail and hike 4 miles further west toward the Reilly Canyon entrance.

From the South Side Park Entrance, the South Shore Trail leads hikers as well as horseback riders 2.5 miles to Long's Canyon and the surrounding forests. From the Long's Canyon area, hikers can take the 0.75-mile Long's Canyon Trail through the Long's Canyon Watchable Wildlife Area to County Road 53.1, which heads west to connect with County Road 18.3 and cross the Madrid Bridge back to Colorado Highway 12. Hikers should be aware that hunting is permitted between Labor Day and Memorial Day in posted areas. Check with the park office concerning season and regulations.

Mountain biking is permitted on all trails in the park. In winter, cross-country skiing takes place on the north side trail system, with ice fishing available throughout the lake.

In Long's Canyon on the southwest end of the park, the Watchable Wildlife area features a wetlands habitat on Long's Creek. A helpful brochure designed to enhance the observing of wildlife is available at the park office. Ask for the "Colorado's Watchable Wildlife" brochure. Bird-watchers can also pick up the pamphlet "Birds of Trinidad Lake State Park," which lists the species commonly seen in the park, such as hummingbirds, great blue herons, red-tailed hawks, great horned owls, Canadian geese, western grebes, and wild turkeys. Larger animals commonly seen include cottontail rabbits, ground squirrels, mule deer, coyote, and black bear.

No visit to Trinidad Lake State Park would be complete without driving the famed "Highway of Legends," Colorado Highway 12, which takes visitors out of the park. This 120-mile round trip has been designated a Colorado Scenic and Historic Byway. Along the route, travelers can visit many charming mountain towns steeped in the history of the area . . . La Veta, Cuchara, Segundo. These towns reflect the influence of gold, coal, and the Spanish heritage on the region. Visitors also are treated to some spectacular scenery, especially the majestic Spanish Peaks just east of Cuchara. Museum goers enjoy the historic museums located in Trinidad, including the Louden-Henritze Archeology Museum, the Aultman Museum, and the Baca and Bloom House and Pioneer Museum. Information on these museums can be obtained by calling the Baca House (see appendix A).

View from atop Grand Mesa near Vega State Park

WEST REGION

▲Western Colorado is a timeless place. It wears colorful splashes of ancient Indian cliff dwellings, red- and rust-tinted volcanic mountains, shimmering slopes of green and yellow aspen groves, and sky blue lakes scattered like so many topaz gemstones across the landscape. This is a place that stimulates the senses and the imagination, a land that impresses while healing the soul. J. N. Macomb, one of the first explorers to survey the western slope of Colorado (the topography that sweeps down the west slopes of the Rockies and out into the plateau/mesa country that reaches into Utah), observed in 1859, "There is scarcely a more beautiful place on the face of the earth" (quoted in a state park brochure). The fourteen West Region state parks all reaffirm this claim, from the high-mountain Sylvan Lake to the Grand Mesa–surrounded Vega reservoir, to the southwestern Mancos Lake sitting in the shadow of the spectacular San Juan Mountains. Every park offers a unique expression of the far-reaching natural beauty found in the region's many national forests, mountain ranges, canyon gorges, high mesas, plateaus, and powerful rivers.

The West, synonymous with majestic vistas, diversity of nature, rugged scenery, and wide-open spaces stretching to far horizons, is fully realized in the West Region of Colorado. The Colorado Plateau occupies most of the western fourth of the state, and contains Navajo, Ridgway, Sweitzer Lake, Vega, Mancos Lake, Highline, and Crawford state parks. Also on the Colorado Plateau is the Grand Valley, a drainage for the Colorado River located near the western border with Utah. The Colorado River State Park sites at Corn Lake, Connected Lakes, and Island Acres are located in the Grand Valley and, along with Rifle Gap, Rifle Falls, and Harvey Gap state parks, are on or near the Roan Plateau, which encompasses the famous Book Cliffs that stretch an additional 50 miles into eastern Utah. From the Continental Divide, the north–south mountain ridge running through the middle third of the state, the western slope of the Rocky Mountains sweeps down and west. In this more mountainous region are Paonia and Sylvan Lakes State Parks. The high-country San Juan and La Plata Mountains in southwest Colorado; the Black Canyon of the Gunnison in the east-central portion of the West Region; the Colorado River; the colorful Southwest canyon country of Grand Mesa and the Uncompahgre Plateau south of the Colorado River, and the high desert and low foothills near Grand Junction; the Maroon Bells-Snowmass, West Elk, Lizard Head, Weminuche, Raggeds, and Mountain Sneffels wilderness areas near the west-central part of the state—these areas, scenic beyond belief, are diverse, colorful, and inviting.

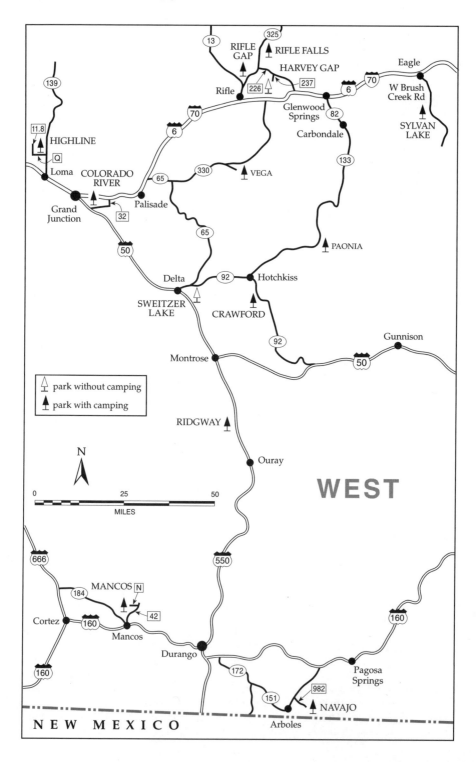

The climate of the West Region tends to be milder as the land slopes down from the Continental Divide and into eastern Utah. Winters in the Grand Valley and on the Colorado Plateau are far less severe than in the higher alpine and subalpine zones in the center of Colorado. The San Juan Mountains, however, endure harsh winters. The west slope—considered most of the West Region—can be hot during the summer, but milder in spring and fall, like its counterpart, the Colorado eastern plains. Rainfall is sparse, except near the upslope of mountains, and much of the area is regarded as high desert.

The flora of this region (except for the subalpine and alpine areas near the Continental Divide) is largely shrubland. Sagebrush, greasewood, mountain mahogany, Gambel oak, saltbush, and cactus are prevalent. The grasses in the West Region are not nearly as prairielike as those on the eastern plains, but Junegrass, blue grama, and wheatgrass are often seen.

The wildlife of the West Region includes some species also found on the eastern plains. Lizards, rattlesnakes, Gambel's quail, roadrunners, eagles, hawks and owls, elk, mule deer, chipmunks, coyote, gray fox, black bear, and bighorn sheep make their home from the lower plateau and valley areas 60 to 80 miles east of the Utah border all the way up to the Continental Divide east of Aspen.

The West Region is a diverse mix of high-country mountains and their famous

Farmlands reminiscent of Switzerland along the eastern border of Harvey Gap State Park

149

resort towns of Aspen, Snowmass, Telluride, and Crested Butte. At the same time, it offers colorful Southwest canyon country at Grand Junction, Cortez, and Montrose.

Some of Colorado's most scenic highways are found in the West Region. The Alpine Loop Backcountry Byway near Silverton in the west-central Rockies, the San Juan Skyway in the state's southwest corner, and the West Elk Scenic and Historic Byway 80 miles east of Grand Junction and south of Interstate 70 are just a few of the many beautiful routes visitors can drive on their way to some of the state's finest recreational opportunities. The major highways of the West Region include Interstate 70, Highway 50, Highway 92, and Highway 160, all running east–west, and Highways 50, 550, and 133 running north–south.

Mancos State Park invites a pilgrimage north along the San Juan Mountains via the historic San Juan Scenic Skyway until one reaches Ridgway State Park. Along the way, travelers see some of the most awesome mountain scenery in America, from Molas Pass down through Silverton and Ouray. Once at Ridgway Reservoir, visitors can look south and admire the stunning vistas they viewed from afar.

Sweitzer Lake, Vega, Highline, Rifle Gap, Rifle Falls, Harvey Gap, and Crawford are state parks found in the high desert and low foothills near Grand Junction that cater to families, picnickers, fishermen, and boaters. Colorado River State Park's three sites serve the boating and rafting needs of those seeking whitewater adventure, while the gentle high-alpine Sylvan Lake offers a real retreat from city distractions.

From Crawford State Park's cattle country to Rifle Falls State Park's famous triple waterfall, visitors have plenty to see and do, much to explore and enjoy. Navajo State Park's large reservoir borders New Mexico and resembles a toned-down version of Utah's Lake Powell, with its surrounding mesas and plateaus. Harvey Gap State Park occupies a plateau and valley region looking out upon the central Rockies to the east and southeast, while Paonia State Park is a sliver of water in a

Old covered wagon at a Colorado ranch

Hahns Peak looking north from Steamboat Lake

steep, high-country valley just west of the Ragged Mountains.

Hikers wanting to see the scenic masterpieces of this West Region are treated to perhaps the most beautiful section of the Colorado Trail, which extends from Denver to Durango and now connects to Mancos State Park further west. The trails found in the San Juan and La Plata Mountains; atop Grand Mesa and along the Uncompahgre Plateau and Colorado National Monument; and in the Maroon Bells-Snowmass, West Elk, Lizard Head, Weminuche, Raggeds, and Mountain Sneffels Wilderness Areas are trails hikers dream of. These areas have enough trails to last a lifetime and to give a lifetime's worth of meaning to the hiking experience. This is the region of Colorado that made llama trekking famous. And with so many places to see, sometimes it does help to have an animal companion carry the load!

Native American heritage is displayed in dozens of famous Anasazi sites such as Hovenweep National Monument, Chimney Rock, and Mesa Verde National Park. Ghost towns, mining towns, ski resorts, historic districts . . . all offer an alternative to countless fishing, boating, hiking, mountain biking, and many other outdoor recreational enjoyments found in this part of the state.

The Colorado state parks in the West Region provide a perfect destination for visitors wanting to journey from section to section of western Colorado. It is a place where you take your time to see the wonders time has created. The land brings visitors back year after year, and always with the same feeling that so much remains yet to be discovered!

SYLVAN LAKE STATE PARK

Hours/Season: Overnight; year-round
Area: 115 acres; 40 surface water acres
Facilities: 50 campsites, 9 picnic sites, boat ramp
Attractions: Camping, picnicking, photography, fishing, boating, hiking, mountain biking, cross-country skiing, ice skating, ice fishing
Nearby: Holy Cross Wilderness Area, Eagle's Nest Wilderness Area, Eagle–Vail Valley
Access: From Eagle on I-70, east of Glenwood Springs, exit and go south through the town of Eagle on Main Street to West Brush Creek Road; turn right and go 16 miles to the park entrance

The drive up West Brush Creek Road to Sylvan Lake State Park is another of those incredibly scenic byways that capture so much of the beauty that exemplifies Colorado. Quiet-running West Brush Creek runs the length of the canyon into Sylvan Lake, and leads you past gentle mountain ranches, free-running horses, and magnificent stands of aspen on the surrounding mountains, which are captivating in their own right. As the road takes you higher, the mountains of the Sawatch Range begin to close in on you, until you finally reach the secluded meadows and wooded mountains that envelop Sylvan Lake.

What was at one time a mink farm was acquired by the state in 1962 and became

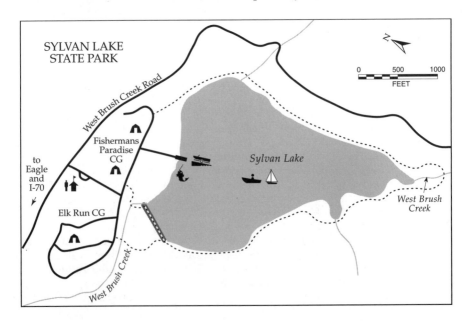

Sylvan Lake with surrounding mountains

part of the park system in 1987. Located at 8,500 feet, Sylvan Lake is a true alpine park. Expansive pine and fir forests converge at the lake's edge from the surrounding White River National Forest to provide a secluded mountain retreat. The lake is often touted as one of western Colorado's best-kept secrets.

Campers enjoy restful sojourn, with 30 campsites available at Elk Run campground, to the right of the park entrance, and 20 more at Fisherman's Paradise campground, to the left of the park entrance. These sites allow for tents, trailers, and campers, with some pull-through sites for larger units.

The picnic sites at Sylvan Lake are at the north end of the reservoir, just south of the residence building. Currently there are nine picnic tables, but plans call for the addition of more sites as well as changing the residence building into a cabin for public overnight use.

Nonmotorized boats and boats with electric motors are allowed on the lake; gasoline-powered motors are not permitted. The boat ramp is just south of Fisherman's Paradise campground. Boaters enjoy stable water levels throughout the summer. The lake is quiet and uncluttered, as no competing water sports are permitted. Because of the high elevation, the temperature cools early in the evening, even in the summer. Boaters should dress accordingly.

Local fishermen know Sylvan Lake for its tranquil atmosphere that is as hushed as the inside of a cathedral. Life is slowed down at the lake. Quiet, cool early mornings waiting for the brook and rainbow trout to bite slip effortlessly into lazy sun-filled afternoons, watching the billowing white cumulus clouds that often build over the Rockies. This is the stuff of which summers are made. As late afternoon fades to the purple twilight of dusk, the day's catch is gathered and iced, leaving fond memories of another day well spent at Sylvan Lake. Ice fishing is also permitted at the lake in winter.

Hiking trails circle the lake from both campgrounds. The trail, almost 1 mile long, hugs the shoreline; in places it enters the woods before returning to the lakeshore. Biking is allowed on the roads into the park. More serious bikers ride the forest service roads off West Brush Creek Road. Cross-country skiing is permitted anywhere in the park, although there are no groomed trails.

Outdoor photography enthusiasts find mountains (literally) of possible subject matter. The reflections in the lake, the fact that few boats are ever on the lake at one time, the abundance of forest and mountains, the pristine clear water . . . all conspire to make Sylvan Lake a choice alpine setting. Afternoon clouds contribute to the mix and frame many possible shots with added depth. As the seasons change, so do the opportunities for capturing the nuances of nature's shift from greens to yellows, browns, and, finally, grays and white, with the azure blue of Colorado's skies providing its supportive backdrop.

Wildlife is abundant, both for viewing and photographing. Mule deer, beaver,

The Flat Tops Wilderness along Highway 131 north of Sylvan Lake

elk, and waterfowl are just a few inhabitants of Sylvan Lake that are often spotted. In White River National Forest, located near the park, "there are more hiking trail-miles available within 40 miles of Sylvan Lake than can scarcely be believed." Information on the trails within White River National Forest is available by calling the headquarters office (see appendix A). Just over the pass, east of Sylvan Lake, is the Holy Cross Wilderness Area, and nearby are the Hardscrabble Mountains and the Eagle's Nest Wilderness Area. I found a superb hiking map, well marked with all the trails in this area, titled "Vail and Eagle Valley . . . Mountain Biking and Recreation," available in the towns of Eagle, Avon, and Vail. You can get this map by calling the Eagle Valley Chamber or the Vail Resort Association (see appendix A). Outdoor recreation of every kind abounds in and near the Eagle–Vail Valley. You can river-raft the Colorado or Eagle River, fish dozens of mountain streams and lakes, hike and mountain bike, and, of course, ski.

PAONIA STATE PARK

Hours/Season: Overnight; year-round
Area: 1,507 acres; 334 surface water acres
Facilities: 15 campsites, 4 picnic sites, boat ramp
Attractions: Camping, picnicking, interpretive programs, outdoor photography, fishing, boating, waterskiing, jet skiing, sailboarding, horseback riding, cross-country skiing; *no drinking water*
Nearby: Ragged Wilderness Area, Maroon Bells-Snowmass Wilderness Area
Access: From I-70 at Glenwood Springs, take Highway 82 south 12 miles to Carbondale, then take Highway 133 south for 46 miles

Paonia State Park is an alpine lake setting at 6,500 feet elevation. The park is surrounded to the east by the spectacular Ragged Mountains, whose close proximity gives visitors the feeling of enclosure. This is accented by the fact that the lake is a long, narrow crescent with mountains rising out of the waters to fill up the small valley that the lake rests in. Gunnison National Forest in many places borders right to the lake's edge. If you are looking for a sense of privacy, an out-of-the-way mountain lake retreat, Paonia is the place. The park leans more to the rustic side, with few amenities. However, plans are being drawn for adding to already existing campsites and picnic facilities, and for improving the available parking areas. For some outdoor enthusiasts, the simple and uncomplicated fare at Paonia is a plus when it comes to a backcountry experience.

All the present amenities are located at the north end of the lake, mostly on the eastern side of the reservoir. This area can be cooler than expected, as the sun takes a while before rising high enough to warm this side of the lake.

Paonia State Park is situated 16 miles east of the mining town of Paonia. This area has long been a coal mining center, and coal chunks can sometimes be seen along the sides of the road as one drives through Paonia. In 1960 a dam was constructed to provide additional water and irrigation resources for the lower valley towns that follow Highways 133 and 92 down to the farming community of Delta, southeast of Grand Junction. In 1967 Colorado State Parks agreed to manage the area for the U.S. Bureau of Reclamation.

The park has fifteen campsites, located in two separate campgrounds. Spruce campground is next to Highway 133 and offers eight campsites in a beautiful

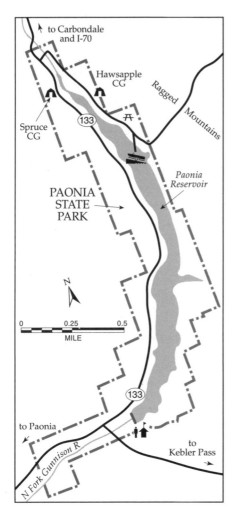

sylvan setting of majestic blue spruce trees, with a babbling stream nearby. Hawsapple campground is located across the East Muddy Creek and is more popular with water-skiers. All campsites have a picnic table and a fire ring, and vault toilets are nearby. However, no drinking water is available in the park, so campers must bring their own supplies.

Picnic sites are at the end of the park road that crosses the river to Hawsapple campground. This is also where the boat launch is located. Supplies for picnickers, boaters, campers, and fishermen can be found at Crystal Meadows Ranch, located just south of the dam on the Kebler Pass Road. It is best, however, to bring all serious supplies with you . . . especially gear of a more specific nature. If you plan a long camping stay, then food supplies, especially, need to be brought with you.

Boaters find the mountain and forest setting beautiful and inspiring. The lake is long and very narrow, which makes for fast runs down the entire length of the reservoir. As boaters travel from south to north, the towering Ragged Mountains fill the eastern horizon. The enclosed feeling generated by the towering, nearby mountains is one of the unique features of this park.

Fishing is highlighted from late June until late August, when northern pike and rainbow trout are occasionally caught. Good fly fishing is found by driving to the confluence of Muddy Creek and Anthracite Creek below the dam. The latter creek's name reflects the coal mining legacy of the area. Visitors driving to Paonia State Park from the southwest see large standing deposits of coal in and around the town of Paonia.

There are no hiking trails at Paonia State Park, but horseback riding and cross-country skiing can be done on an informal basis along the shore of the lake; no groomed cross-country ski trails exist in this park.

Some wildlife, such as chipmunks, squirrels, rabbits, and an occasional mule deer or elk, can be seen around the lake. Any walks up and into the surrounding forests are sure to offer some encounter with wildlife. Black bear sometimes visit the area, so take precautions in food storage and camp cleanliness.

Hikers may wish to visit the trail systems in the nearby Ragged Wilderness Area; call Gunnison National Forest (see appendix A). Traveling further east, hikers and

Views east across Paonia Reservoir toward the Ragged Mountains

other outdoor recreation enthusiasts might visit the Maroon Bells-Snowmass Wilderness Area located in Gunnison/White River National Forest area (see appendix A).

RIFLE GAP STATE PARK

Hours/Season: Overnight; year-round
Area: 1,541 acres; 359 surface water acres
Facilities: 46 campsites, 14 picnic sites, boat ramp, dump station
Attractions: Camping, picnicking, swimming, boating, waterskiing, sailing, jet skiing, fishing, biking, horseback riding, cross-country skiing, ice skating, ice fishing
Nearby: Flat Tops Wilderness Area
Access: From the Rifle interchange on I-70, west of Glenwood Springs, take CO 13 north, go through Rifle and continue 3 miles, then turn right on CO 325 and go 6 miles to the park

Rifle Gap State Park is reached by a scenic byway, Colorado Highway 325, which runs north from the town of Rifle. This beautiful drive takes you through a quaint farm valley, bordered east and west by a red-rock canyon overflowing with verdant grasslands and trees. As you approach the park, you pass through a

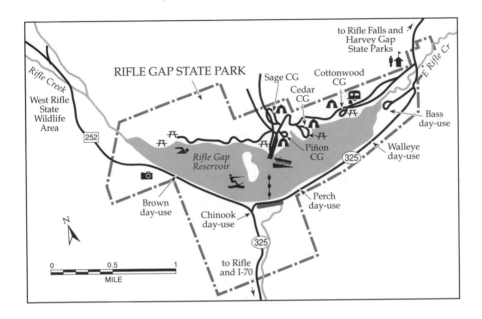

narrow section of canyon, a "gap" in the mountain that looks down toward the town of Rifle. Hence the name.

The area was devoted to cattle ranching during the late 1800s. The small town of Austin, with its schoolhouse, occupied the land from 1887 to 1958, but was forced to relocate when plans were drawn by the U.S. Bureau of Reclamation for the construction of the Rifle Gap Reservoir. This project was completed between 1964 and 1968, and the area was turned over to Colorado State Parks in 1967.

As you pass through the "gap" and begin the drive around the Rifle Gap Reservoir, you know at once that this is a water-sport park that virtually dominates the small lowland depression that it occupies. Everywhere you look, you see Rifle Gap Lake filling the landscape. Lying at an elevation of over 6,000 feet, the clean, clear waters of this state park are famous for offering some of the best boating, swimming, waterskiing, and even scuba diving in this part of Colorado. Western winds blow across the lake from the incoming weather of the northwest or Pacific, and ensure sailing enthusiasts all the action they can handle.

Camping is especially scenic at Rifle Gap. Sage, Piñon, Cedar, and Cottonwood campgrounds are all located along the northern shore of the lake, and each offers a spectacular view down-canyon, looking through Rifle Gap toward the distant Rocky Mountains to the south. The lake is quite open to the surrounding mountains, and allows you to really appreciate the beauty of the expansive lake. There are forty-six campsites at the reservoir, and they can accommodate tents, small trailers, and pickup campers, with some pull-through sites for larger units.

The picnic areas at Rifle Gap are located on the north side of the reservoir. Picnic tables can be found at the Cottonwood and Cedar campgrounds along the north shore and at the swim beach in the northwest portion of the park at the end of the access road. These sites are exposed, offering no shade.

A two-lane boat ramp is located just west of the Piñon campground. The water is considered quite smooth for boating, clear, and even somewhat warm during the summer, with water temperatures sometimes reaching 70°F.

Fishing is permitted anywhere on the lake. However, some day-use-only fishing

Rifle Gap Reservoir from Cottonwood Campground

areas are located on the south side of the lake, beginning with Chinook day-use area to the left of Highway 325, on County Road 252 as you enter the reservoir area. To the right, on Highway 325, are Perch, Walleye, and Bass day-use areas. In Rifle Gap State Park, the catch is often these fish (excluding perch), along with rainbow and German brown trout, channel catfish, and smallmouth and largemouth bass.

Hiking is limited to walks around Rifle Gap on the road that hugs the northern shoreline. The views of the nearby mountains are engaging, with the snowcapped Rockies highly visible until the snowmelt of summer asserts itself. Biking and horseback riding are allowed on the roads into and through the park. In winter, cross-country skiing is popular at Rifle Gap State Park. Other winter sports available at Rifle Gap include ice fishing and snowmobiling.

The wildlife around the lake include deer, elk, beaver, chipmunks, rabbits, bobcats, and weasels. Blue heron, hummingbirds, and a wide array of waterfowl are often seen at the reservoir.

Near the park is White River National Forest, which offers many miles of hiking trails. For information, call the district office located in Rifle (see appendix A). Additional trails to the north on BLM lands are also available for biking and horseback riding. Another nearby hiking destination worth visiting is the Flat Tops Wilderness Area located to the northeast of Rifle Gap. This area looks just like it sounds . . . a series of mountain ranges and elevated land all showing the distinct feature of being somewhat flat-topped. For information about the Flat Tops Wilderness Area, call Medicine Bow Routt National Forest (see appendix A).

Although the only skiing available at Rifle Gap State Park is cross-country, the park is situated near several major ski resorts. Some 65 miles south are Aspen and Snowmass, while to the southwest is Powderhorn.

RIFLE FALLS STATE PARK

Hours/Season: Overnight; year-round
Area: 200 acres
Facilities: 18 campsites, 9 picnic sites
Attractions: Camping, picnicking, spectacular scenic waterfall, fishing, hiking, biking, cross-country skiing
Nearby: Flat Tops Wilderness Area
Access: From the Rifle interchange on I-70, west of Glenwood Springs, take CO 13 north, go through Rifle and continue for 3 miles, then turn right on CO 325 and go 9.8 miles to the park

Rifle Falls State Park is one of the most serene and beautiful of all the Colorado state parks. The drive into the park takes you through a colorful canyon that slowly narrows into an almost gardenlike setting that eventually becomes the park. No great and expansive lake here; instead, visitors find a lush and peaceful hideaway, surrounded by gentle, highly vegetated canyons, accented by a running creek and a rich abundance of box elders, narrow-leaf cottonwoods, hawthorns, chokecherries, and wild columbines (the Colorado state flower). Photographers enjoy the lush setting (some have compared it to Costa Rica), and hikers find the cooler canyon-and-streamside trail a real respite from a hot Colorado summer's day.

As early as 1884, Rifle Falls was a tourist attraction for the area. James Watson

Caves along the trail leading from Rifle Falls

developed the Rifle Falls Ranch and charged admission for viewing the caves and falls. From 1890 to 1922, the Zerbe Resort, consisting of cabins for overnight tourists, was operated by Allan Zerbe. The falls were tapped as a source of hydroelectric power for the nearby town of Rifle from 1908 to 1959. Recreation became the focal point of the property once again when Colorado State Parks opened the area as a state park in 1966.

Scattered along the canyon valley to the north of the park entrance are beautiful camping sites set on grassy lawns that accommodate tents and recreational vehicles. The creek makes a tranquil backdrop for campers.

Picnic sites are located to the north of the park entrance, with many of them walk-in sites. A favorite picnic basket with all the trimmings and two, three, or more days to get away from it all and rest within this tranquil setting . . . what more can you ask for from a visit into Colorado's scenic countryside?

Surprise! As you rest awhile you will be sure to hear the distant sound of what might be a gentle thunder. If you begin walking north—on the Squirrel Trail from the campground, or from one of many connecting trails from the picnic area—you soon find the noise growing louder. Walking just a bit further brings you around a group of trees and reveals a spectacular triple waterfall! The falls is the famous Rifle Falls created by East Rifle Creek splitting into three distinct waterways as it plunges down onto the canyon floor. Of course, you brought your camera! A fair number of outdoor photographers surround the falls and patiently maneuver for the perfect shot. Movie crews and famous nature photographers from around the country make the trek yearly to capture the lush grotto setting of Rifle Falls.

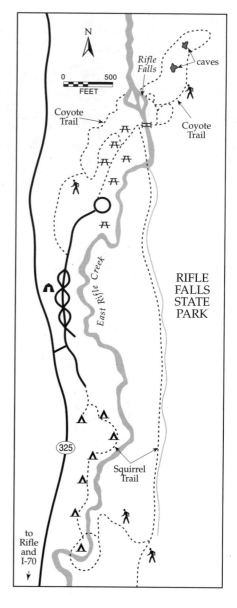

Visitors can stay and rest beside the falls or continue on the Coyote Trail, which begins to the right just after the falls. In just a few short yards, another incredible natural wonder is discovered: a series of dark caves in the limestone cliff that the trail follows alongside. At first the caves are small and suggest a possible residence for coyote, fox, or other large ground animals. But soon visitors come to a huge

Rifle Falls

90-foot hollow that takes a flashlight (and some courage!) to begin exploring. This limestone cave brings out the spelunker in anyone, enticing them to come discover the wonders within. Continue following the trail until it comes back on itself and leads you once again past the thundering Rifle Falls. If this gentle but fun-filled hike does not bring out the kid in someone, then nothing will!

East Rifle Creek provides some great stream-fishing opportunities. Rainbow and brown trout, some up to 19 inches long, have been caught, with the average size being 10 to 12 inches.

Biking is allowed on all roads and trails in the park. Cross-country skiing occurs anywhere in the park during winter, but there are no groomed trails.

On a good wildlife observation day, visitors might see beaver, chipmunks, rabbits, and mule deer, with an occasional red-tailed hawk keeping watch above.

Additional hiking can be found in the Bureau of Land Management lands that border on the park. Information is available by calling the nearest BLM office, in Grand Junction (see appendix A). Even more hiking opportunities are found 20 to 30 miles north and northeast in the Flat Tops Wilderness Area and White River National Forest. The road into Rifle Falls joins an all-weather road that heads north into the Little Box Canyon and Three Forks campgrounds. From there, hikers can connect to dozens of forest and all-weather roads that lead for miles into the backcountry wilderness and onto countless hiking trails. When you call for information at the Rifle Ranger District Office (see appendix A), ask for both the White River National Forest map and USGS topo maps for Rifle Falls, Triangle Park, and Meadow Creek Lake.

HARVEY GAP STATE PARK

Hours/Season: Day-use 6:00 A.M. to 10:00 P.M.; night fishing (no overnight camping); year-round
Area: 160 acres; 160 surface water acres
Facilities: 30 picnic sites, boat ramp
Attractions: Picnicking, fishing, swimming, boating, sailboarding, cross-country skiing, ice fishing
Nearby: Maroon Bells-Snowmass Wilderness Area
Access: From the Rifle interchange on I-70, west of Glenwood Springs, take CO 13 north, go through Rifle, and continue for 3 miles; turn right onto Highway 325 and go 7 miles to CR 226; turn right and go 4 miles to CR 237; turn right and go south 1 mile to the park entrance

Harvey Gap State Park is one of those get-away-from-it-all recreational destinations. The visitor is welcomed by a beautiful array of surrounding mountains, with a look to the east onto rolling farm fields nestled beneath the distant Rockies . . . a Swiss-like picture in western Colorado. No camping is allowed at the park, but night fishing is allowed and day use can be very busy.

The park exists as the result of a dam constructed in 1902, replacing the original

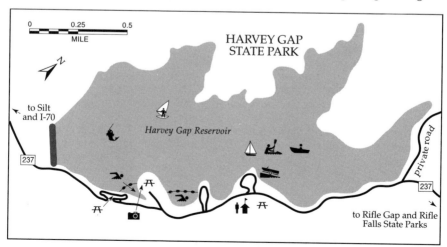

HARVEY GAP
STATE PARK

0   0.25   0.5
MILE

to Silt
and I-70

Harvey Gap Reservoir

237

private road

237

to Rifle Gap and Rifle
Falls State Parks

Harvey Gap Reservoir/Lake from the north shore

one built in 1890. Colorado State Parks has developed the recreational aspects of the Harvey Gap Reservoir, but left in place its quiet look and feel. At Harvey Gap, you are in the backcountry.

There are three picnic areas, with the sites generously spread out along the reservoir, all equipped with grills, and some are scenically placed on a beautiful overlook above the lake. The quiet, uncrowded conditions make for a perfect family outing.

Although boating is an avid pastime at the lake, there is a 20-horsepower maximum for motors permitted on the lake. Thus no waterskiing is allowed. Boaters find the views magnificent. The west side of the lake is virtually undeveloped, with no road access, so boaters wanting to head for quieter waters merely have to head toward the western shore. The boat ramp is located at the picnic area near the entrance station.

Harvey Gap State Park is well situated to catch the prevailing winds blowing out of the west and northwest. This makes this park a premier windsurfing destination. The absence of strong wakes from water-skiers adds to the quality of the windsurfing, as well.

Swimmers find two buoy-protected areas for swimming, and because of the depth and clarity of the water, even scuba diving is a sport well suited for Harvey Gap State Park.

Fishing is the major draw at the lake, and it is generously stocked with a variety of both cold- and warm-water fish, including rainbow trout, crappie, catfish, and smallmouth bass. While rainbow trout are best caught during the cooler months, trout, tiger muskie, and northern pike fishing is good year-round. The fishing is tranquil in the west area of the lake. Ice fishing is permitted anywhere on the reservoir in the winter.

There are no hiking trails at Harvey Gap State Park, but cross-country skiing is allowed, although there are no groomed trails.

Wildlife observers can spot mule deer, beavers, chipmunks, rabbits, bobcats, and weasels, with a variety of ducks, waterfowl, eagles, and hawks often seen. The atmosphere at Harvey Gap is one of quiet isolation. Visitors seeking a more rustic, less developed recreational experience find it at Harvey Gap State Park.

Visitors wishing to do some hiking in the area have an excellent opportunity to do so in the nearby Maroon Bells-Snowmass Wilderness Area. From Harvey Gap State Park, travel south for a few miles until you reach Interstate 70, then drive east to Glenwood Springs and take Highway 82 south to the alpine and ski resort towns of Snowmass Village and Aspen. Perhaps the most photographed scene in all of Colorado is located just a few miles from Aspen . . . the 14,000-plus-foot Maroon Bells mountain area. Not far from here are several other fourteeners, including Snowmass Mountain, Pyramid Peak, and Castle Peak. The hike to Maroon Bells and Maroon Lake can be accessed with the help of bus service that takes you to the trailhead. The trail winds up a scenic valley and past a beautiful alpine lake, and eventually reaches the lower part of the mountains; most tourists come this far, then return to the trailhead . . . photographs in hand! One of the great hikes in Colorado links the Maroon Bells area with the alpine resort town of Crested Butte, located southwest of Aspen. This is a long day's hike, best made as a shuttle between resorts. Information on hikes in this area can be obtained by calling the Maroon Bells-Snowmass Wilderness Area and Gunnison/White River National Forests (see appendix A).

VEGA STATE PARK

Hours/Season: Overnight; year-round
Area: 898 acres; 900 surface water acres
Facilities: 110 campsites, 42 picnic sites, group picnic area, dump station, 3 boat ramps
Attractions: Camping, picnicking, interpretive programs, boating, waterskiing, sailboarding, jet skiing, fishing, hiking, biking, horseback riding, cross-country skiing, ice skating, ice fishing, winter camping
Nearby: Grand Mesa
Access: From I-70 about 12 miles east of Grand Junction, go south on Highway 65 10 miles, then east on CO 330 for 11 miles to the town of Collbran; continue for 12 miles past Collbran to the park entrance

The drive along the Scenic Byway of Highways 65 and 330 to Vega State Park is part of the enjoyable outdoor experience the park first offers. Visitors make their way from the colorful mesa and plateau areas north along a beautiful valley accented by low mesas and bluffs, with the towering flat top of Grand Mesa filling the southern horizon. The drive brings visitors out of the lower, more desertlike valley into a subalpine forest and meadow region situated at 8,000 feet. The land around the park offers summer visitors an abundant wildflower display.

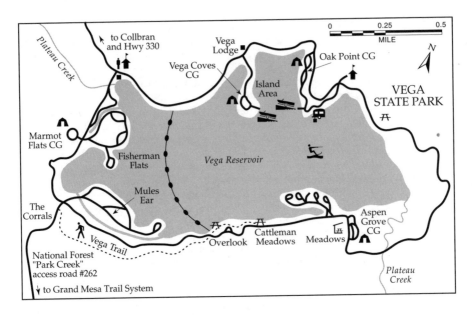

The Vega Reservoir area is rich in history and natural beauty. A marker at the lake salutes the Dominguez-Escalante expedition of 1776 that passed through this area . . . the same expedition that explored much of southern Utah to the west. The name Vega is the Spanish word for "meadow," reflecting the fact that from the late 1800s until 1962, cattle ranchers grazed their herds on the expansive meadow grasses surrounding the area that was to eventually become the state park.

Vega State Park offers 110 camping sites considerately spaced along the shore of Vega Reservoir. Marmot Flats Campground is located south of the entrance station, with views down the entire length of the lake. Vega Coves and Oak Point campgrounds are situated near each other along the north shore, with a boat ramp between them. Aspen Grove Campground occupies the southeast section of the park, next to Plateau Creek. Each campground is scenically located, and can accommodate recreational vehicles and tents. A dump station can be found in the Oak Point Campground. Supplies are available in the town of Collbran, 12 miles west of the park entrance.

Picnickers enjoy fantastic mountain and forest scenery from the forty-two picnic sites found mostly along the south shore of the lake; Overlook and Cattleman Meadows picnic areas are connected to the Marmot Flats Campground by Vega Trail. Meadows group picnic area can host up to 200 people and comes complete with its own ballfield. Vega is an out-of-the-way mountain lake in a verdant sylvan setting, perfect for summer picnicking!

Because Vega is an alpine-type lake, waterskiing usually begins in early June and ends by mid-August, depending on the water level. Always contact the park office (see appendix A) as to weather, temperature, and water conditions. Other water-sports enthusiasts find Vega's cool mountain temperatures a welcome relief from the Grand Valley's 100-degree heat in July and August. Water-skiers are required to ski counterclockwise inside the buoys to avoid disrupting the fishing on the lake's west end, around Fisherman Flats.

Fishermen enjoy the largest body of water in the Grand Valley area when they fish at Vega State Park. Famous as a well-stocked trout fishery, Vega Reservoir is the last

View east across Vega Reservoir from Angler's Stairwell

lake in the Grand Mesa region to freeze in the fall and the first to thaw in the spring.

Winter sports are very popular at Vega. They include ice fishing, ice skating, cross-country skiing, and snowmobiling. The area is less crowded than during summer and the snow on Grand Mesa makes for a spectacular scenic backdrop.

The self-guiding Vega Trail (2 miles) with interpretive view stations highlights the flora and fauna of the region while escorting visitors through forests of aspen and other high-altitude vegetation. The trail begins at the park road south of Marmot Flats campground, and ends at Cattleman Meadows picnic area. Biking is allowed throughout the park. Horseback riding is permitted only on the roads through the park.

Wildlife in the area includes deer, elk, beaver, waterfowl, weasel, blue grouse, and even wild turkey.

Hikers and visitors with motorized bikes can access the higher and quite extensive trail systems of Grand Mesa above the park by taking the national forest "Park Creek" access road #262 found at the southwest corner of the park. This road brings visitors into the 650-mile trail system found atop Grand Mesa. Information on these trails can be received by calling the Grand Mesa–Uncompahgre and Gunnison National Forest Headquarters in Delta (see appendix A). Downhill skiers are just 45 minutes from the famous Powderhorn Ski Resort (see appendix A), which offers recreational opportunities in summer as well as in winter.

COLORADO RIVER STATE PARK:
ISLAND ACRES

Hours/Season: Overnight; year-round; Day-use open from 7:00 A.M. to 10:00 P.M.
Area: 120 land acres; 10 surface water acres
Facilities: 60 campsites, 50 picnic sites, dump station, group picnic area
Attractions: Camping, picnicking, interpretive programs, fishing, boating, swimming, hiking, biking, cross-country skiing, ice skating, ice fishing
Nearby: Dinosaur sites; Uncompahgre Plateau; Kokopelli's Trail, Tabegauche Trail (mountain biking); Unaweep/Tabeguache Scenic and Historic Byway, Grand Mesa
Access: From I-70 5 miles east of Palisades, take exit 47

Island Acres is the eastern anchor of the Colorado River State Park system. Island Acres is composed of four lakes nestled along the Colorado River in scenic DeBeque Canyon. Island Acres is one of the few state parks located within the scenic splendor of a plateau and mesa canyon. As this canyon was shaped and eroded by the Colorado River, a large island was left in the middle of the river, but a dam built in the 1950s caused the true island characteristics of the area to disappear. Campers, fishermen, picnickers, hikers, and bikers are all treated to the combined magic of the majestic Colorado River winding its way beneath the colorful rock formations of DeBeque Canyon.

A flock of geese emerging from Lake #3

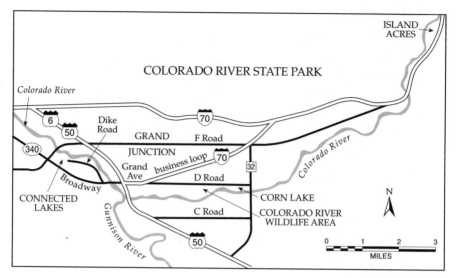

Island Acres enjoys its own unique history, reflecting the changes in western Colorado. Before irrigation made farming, settlement, and other economic use of the area possible, trappers, explorers, and the native Ute Indians used the area as a campsite. From the early 1900s until 1967 the area was known as Island Ranch, and was used as a peach orchard and livestock ranch. Indeed, the entire Grand Valley around Grand Junction is now a highly productive fruit and vegetable agricultural area which has expanded to include vineyards and the production of fine wines. The Division of Parks and Outdoor Recreation began developing the area for recreational use in 1967.

Camping is available at several locations throughout the park. Lush grassy areas provide inviting campsites that can accommodate either tents or recreational vehicles. This area also allows visitors to see great down-canyon views of DeBeque Canyon.

Picnickers are treated to the same cool setting. Picnicking is available in the

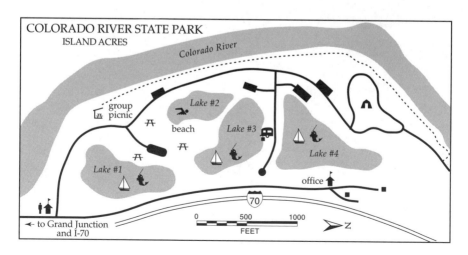

169

southwest section of the park near Lake #2, in the shade of a cottonwood grove. A group picnic site is just left of the entrance road, 0.1 mile after entering the park. During a hot western Colorado day, Island Acres offers a true oasis to escape to and laze away the day, lulled by the sounds of the ever-present Colorado River.

Boating is restricted to non-motorized boating at three of the four Island Acres lakes. Lake #2 is set aside for swimming only, and features a large sandy beach. Where else can you sun and swim, basking in the shadow of colorful canyons and a nationally famous scenic river?

Fishing is allowed on all the lakes at Island Acres except Lake #2. Access to the Colorado River is just a short walk away from any of the lakes. Trout and channel catfish are the prize river catches.

Hiking at Island Acres consists of a 0.75-mile self-guided nature trail that takes you along the edge of the Colorado River from the group picnic area at the south end of the park to the campground at the north end.

Because of the riparian habitat found along the Colorado River, wildlife observers may see Canadian geese, hawks, bald eagles, blue herons, and a variety of ducks. Sometimes mule deer, cottontail rabbits, and weasels make their appearance, but these are best viewed during the early morning or late evening hours.

Although the hiking trails at Island Acres are limited, the park is just a few miles northwest of one of the great hiking destinations in western Colorado: Grand Mesa. For a description of this and other nearby attractions see the Colorado River State Park write-up in this section.

Picnic grounds at Island Acres State Park

COLORADO RIVER STATE PARK:
CORN LAKE, CONNECTED LAKES

Hours/Season: Day-use; 7:00 A.M. to dark; year-round

Area: *Corn Lake* 20 acres, 15 surface water acres; *Connected Lakes* 100 acres, 22 surface water acres

Facilities: *Corn Lake* 20 picnic sites, boat ramp; *Connected Lakes* 24 picnic sites, boat ramp

Attractions: *Corn Lake* picnicking, interpretive programs, fishing, hiking, biking, cross-country skiing, ice skating, ice fishing; *Connected Lakes* picnicking, interpretive programs, fishing, boating, sailboarding, hiking, biking, cross-country skiing, ice skating, ice fishing

Nearby: Dinosaur sites; Uncompahgre Plateau; Kokopelli's Trail, Tabegauche Trail (mountain biking); Unaweep/Tabeguache Scenic and Historic Byway, Grand Mesa

Access: *Corn Lake* from westbound I-70 in Grand Junction, near the western border with Utah, take exit 37 (I-70 business loop) to 32 Road, turn left, and go 2 miles; *Connected Lakes* from I-70 in Grand Junction, near the western border with Utah, take Highway 6/50 exit south 2 miles to Grand Avenue; turn right and continue for 1 mile to Dike Road; turn right and go 1 mile to the park entrance

Colorado River State Park follows the Colorado River for its long and scenic journey through the Grand Valley and its major city, Grand Junction, at the western border of Colorado. From Island Acres (managed by Colorado River State Park) at the eastern end of this section of the river, to the boat launch in the town of Loma at the western end, Colorado River State Park links the various hiking/biking trails in the area along the river corridor. Along this beautiful trail system are a number of small park picnic sites and fishing areas which together make up Colorado River State Park.

The park came about as a result of the efforts by the Grand Junction/Mesa County Riverfront Commission to restore the famed Colorado River corridor in

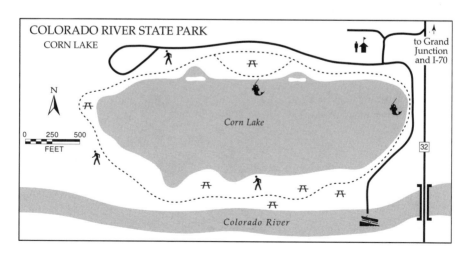

Mesa County and make it a useable recreational resource by improving public access. The section known as Corn Lake was acquired by the state in 1991. The area is popular for picnicking, as several cool and inviting picnic sites are available both at the lakeshore and along the Colorado River. Picnickers can enjoy the fantastic view of the roaring Colorado River and wave to the many boaters and rafters as they make their way downriver. Just west of Corn Lake is the Colorado River Wildlife Area. When the wildlife area is open to public use, sometime in 1995 or 1996, it will feature different types of food crops and habitat for wildlife species. During the 1970s and '80s, the area now known as Connected Lakes was a gravel operation for The United Companies of Grand Junction. The property was first given to Mesa County but was later deeded to Colorado State Parks. The gravel pit areas were transformed into lakes and the entire area opened as a state park in 1993.

Picnicking at Corn Lake is available in the cottonwood trees south of the lake and between the Colorado River, and at the west end of the lake. On the north side of the lake, picnic sites are being developed with landscaping and trees. On a hot day, picnickers often just pull a picnic table out of the open grassland to the comfort of a shady cottonwood. At Connected Lakes, the picnic sites are located mostly around the lakes, under box elder and cottonwood trees, or out in the open grasslands. Shaded picnic areas are located at the handicapped-accessible fishing platform at Dike Road and Connected Lakes.

All boating is prohibited on Corn Lake itself, but the Corn Lake site offers river rafters and boaters a direct launch site into the Colorado River. This section of the Colorado is enjoyed for the scenic vistas seen along the river, from Grand Junction past the Colorado National Monument and out into the Castle Valley and Moab sections in eastern Utah . . . the famed "Westwater" section of the Colorado River. At Connected Lakes, hand-propelled craft and boats with electric trolling motors are allowed. Swimming is not currently permitted at either the Corn Lake or the Connected Lakes site.

The fishing is very good at Colorado River State Park, due to the efforts of the Colorado Division of Wildlife. Corn Lake is stocked with a generous supply of rainbow trout, along with bass, bluegill, catfish, and crappie. The best rainbow trout fishing times are from March to May, and September through October. Corn Lake offers a wheelchair-accessible concrete fishing pier. Duke Lake and Connected Lakes are

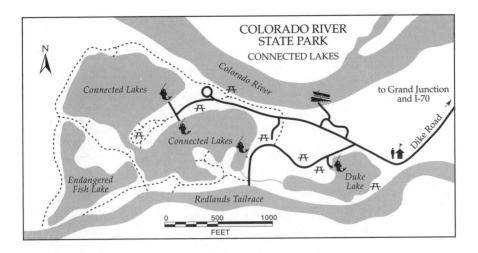

Entrance sign at Corn Lake

among the few lakes in western Colorado stocked strictly with warm-water fish. Connected Lakes offers four sheltered, accessible fishing sites. Fishing is allowed year-round, and if it is cold enough, ice fishing is allowed anywhere in the park. It rarely gets cold or snowy enough for other winter activities.

Corn Lake has a mile-long trail around the lake and along the Colorado River; plans for 1995–96 call for this trail to tie in with the nearby Colorado River Wildlife Area. The Connected Lakes site has over 4 miles of both paved and hard-packed trails that circle the two lakes, with a connecting trail that runs between the lakes along the Redlands Canal and the Colorado River.

Because of the riparian habitat found along the Colorado River, wildlife observers at the Colorado River State Park sites might see Canadian geese, hawks, bald eagles, blue herons, and a variety of ducks. Sometimes mule deer, cottontail rabbits, and weasels make their appearance, but these are best viewed during the early morning or late evening hours. At the soon-to-be-opened Colorado River Wildlife Area, waterfowl and upland game birds in the area will use the various habitats for feeding and nesting. As it now stands, shorebirds, waterfowl, osprey, dove, quail, and bald and golden eagles can be seen on Corn and Connected Lakes and along the river shore, especially in the early morning and evening. Larger land animals, such as mule deer, skunk, rabbits, and beaver are also common to the park.

The Grand Valley, at the heart of Colorado River State Park, offers many additional recreational opportunities. The area surrounding Colorado River State Park was once home to the smallest and largest dinosaurs ever seen on earth. Just west of the parks is an area offering walking tours through some of the more famous dinosaur sites. The Grand Junction Visitor and Convention Bureau has a brochure highlighting these tours, with a map showing directions to the sites. Riggs Hill is the site of the earliest discovery of Brachiosaurus remains. Dinosaur Hill and Rabbit Valley are other sites to visit, with the latter boasting of the "Trail Through Time," a 1.5-mile walk through rich dinosaur deposits and a working dinosaur quarry. For information about activities in the Grand Junction area, call the Visitor and Convention Bureau (see appendix A).

View of Corn Lake from the north shore

Mountain bikers are treated to one of the country's greatest mountain biking trails, the famed Kokopelli's Trail, running 128 miles from Grand Junction to Moab, Utah. Additionally, the Tabegauche Trail crosses the Uncompahgre Plateau from Montrose to Grand Junction. These are two premier mountain biking trails that must be biked to be believed! Information and maps can be obtained by calling the Bureau of Land Management or the Colorado Plateau Mountain Bike Trail Association (see appendix A).

Although the hiking trails at Colorado River State Park are limited, the park is just a few miles west of one of the great hiking destinations in western Colorado: Grand Mesa. Grand Mesa is the largest flat-topped mountain in the world, a virtual 10,000-foot-high island-in-the-sky. Atop the mesa over 200 lakes are scattered throughout pine forests, offering (along with the many streams feeding the lakes) prime fishing locations. Hikers are especially rewarded by more than 650 miles of scenic hiking trails found on the mesa. During the winter these trails second as beautiful cross-country ski trails. A designated Scenic Byway leads to the top of the mesa, from where visitors can view the Alp-like San Juan Mountains to the south. Take exit 49 off Interstate 70, and follow Highway 65 the length of the byway to Cedaredge. Hikers and other outdoor recreation enthusiasts can get information by calling the U.S. Forest Service (see appendix A).

The Uncompahgre Plateau, which extends southeast from Grand Junction, also offers hikers many trails found atop the plateau in Uncompahgre National Forest. Hikers should contact both the Grand Junction Bureau of Land Management Office and the Grand Mesa–Uncompahgre and Gunnison National Forest (see appendix A).

Another nearby treasure is the Unaweep/Tabeguache Scenic and Historic Byway. By following Colorado Highways 141 and 145 south of Grand Junction, you travel through the "last remote vestiges of our Western heritage" (state park brochure). This 133-mile tour winds past 1,200-foot granite walls rising from green fields, slickrock canyons, and high-desert landscape . . . once home to the Ute Indians and the outlaw Butch Cassidy.

HIGHLINE STATE PARK

Hours/Season: Overnight; year-round

Area: 580 acres; 174 surface water acres

Facilities: 25 campsites, 64 picnic sites, group picnic area, dump station, bathhouse, boat ramp, jet ski rental

Attractions: Camping, picnicking, fishing, boating, sailing, swimming, waterskiing, sailboarding, hiking, biking, horseback riding, wildlife observation, ice skating, ice fishing

Nearby: Colorado National Monument

Access: From I-70 just west of Grand Junction, take the Loma exit, onto CO 139; go north 5 miles to Q Road, turn left and go west 1.2 miles to 11.8 Road, then turn right and go north 1 mile to the park entrance

The natural backdrop for Highline State Park is the stunning mesa and canyon country surrounding the Grand Junction area, known as Grand Valley. To the south is the spectacular Colorado National Monument. These 32 square miles of uplifted plateau and dozens of scoured-out canyons comprise an area as colorful as its geological cousins, the Grand Canyon in Arizona and Canyonlands National Park in Utah. To the northeast and east are the imposing purple-gray Book Cliffs, standing like massive sentinels over the city of Grand Junction, and to the far east is the huge flat-topped Grand Mesa.

Highline State Park is the recreational magnet for water-sports, boating, and fishing enthusiasts in Colorado's far western Mesa County. The park consists of two lakes, Highline Lake and Mack Mesa Lake, completed in 1969 and added to the state's recreational park inventory.

Before the construction of the state park, the area was strictly farmland with limited ranching. The nearby town of Fruita hints of the early Mormon agricultural influence of the late 1800s; fruit was a primary agricultural product that has since

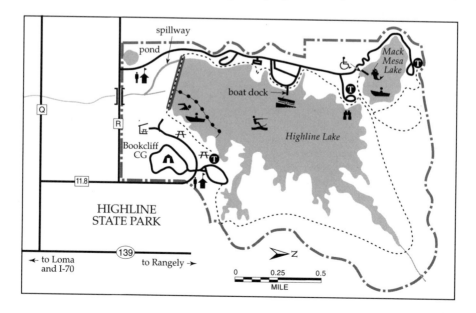

Picnic area east of Highline Lake

given way to corn, wheat, alfalfa, and vegetables. In the late 1960s a governor's commission visited the West Slope (the area of Colorado that sweeps west down from the Continental Divide to Utah) and asked the people of the area what they needed. Their answer: "A lake for recreation." By 1969 their wish was granted with the opening of Highline State Park.

Campers can enjoy twenty-five grassy campsites in Bookcliff campground that accommodate both tents and recreational vehicles. Showers are also available. While there is just one handicapped-accessible campsite, all campsites are level with graveled pads and lawn. Highline State Park offers campers the home base they might need for exploring all the recreational opportunities and natural wonders of the area.

The park is more like a friendly city park, with plenty of shade trees adding a cozy atmosphere to the many picnic areas situated on flowing, deep green lawns. The grassy knolls reach out and touch the main attraction: inviting Highline Lake. A group picnic facility is also available in the grassy area located southeast above the lake. This group picnic area can serve up to 150 picnickers, and conveniences include a large fire grill, covered eating area, and modern rest rooms. Because this facility is so popular, groups should reserve the area in advance by calling the park office (see appendix A).

The park rangers offer, by appointment only, interpretive programs that focus both on the wildlife and the rich geological surroundings of the park.

Boaters find Highline Lake a fine waterskiing area, and the winds blowing from the west give a lift to the sport of sailboarding. The lake offers some scenic protected coves, as well as its relaxing backdrops of canyon and mesa. All boats are required to carry approved life jackets, and a throwable ring buoy if the boat is 16 feet or longer. A whistle or horn and at least one fully charged fire extinguisher for gasoline-motorized boats are also required. The boat launch is located on the lake's west shore, opposite the campground.

Highline offers some unique fishing opportunities. Mack Mesa Lake is famous for its fine early season trout fishing, on a lake where only hand- or electric-powered boats are permitted. A fishing jetty with wheelchair stops is located on the southwest side of Mack Mesa Lake. Highline Lake, just a few yards away, has excellent warm-water fishing, featuring catfish and crappie. During the winter, ice fishing is a possibility, although the waters in the lake enjoy an earlier ice-off than the higher alpine state park lakes.

A swimming area is located on the southeast shore of Highline Lake near the dam. However, no lifeguard is provided. The warm summer months bring the water temperature up to a comfortable level, and the beautiful grassy lawns under protective shade trees offers a cool respite from the hot, direct sun. The swim area at Highline Lake, located just 50 to 75 yards from the parking lot, is handicapped-accessible with assistance; the beach house, rest rooms, and group shelter in this area are all handicapped-accessible. A concrete walkway along the lakeshore is also handicapped-accessible.

The park has 3 miles of hiking trails that connect with extensive trail systems in the nearby Bureau of Land Management area. The main trail in Highline State Park begins at the parking lot north of the Bookcliff campground and winds around the eastern portion of the park through the grasslands near the lake. It swings around the north end of the lake, passing just south of Mack Mesa Lake, and ends near the boat ramp parking area on the west side of the lake. Another short trail (0.5 mile) begins along the southern edge of Mack Mesa Lake and travels north a short distance before ending next to a small hill. The trail around the lake also has a trailhead near the south swim area that crosses over the dam and skirts the west edge of Highline Lake before ending at the boat ramp parking area. None of these trails are currently named.

Even when the summer's rich offering of water sports lessens with the coming of winter, Highline saves some of its finest moments for wildlife observation in the off-season months. From 5,000 to 10,000 birds winter on Highline Lake, while over 150 species of birds can be observed at various times throughout the year. Birds such as snowy egret, golden eagle, great blue heron, white pelican, whooping crane, and bald eagle are familiar visitors. A bird-watching overlook is located on the narrow bit of land between the two lakes.

Hiking opportunities abound near Highline State Park. Interested hikers, mountain bikers, ski enthusiasts, and equestrians can ask the main Colorado State Parks office (see appendix A) for the "Western Slope and Mountains" trail guide from the Urban Trails in Colorado program. This informative guide/map illustrates key trail use areas in the western part of Colorado.

Colorado National Monument, less than 30 miles from Highline State Park, is an incredible hiking plateau that offers almost 90 round-trip miles of trail. The views of the valley below and the surrounding distant mesas are breathtaking. In addition to hiking, visitors can enjoy camping, picnicking, horseback riding, mountain biking, rock climbing, and cross-country skiing. For more information, call Colorado National Monument (see appendix A).

Along with the fascinating geological history of the creation of Colorado National Monument, human history has also played its part. In 1906, John Otto, a newcomer to the area, fell in love with the plateau and canyon country. In 1907 he wrote, "I came here last year and found these canyons, and they felt like the heart of the world to me. I'm going to stay . . . and promote this place, because it should be a national park" (quoted in a state park brochure). He lived alone in the desolate

Highline Lake from the southeastern shore

canyon country he loved, urging local citizens to ask Washington, D.C. to set aside the area as a national park. Meanwhile, he built miles of difficult trail with his own hands through the proposed park so that others could enjoy what he so loved. In 1911 Colorado National Monument was created . . . with John Otto named as the park's caretaker, a job he enjoyed until 1927, for a salary of $1 a month!

CRAWFORD STATE PARK

Hours/Season: Overnight; year-round
Area: 337 acres; 397 surface water acres
Facilities: 53 campsites, 19 picnic sites, boat ramp, dump station
Attractions: Camping, picnicking, interpretive programs, swimming, boating, waterskiing, sailboarding, jet skiing, fishing, hiking, horseback riding, cross-country skiing, ice skating, ice fishing, snowmobiling
Nearby: Black Canyon of the Gunnison National Monument, West Elk Wilderness Area, Gunnison River Territory
Access: From US 50 in Delta, south of Grand Junction, take CO 92 east to Hotchkiss; veer right to stay on CO 92; drive 10 miles to Crawford, then 1 mile south to the park entrance

⅄ Crawford State Park lies just west of the spectacular West Elk Wilderness Area, in the middle of the North Fork cattle country. As I drove through Crawford, I had to negotiate a huge herd of cattle being tended by a local cowboy as he drove his charges straight down the middle of the highway! Park officials later informed me that this was a common occurrence on many a spring or fall day. Cattle and horse ranches and farms surround the park, lending an authentic "out West" flavor to this part of Colorado. The West Elk Wilderness Area is 9 miles east of the park, with the towering Mount Lamborn, Land's End, and the volcanic plug known as Needle Rock forming a beautiful mountain backdrop. Just 12 miles to the south is the famous Black Canyon of the Gunnison National Monument. Together with the gentle, rolling green hills, Crawford State Park is scenically well endowed. And at 6,600 feet elevation, Crawford Lake and surrounding land areas offer a cool retreat from the hotter Grand Valley lowlands just 30 miles west.

The area around Crawford State Park has been associated with cattle ranching and farming since the late 1800s. In the early part of the 1960s, farming had grown to the point that the federal Bureau of Reclamation built a dam to increase the supply of irrigation water. In 1967 Colorado State Parks began building up the area as a recreational destination for the areas east of Grand Junction.

The facilities at Crawford are generously spaced from each other. If you have come to get away from it all, the open spaciousness of this park should be well to your liking. Things are simple at Crawford State Park, and even the development plans continue to honor the atmosphere of wide-open spaces the park provides.

Crawford offers 53 modern campsites, which can accommodate tents and recreational vehicles, in three campgrounds along the east shore. The scenery of the mountains and lake add to the relaxed camping experience. Each site provides tables, grills, and parking pads, with water hydrants located in two of the three campgrounds. Campgrounds are patrolled to ensure quiet after 10:00 P.M. A dump station is located in the center campground for the dumping of waste and sewage. Campers can obtain supplies in the town of Crawford, 1 mile north of the lake.

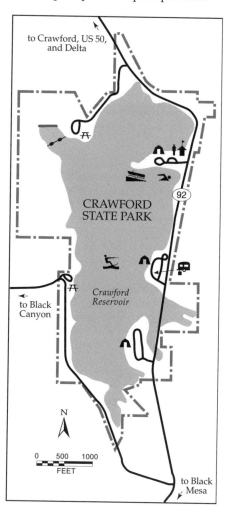

Picnic sites are located along the north and west shore. The site at the north shore sits by itself, with only a restroom facility nearby. If you are looking for privacy, this is the place for that quiet summer picnic. This site also offers a view down the entire length of the lake. The west-side facility is also isolated, and gives a clear view across the lake toward the soaring mountains of the West Elk Wilderness Area.

Boating is a thrill at this park, with the views unspoiled and plenty of room to cruise the lake. The waters of Crawford Lake are fresh-looking and very clean. Boaters with water-skiers are required to ski counterclockwise inside the buoys. The waterskiing season begins in mid-May and ends in mid-September, but it is always a good idea

179

Picnic area along the north shore of Crawford Reservoir

to check with the park concerning weather and temperature conditions. The only boat ramp is located at the northernmost campground area, near the park's headquarters. There is also a swimming beach near the headquarters.

Fishermen find Crawford an excellent perch fishery. Largemouth bass and rainbow trout are also stocked in the lake, and record-size catfish have been caught. Fishing is allowed anywhere on the reservoir, but use or possession of minnows or fish for bait is prohibited. Ice fishing during winter is permitted wherever the ice is thick enough.

There is currently only one hiking trail at Crawford State Park; the Indian Fire Nature Trail meanders 0.25 mile along the west shoreline and loops back to the parking lot. Horseback riding is allowed in undeveloped areas. Cross-country skiing is allowed anywhere that enough snow accumulates, though there are no groomed trails at Crawford State Park.

Crawford Lake is a migration and nesting stopover for waterfowl. Western grebes, Canadian geese, and dozens of other species can be seen at various times throughout the year. In the early morning or late evening, beavers, rabbits, and mule deer are often seen along the lakeshore. And, of course, there are always the cattle and horses nearby to show the kids if a wild critter fails to appear!

Visitors wanting to explore other recreational opportunities nearby can easily access the Black Canyon of the Gunnison National Monument. This magnificent canyon was formed by the carving force of the Gunnison River, creating a 53-mile-long gorge that some canyon lovers feel is the most all-around masterpiece of canyon topography in North America, save for the Grand Canyon in Arizona. From Crawford State Park, take the North Rim Road just south of the park for 12 miles to the monument's North Rim ranger station and campground. Only 12 miles of the canyon are in the confines of the monument, but visitors to the North Rim can hike along the top by taking either the Deadhorse Trail or the North Vista Trail. Rock climbers find this canyon a challenging adventure, as does anyone taking the wild white-water rafting trips on the Gunnison River offered by many concessionaires. For information on this spectacular canyon, call the superintendent's office (see appendix A).

Hikers and other outdoor enthusiasts who wish to explore the many trails found near Crawford Lake in the West Elk Wilderness Area can contact the office for Gunnison National Forest (see appendix A) and ask specifically for West Elk information.

East of Crawford is the region known as the Gunnison River Territory, comprising many of the outdoor opportunities found in the lands drained by the Gunnison River. Here are the famous mountain towns of Crested Butte and Gunnison and the state's largest man-made lake, Blue Mesa. Information on river rafting, fishing, hiking, and visits to historic mining towns are found in the Gunnison River Territory free brochure (see appendix A).

Equestrians, as well as hikers, should look for the North Fork Trails Network Hiking and Horseback Riding Trails Guide. This guide highlights eleven scenic trails surrounding Crawford State Park and lists trail descriptions, access routes, distance, and elevation. Ask the Delta County Area Visitor Bureau (see appendix A).

SWEITZER LAKE STATE PARK

Hours/Season: Day-use; 8:00 A.M. to 5:00 P.M. Oct.–April, 8:00 A.M. to 10:00 P.M. May–Sept.
Area: 73 acres; 137 surface water acres
Facilities: 32 picnic sites, boat ramp, swim area
Attractions: Picnicking, swimming, boating, waterskiing, jet skiing, sailboarding, fishing, hiking, ice skating, ice fishing
Nearby: Grand Mesa
Access: From Grand Junction on I-70, near the western border with Utah, drive south on US 50 to Delta and continue another 1.5 miles to the park

▲ The natural setting for Sweitzer Lake is magnificent. To the south, the snowcapped San Juan Mountains strech across the horizon. To the north, the 10,000-foot-high island in the sky known as Grand Mesa dominates the vista, while to the west the canyon country of the Uncompahgre Plateau fills the view. The spectacular West Elk Mountain Range completes the skyline to the east. This part of Colorado has many recreational options in all directions; however, a good starting point is the gentle, quiet Sweitzer Lake.

Sweitzer Lake State Park is the result of a land donation made by the Morgan Sweitzer family to what is now the Division of Wildlife. Since 1972, the area has been administered by Colorado State Parks.

The lake is often referred to as the "oasis on the edge of the desert," the desert being a low-rainfall region located 30 miles east of the lake and all the way west into Utah. The Audubon Society uses Sweitzer Lake as a bird sighting area and a waterfowl observation site. Almost 180 species of birds have been spotted near the area.

Picnic area at Sweitzer Lake State Park

Sweitzer Lake provides a tranquil spot for picnicking, with four picnic areas located around the lake's west and south shores. The scenery adds to the day's pleasure, while kids can enjoy the swimming area just south of the boat ramp. Picnic, fishing, and boating supplies are available in the town of Delta, located just 1.5 miles north of the park.

The scenic setting of Sweitzer Lake offers boaters beautiful views in all directions. Sailing, canoeing, power boating, and waterskiing are popular pastimes at the lake. The boat ramp is located at the west end of the lake near the dam and the park entrance. At the east end of the lake, boaters are asked to observe a no-wake zone, for the consideration of the nearby waterfowl area. Boaters are required to follow the Colorado boating statutes and regulations (brochures are available at the entrance station and park headquarters).

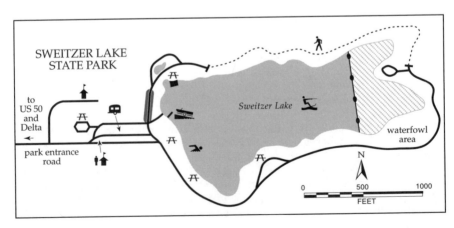

Fishing is good at the lake, but some important considerations do exist. This lake is generally thought of as a good fishing spot for youngsters. Channel catfish, blue catfish, perch, bluegill, and carp are caught in these waters. *However, fish in this lake contain dangerous levels of selenium and are not edible.* Kids can learn some fishing skills at Sweitzer, but no fish should be kept! Ice fishing is allowed anywhere in the park during the winter, but rarely is the ice thick enough to safely go out on it.

The only hiking trail in the park is the canal road connecting the northwest picnic area with the waterfowl area at the northeast end of the lake. Cross-country skiing is allowed anywhere in the park, although there are no groomed trails and snowfall is rarely deep enough for skiing.

Because this area is on the migratory path for wintering birds, visitors can view scores of different species throughout the year. Pelicans, swans, eagles, and many native duck are just a few of the waterfowl seen at the lake. Larger animals living near this area include mule deer, rabbits, raccoons, mink, muskrat, and pheasant.

Plenty of good outdoor recreation outlets can be found nearby in Delta, with many offering brochures and tips on the other fishing, boating, picnicking, and hiking opportunities available nearby.

Hikers have many trails that can be accessed within 50 miles of Sweitzer Lake. The nearest area is the massive Grand Mesa (see appendix A). This huge plateau has over 200 lakes atop it, with more than 650 miles of hiking trail stretching across its broad, flat top. A Scenic Byway leads you to the top of Grand Mesa via Highway 65. Once there, you might also choose to visit Powderhorn Ski Resort (see appendix A), open in both winter and summer. To obtain the Colorado State Parks' brochure titled "Western Slope and Mountains" in their Urban Trails in Colorado series, call the Denver office (see appendix A). This brochure is also available at Colorado Welcome Centers statewide.

RIDGWAY STATE PARK

Hours/Season: Overnight; year-round (major facilities open May through September)

Area: 2,200 land acres; 1,000 water acres

Facilities: 283 campsites, 70 picnic sites, group picnic area, dump station, laundry, bathhouse, snack bar, boat ramp, marina, fish-cleaning station, swim beach, hiking trails, playgrounds

Attractions: Camping, picnicking, group picnicking, hiking, fishing, ice fishing, visitors/nature center, interpretive programs, nature hikes, boating, waterskiing, swimming, horseback riding, cross-country skiing, ice skating, ice fishing

Access: From US 550 in Montrose, 60 miles south of Grand Junction, go south 20 miles

Ridgway State Park offers some of the finest scenery in Colorado to complement the outstanding recreational opportunities found in the park. The entire southern horizon is filled by the sweeping, snowcapped San Juan Mountains and Sneffels Range, a magnificent collection of fourteeners that has inspired this part of Colorado to be known as the "Switzerland of America."

Ridgway Reservoir, formed by the damming of the Uncompahgre River, rests

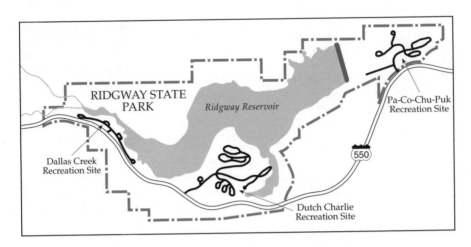

comfortably between the lower green foothills of the Uncompahgre River Valley, 20 miles south of Montrose. Ridgway is one of the most modern and newest of all Colorado's state parks. The park is comprised of three different recreational areas: Pa-Co-Chu-Puk Recreation Site, Dutch Charlie Recreation Site, and Dallas Creek Recreation Site.

The area surrounding the state park opened to development in the 1860s with the silver and gold boom in Ouray and Silverton, in the mountains south of Ridgway. By 1890 the boom had subsided. Ranching and farming took hold and

Group picnic area at Ridgway State Park

View of the San Juan Mountains looking south from Ridgway State Park

continue to impact the economy of the valley. After World War II, recreation began growing as a viable part of the economy. Ridgway Dam was constructed during the 1980s, and the Dutch Charlie site of the Ridgway State Park opened in 1989, followed by Dallas Creek in 1992 and Pa-Co-Chu-Puk in 1994.

Visitors coming to the park from the north on Highway 550 first come to the Pa-Co-Chu-Puk site. The most recent recreational site at Ridgway to open, Pa-Co-Chu-Puk is situated along the banks of the Uncompahgre River. This site offers 81 level campsites with full utility hookups and a camper services building with a laundromat and soda machines. In addition, there are walk-in campsites across the river from the fishing ponds, via a pedestrian bridge.

This section of Ridgway Park offers six day-use picnic areas along the river. A very modern and attractive group picnic area (suitable for weddings, reunions, etc.) can accommodate up to 200 people. This picnic site is equipped with shade shelters, redwood decking, cooking facilities, rest rooms, horseshoe pits, a playground, sand volleyball court, and stage. Call the park office to reserve this very beautiful and popular attraction (see appendix A).

The fishing is especially good at this site along the river. The catch-and-release rule is in effect, requiring that all fish caught be immediately returned to the river; only artificial flies and lures are permitted. Two scenic trout ponds are also located near the river; fish that are caught from these are allowed to be kept, and fishing with bait is permissible.

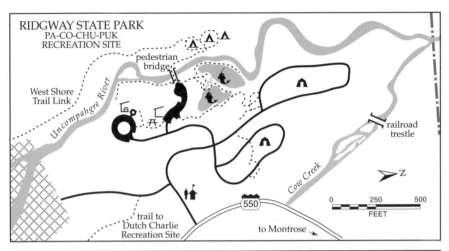

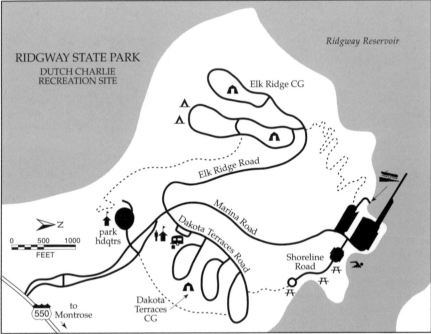

The Ridgway Dam is located just upstream from Pa-Co-Chu-Puk. The trail to the top of the dam can be reached by crossing the pedestrian footbridge near the fishing ponds and following the west side of the river. Once at the paved road on the dam, visitors are cautioned to stay only on the road. The dam offers great views and good fishing. Some areas around the site are closed, so caution is advised.

Just down the highway from Pa-Co-Chu-Puk is the Dutch Charlie site, which is the original Ridgway State Park recreation site that opened in 1989. This section of the park, located on a large point on the reservoir, is nearly surrounded by water, but steep bluffs on the north and west sides limit water access to the northeast side.

Visitors have two scenic campgrounds from which to choose. Dakota Terraces is located just opposite the entrance station, within walking distance of the swim beach on the lake. Elk Ridge occupies the higher ground above the park and rests in a piñon-juniper forest affording a panoramic view of the nearby San Juan Mountains. In the two campgrounds combined, there are 187 modern, clean campsites, including ten walk-in tent sites. These campgrounds can accommodate recreational vehicles and tents. All sites, except the tent sites, have electrical hookups, and a campers service building nearby offers modern rest rooms, hot showers, and laundry facilities.

Most of the thirty picnic sites at Dutch Charlie are sheltered, with the most popular sites found near the swim beach and playground area.

Several innovative volunteer programs are available at Ridgway State Park. These include boat patrol rangers, park naturalist, campground host, trail construction crew leaders and workers, and visitors center assistant. Check with the park office for details (see appendix A). The visitors center displays skeletons of wildlife, park habitat, and geology interpretations, and offers a wide selection of books dealing with outdoor topics. You can pick up a booklet on the self-guided nature trail that begins as you leave the center; topics covered include an excellent discussion about the mountains and geology of the region.

Boaters find a full-service marina at Dutch Charlie, just beyond the swim beach, complete with boat and slip rentals and a four-lane concrete boat ramp. Waterskiing, sailing, and sailboarding are popular; however, boaters are cautioned to observe the no-wake areas located on the reservoir. The combination of clear summer skies and a freshwater lake surrounded by plateaus and alpine mountains makes boating especially pleasurable at Ridgway.

The swim beach at the northeast end of the site is the only place in the park where swimming is permitted. Showers, changing rooms with lockers, a deluxe playground, and a volleyball court add to the enjoyable beach amenities. The mountain park setting at Dutch Charlie also makes a delightful backdrop for beach-goers.

Some wildlife can be observed in this section of the park and the visitors center

The San Juan Mountains at Molas Pass south of Ridgway State Park

offers bird-watchers a checklist on the birds commonly seen. The best wildlife observations take place during the winter.

Just down the highway from Dutch Charlie is the Dallas Creek Site. This area occupies the small but very scenic southern tip of Ridgway Reservoir and the outlet of the Uncompahgre River. This section of the park offers expansive views northwest through the entire length of the reservoir toward the Uncompahgre Plateau, forming the western border of the lake. Dallas Creek is an open-space site, offering shoreline parking, fishing, and picnicking.

Picnic sites are neatly arranged along the east shore, with the Deer Run picnic area offering sheltered tables and a playground. More secluded sites can be found near the confluence area and are accessible by a gravel trail. Dallas Creek Recreation Site is cool, lush, and open . . . just right for a scenic picnic lunch!

Fishermen come to cast their lines from shore for the rainbow and brown trout that inhabit the Uncompahgre River, Dallas Creek, and the Ridgway Reservoir. Fishing is also permitted from the pedestrian bridges over the river and creek, but anglers are cautioned to respect the rights of the hikers that access this same area.

Over 4 miles of hike/bike trails meander around Dallas Creek, and connect this site with Dutch Charlie. A walking trail parallels the lakeshore drive, allowing for closer inspection of the reservoir.

Within an easy drive of Ridgway State Park are enough trails to fill an entire summer's agenda. One of the best publications available, found at the Dutch Charlie visitors center, is titled "Hiking Trails of Ouray County." Information on San Juan National Forest is available by calling Durango (see appendix A). The Montrose Chamber of Commerce also has many excellent recreational brochures (see appendix A).

MANCOS STATE PARK

Hours/Season: Overnight; year-round
Area: 334 acres; 216 surface water acres
Facilities: 33 campsites, 12 picnic sites, group picnic area, boat ramp, dump station
Attractions: Camping, picnicking, interpretive programs, boating, sailboarding, fishing, hiking, biking, horseback riding, cross-country skiing, ice fishing
Nearby: Mesa Verde National Park, Ute Mountain Tribal Park, Hovenweep National Monument, Crow Canyon Archaeological Center
Access: From Durango, at the junction of US 550 and US 160 in the southwest area (near the Four Corners), take US 160 west 27 miles to the town of Mancos; go north on Highway 184 for 0.25 mile, then turn east onto CR 42; go 4 miles and take CR N to the park entrance

No matter what route visitors take to reach Mancos State Park—down from Grand Junction, east from Durango, or west from Cortez—they pass through some of Colorado's most scenic countryside. Mancos is located on the San Juan Skyway, a national forest and state of Colorado Scenic Byway. The park itself is located a few miles northeast of the town of Mancos. The drive there focuses your attention on the spectacular La Plata Mountains that fill the eastern horizon beyond the state park. The combination of forests, mountains, and streams surrounding Mancos Lake tells you at once that you are entering a very special place.

The San Juan Mountains extend around Mancos Reservoir in all directions. At 7,800 feet, Mancos is a true alpine lake. A lush, quiet, pine and fir forest envelopes the lake, while along the shoreline can be found cottonwoods, bushes, and other wetland-type growth that offer fishermen many secluded and protected coves from which to try their luck. Whatever activity (or non-activity) one chooses to pursue at Mancos, the captivating, beautiful scenery adds to it. This is a tranquil and restful park, absent of any hint of the busy outside world.

Mancos State Park is located only 10 miles northeast of historic Mesa Verde National Park. The early history of the area was tied to the rise and sudden disappearance of the Anasazi Indians. The Spanish settled the area during the 1600s and were influential until the 1800s and the discovery of gold and silver 50 miles to the northeast in Silverton. Ranching, farming, and some lumber operations comprised the main economic staple of the area until the advent of tourism and recreational development after World War II. In 1948 the federal Bureau of Reclamation completed the Jackson Gulch Dam at Mancos in order to supply drinking water for Mesa Verde and the surrounding rural areas. As recreational needs grew, Mancos was added to the state park system in 1988.

Camping is in twenty-four campsites located in a thick ponderosa pine forest on the south side of the reservoir. Vault toilets and drinking water are available, but no electrical hookups. Along the northwest side of the lake are nine campsites, mainly for tent campers, with toilets but no drinking water. All campers are asked to use a dump station located at the exit the campground. The campsites are generously spaced, while the canopy of pine provides a cool shade from warm afternoon sun.

Picnickers enjoy a beautiful mountain and forest backdrop, which on calm days is stunningly mirrored on Mancos Lake. Picnic tables and sites with grills are scattered along the lakefront. A covered group shelter near the entrance station is also available. It is easy for visitors to arrive in midmorning, take the gentle several-mile stroll around the lake, get lost in the solitude of the park, treat themselves to a tasty late-afternoon lunch, and, before they know it, find themselves admiring the last glow of a Southwest sunset.

Boaters are required to operate their crafts at wakeless speeds. No swimming or waterskiing is permitted on the lake. The boat ramp is located near the spillway at the entrance station area. The relaxed boater drifting slowly and effortlessly across a still mountain lake, snowcapped mountains outlining the sky while a lazy meandering cloud floats silently through a deep blue sky . . . an enjoyable and often repeated scene at Mancos Lake!

Fishermen can try their luck from shore or join the "without-a-care-in-the-world boaters club" out on the lake. Rainbow trout is the fish of choice at the lake. The Division of Wildlife generously stocks Mancos with this fish, although other species can also be found. Fishing from shore has its good points, too. Each shaded

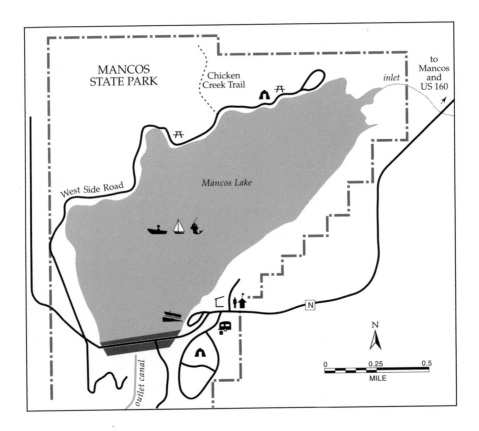

The La Plata Mountains from the West Side Road

cove offers privacy, while the road around the lake allows fishermen to quickly change to another "hot spot."

Hiking consists of walking on the West Side Road along the lakeshore until it joins the Chicken Creek Trail. The lakeside walk is an easy ramble, offering beautiful views of the La Plata Mountains to the east. The scents of pine, cottonwood, wildflowers, and grasses heighten the hiking experience at Mancos. The Chicken Creek Trail, which begins at 7,900 feet elevation, follows the creek bed for the first 5 miles, eventually climbing out of the canyon and the park.

Ice fishing is allowed anywhere on the lake during winter, as is cross-country skiing. Winter camping is permitted in the regular-season campground.

Deer, elk, rabbits, bald eagles and waterfowl, hawks, raptors, and hummingbirds are often seen at Mancos State Park. During the fall, some wood ducks and Canadian geese make an appearance.

Hikers can access an extensive network of trails found in the San Juan National Forest from Mancos State Park's Chicken Creek Trail, and eventually connect with the Colorado Trail, which runs from Durango to Denver. The Chicken Creek Trail connects with Forest Development Road 561 5 miles after leaving the Mancos Reservoir. The trail crosses the road at Transfer Campground and joins with the West Mancos Trail at 8 miles and 8,900 feet elevation. The West Mancos Trail drops down

191

Hiker walking on top of Mancos Dam looking toward the La Plata Mountains

into the spectacular West Mancos Canyon, with sheer walls and cliffs running for over 2 miles. Some of Colorado's largest quaking aspen can be found along this section of the trail. After making its way out of the canyon, the trail circles Hesperus Peak (13,232 feet), the highest peak in the La Plata Mountains, and ends by meeting with the Sharkstooth Trailhead in almost 9 miles.

There are hundreds of miles of hiking trail available within a 60-mile radius of Mancos State Park. These trails offer some of the most scenic vistas anywhere in Colorado, through what many consider to be the Switzerland of America . . . the San Juan Mountains. Information on these trails are available from many sources. Mesa Verde County Visitors Bureau (see appendix A) publishes the "Guide to Scenic Hiking Trails in Mesa Verde County," a free brochure. The trail maps for San Juan National Forest are available by calling the San Juan National Forest headquarters (see appendix A).

Visitors to Mancos State Park who are looking for nearby cultural and recreational offerings have an abundance of choices. The Mesa Verde County Visitors Bureau (see appendix A) publishes a series of informative brochures. The "Guide to Anasazi Sites and Cultural Centers" features Mesa Verde National Park, the Ute Mountain Tribal Park, Hovenweep National Monument, and the Crow Canyon Archaeological Center, all within easy driving distance of Mancos State Park. The "Guide to Scenic and Historic Tours" highlights day trips in the area; mountain bikers find the "Mountain and Road Bike Routes" comprehensive and helpful. All these brochures are free.

NAVAJO STATE PARK

Hours/Season: Overnight; year-round
Area: 2,672 acres; 15,600 surface water acres
Facilities: 71 campsites, 16 picnic sites, group picnic area, visitors/nature center, dump station, showers, snack bar, boat ramp, marina
Attractions: Camping, picnicking, interpretive programs, boating, fishing, waterskiing, jet skiing, sailboarding, hiking, biking, cross-country skiing
Nearby: Chimney Rock, San Juan Wilderness Area, Weminuche Wilderness Area
Access: From Pagosa Springs, on US 160 near the southern border with New Mexico, take US 160 west for 17 miles; turn southwest on CO 151, go 18 miles to Arboles, then go 2 miles south on CR 982

Navajo State Park is the only Colorado state park that straddles two states. The focal point of the park is the magnificent 35-mile-long Navajo Reservoir, with over 15,000 surface water acres, 3,000 of which lie in Colorado, with the other 12,000 acres in New Mexico. The lake resembles Lake Powell in Utah, without the colorful rock formations, the land rising abruptly out of the lake into plateau and mesa formations. From the Colorado side, visitors can look down the lake well into New Mexico. The immensity is bounded by the surrounding high plateaus and mountains.

The lake is the result of the construction of Navajo Dam in 1962 for the purpose of providing irrigation water for the Navajo Indian Reservation. Navajo Dam is located on the San Juan River in northern New Mexico. It stands over 400 feet high and is 0.75 mile long.

Navajo Lake offers a modern campground that looks out across the lake to the nearby New Mexico mountains and plateaus. The setting is serene, simple, and relaxing for anyone needing to get away from it all. The campground has 71 sites, showers, and flush toilets. Many sites have pull-throughs while all can accommodate tents or recreational vehicles. A dump station is located in the campground. Supplies are available in the town of Arboles or at the marina.

Picnicking is offered in one area only, between the marina and the campground. The tables are situated on a bluff overlooking the lake, with some shelter

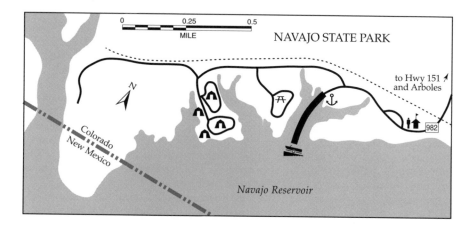

Marina at Navajo State Park

provided. The same peaceful setting that pervades the rest of the park also touches the picnic area.

At the visitors/nature center, exhibits of Indian artifacts excavated from areas now submerged beneath the reservoir are displayed. Archaeology suggests that the area was populated by the Anasazi until the fourteenth century, when they were displaced by the ancestors of modern Ute and Navajo tribes.

Navajo Lake is a boater's paradise. Colorado's largest boat ramp—80 feet wide and 0.25 mile long—is found here. Small coves and inlets offer some secluded spots for fishing or boating. With the lake being as large as it is, boaters easily feel as if the lake is just theirs. All boaters are subject to Colorado boating regulations and statutes, which are available at the entrance station. New Mexico laws and regulations likewise apply to boaters crossing the state line. Both states have a reciprocal agreement honoring current boat registrations and inspection stickers.

A large marina offers boaters a variety of services. Houseboats, fishing boats, runabouts, and pontoon boats can all be rented; dry storage, slip, buoy, and launch-and-retrieve services are available. The marina houses a cafe and store where gas, tackle, supplies, and propane filling can be purchased. The marina is located past the main entrance, left off of County Road 982 before the picnic and camping areas.

Before the dam was built, the San Juan River was often muddy and silt-ridden. Most game fish were almost nonexistent. The dam has changed the river so that water below the dam flows clear and cold, making an ideal habitat for brown, cutthroat, and rainbow trout. Bluegill, catfish, crappie, and largemouth bass can be caught in the shallows and near the lake surface. Deeper waters yield kokanee salmon and many species of trout. During their autumn spawning run, kokanee salmon are permitted to be snagged since they die soon afterward. Highway 151 and County Road 500 to Pagosa Junction have access roads leading to good fishing spots on the San Juan and Piedra Rivers. Visitors planning to cross over into New Mexico and also fish there must have the appropriate licenses for both states.

Hiking in the park is limited to following the abandoned Denver & Rio Grande narrow-gauge railroad bed, or the road that travels the length of the park. This road also serves as the only bike path though the park. In all, 12 miles of "trail" are available. In winter, these same "trails" are open to cross-country skiing, though they are not groomed.

Wildlife is best found in remote areas of the park. Navajo Lake is home to many waterfowl, shorebirds, birds of prey, songbirds, and game birds such as doves, grouse, and turkeys, as well as beaver, mink, elk, deer, and foxes. The visitors center offers a Navajo State Park Bird Checklist that indicates which bird are common or rare at the lake.

Visitors interested in exploring other archaeological Indian sites need only return to Highway 151 and follow it north toward Pagosa Springs. Along the way, 3 miles south of the junction with Highway 160, is the Chimney Rock Indian site. Home to the ancient Anasazi, the "Great House" ruins indicate habitation as far back as 1076 A.D. The site is believed to be the most isolated and remote of the Anasazi communities that can be traced to the Chaco Canyon, New Mexico, community. The Pagosa Ranger Station in Pagosa Springs has on display examples of artifacts excavated from Chimney Rock. For information on this area of San Juan National Forest, call the Pagosa Ranger District (see appendix A).

Hikers can also call for information on the many trails found in the San Juan Wilderness Area, San Juan National Forest, and the Weminuche Wilderness Area. Visitors traveling toward Denver who plan to hike along the way might also ask for trail information in the Wolf Creek Pass and Ski Area northeast of Pagosa Springs.

APPENDIX A

ADDRESSES AND TELEPHONE NUMBERS

COLORADO STATE PARKS

Administrative Office, 1313 Sherman Street, Room 618, Denver, CO 80203; (303) 866-3437

Camping and cabin reservations in the Denver Metro area, (303) 470-1144; outside the Denver Metro area, (800) 678-CAMP

Denver Metro Region

Metro Region Office, 13787 South Highway 85, Littleton, CO 80125; (303) 791-1957

Barr Lake State Park, 13401 Picadilly Road, Brighton, CO 80601; (303) 659-6005

Castlewood Canyon State Park, Box 504, Franktown, CO 80116-0504; (303) 688-5242

Chatfield State Park, 11500 North Roxborough Park Road, Littleton, CO 80125; (303) 791-7275

Cherry Creek State Park, 4201 South Parker Road, Aurora, CO 80014; (303) 699-3860

Eldorado Canyon State Park, P.O. Box B, Eldorado Springs, CO 80025; (303) 494-3943

Golden Gate Canyon State Park, 3873 Highway 46, Golden, CO 80403; (303) 592-1502

Roxborough State Park, 4751 North Roxborough Drive, Littleton, CO 80125; (303) 973-3959

North Region

North Region Office, 3842 South Mason, Room 202, Fort Collins, CO 80525; (970) 226-6641

Barbour Ponds State Park, c/o Boyd Lake State Park, 3720 North County Road 11-C, Loveland, CO 80538; (970) 669-1739

Boyd Lake State Park, 3720 North County Road 11-C, Loveland, CO 80538; (970) 669-1739

Colorado State Forest, Star Route Box 91, Walden, CO 80480; (970) 723-8366

Jackson Lake State Park, 26363 County Road 3, Orchard, CO 80649; (970) 645-2551

Lory State Park, 708 Lodgepole Drive, Bellvue, CO 80512; (970) 493-1623

North Sterling Reservoir State Park, 24005 County Road 330, Sterling, CO 80751; (970) 522-3657

Pearl Lake State Park, P.O. Box 750, Clark, CO 80428; (970) 879-3922

Picnic Rock State Park, c/o Lory State Park, 708 Lodgepole Drive, Bellvue, CO 80512; (970) 493-1623

Stagecoach State Park, P.O. Box 98, Oak Creek, CO 80467; (970) 736-2436

Steamboat Lake State Park, P.O. Box 750, Clark, CO 80428; (970) 879-3922

South Region

South Region Office, 2128 North Weber, Colorado Springs, CO 80907; (719) 471-0900

Arkansas Headwaters Recreation Area, P.O. Box 126, Salida, CO 81201; (719) 539-7289

Bonny Lake State Park, 30010 Road 3, Idalia, CO 80735-9674; (970) 354-7306

Eleven Mile State Park, 4229 Park County, Road 92, Lake George, CO 80827; (719) 748-3401

Lake Pueblo State Park, 640 Pueblo Reservoir Road, Pueblo, CO 81005; (719) 561-9320

Lathrop State Park, 70 County Road 502, Walsenburg, CO 81089; (719) 738-2376

Mueller State Park and Wildlife Area, P.O. Box 49, Divide, CO 80814; (719) 687-2366

San Luis Lakes State Park, P.O. Box 175, Mosca, CO 81146; (719) 378-2020

Spinney Mountain State Park, 4229 Park County Road 92, Lake George, CO 80827; (719) 748-3401

Trinidad Lake State Park, 32610 Highway 12, Trinidad, CO 81082; (719) 846-6951

West Region

West Region Office, 361 32 Road, P.O. Box 700, Clifton, CO 81520; (970) 434-6862

Colorado River State Park, P.O. Box 700, Clifton, CO 81520; (970) 434-3388

Crawford State Park, P.O. Box 147, Crawford, CO 81415; (970) 921-5721

Harvey Gap State Park, c/o Rifle Falls and Rifle Gap State Parks, 0050 Road 219, Rifle, CO 81650; (970) 625-1607

Highline State Park, 1800 11.8 Road, Loma, CO 81524; (970) 858-7208

Mancos State Park, c/o Navajo State Park, P.O. Box 1697, Arboles, CO 81121; (970) 434-6862

Navajo State Park, P.O. Box 1697, Arboles, CO 81121; (970) 883-2208

Paonia State Park, c/o Crawford State Park, P.O. Box 147, Crawford, CO 81415; (970) 921-5721

Ridgway State Park, 28555 Highway 550, Ridgway, CO 81432; (970) 626-5822

Rifle Falls State Park, 0050 Road 219, Rifle, CO 81650; (970) 625-1607

Rifle Gap State Park, 0050 Road 219, Rifle, CO 81650; (970) 625-1607

Sweitzer Lake State Park, 1735 E Road, Delta, CO 81416; (970) 874-4258

Sylvan Lake State Park, c/o Rifle Falls and Rifle Gap State Parks, 0050 Road 219, Rifle, CO 81650; (970) 625-1607

Vega State Park, P.O. Box 186, Collbran, CO 81624; (970) 487-3407

COLORADO STATE AGENCIES

Boulder County Parks and Open Space Department, 2045 13th Street, P.O. Box 471, Boulder, CO 80306; (303) 441-3950

Colorado Division of Wildlife, 6060 Broadway, Denver, CO (303) 297-1192

Colorado Geological Survey, 1313 Sherman Street, Room 715, Denver, CO 80202; (303) 592-5510

Larimer County Parks, (303) 679-4570

COLORADO TOURISM ORGANIZATIONS

Bicycle Colorado, P.O. Box 3877, Littleton, CO 80161-2655; (303) 798-1429

Boulder Off-Road Alliance, 1420 Alpine Avenue, Boulder CO 80304; (303) 444-4196

Coal Creek/Rock Creek Trails Foundation, 488 Owl Drive, Louisville, CO 80027; (303) 441-3900

Colorado Association of Campgrounds, Cabins, and Lodges, 5101 Pennsylvania Avenue, Boulder, CO 80303; (303) 499-9343

Colorado Horsemen's Council, P.O. Box 1125, Arvada, CO 80001; (303) 469-5863

Colorado Llama Outfitters and Guides Association, 30361 Rainbow Hills Road, Golden, CO 80401; (303) 526-0992/(800) 462-8234

Colorado Mountain Club, 710 Tenth Street, Golden, CO 80401; (303) 279-3080

Colorado Plateau Mountain Bike Association, (907) 241-9561

Colorado River Outfitters Association, P.O. Box 1662, Buena Vista, CO 81211; (719) 369-4632

Colorado Tourism Board, 1625 Broadway, Suite 2320, Denver, CO 80202; (303) 592-5510

The Colorado Trail, P.O. Box 260876, Lakewood, CO 80226-0876

The Colorado Trail Foundation/Friends of the Colorado Trail, 548 Pine Song Trail, Golden, CO 80401; (303) 526-0809

Crested Butte Mountain Bike Association, P.O. Box 1133, Crested Butte, CO 81224; (970) 349-5409

Delta County Area Visitor Bureau, (970) 874-8616

Eagle Valley Chamber, (970) 328-5220

Grand Junction Visitor and Convention Bureau, (800) 962-2547

Gunnison River Territory, (800) 323-2453

Hahns Peak USFS Ranger District Office, (970) 879-1870

The Lookout Mountain Nature Center, c/o 700 Jefferson County Parkway, Suite 100, Golden, CO 80401; (303) 526-0594

Loveland High Plains Arts Council, (800) 551-1752

Mesa Verde County Visitors Bureau, (800)-253-1616

Montrose Chamber of Commerce, (800)-873-0244

Mountain and Road Biking Association of Rocky Flats, 13533 West 21st Avenue, Golden, CO 80401; (303) 278-4988

North American Trail Riders Conference, 10590 Egerton Road, Colorado Springs, CO 80908; (719) 495-2906

North Park Chamber of Commerce, (970) 723-4600

Park County Tourism, (719) 836-2771, ext. 279

Pikes Peak Area Trails Coalition, P.O. Box 34, Colorado Springs, CO 80901; (719) 635-4825

Powderhorn Ski Resort, (800) 241-6997

Prairie Development Corporation, (719) 348-5562

Rocky Mountain Backcountry Horsemen, (719) 783-9446

San Juan Hut to Hut System, P.O. Box 1663, Telluride, CO; 81435; (970) 728-6935

Steamboat Springs Chamber Resort Association, (970) 879-0880

Summit Huts and Trails Association, P.O. Box 2830, Breckinridge, CO 80424; (970) 453-9615

Tenth Mountain Trail Association, 1280 Ute Avenue, Aspen, CO 81611; (970) 925-4554

Vail Resort Association, (970) 476-1000
Volunteers for Outdoor Colorado, 1410 Grant, B105, Denver, CO 80203; in
    Denver, (303) 830-7792; outside of Denver Metro area, (800) 925-2220
Walden Town Hall, (970) 723-4344
Walsenburg Golf Club, (719) 738-2730
Wilderness on Wheels Foundation, (303) 988-2212

FEDERAL AGENCIES

Black Canyon of the Gunnison National Monument, (970) 249-7036
Flat Tops Wilderness Area, (970) 879-1722
Maroon Bells-Snowmass Wilderness Area, (970) 874-7691
National Park Service, P.O. Box 25287, Denver, CO 80225; (303) 969-2000
Pawnee National Grassland, (970) 353-5004
Rocky Mountain National Park, Estes Park, CO 80517-8397; (970) 586-3565
U.S. Bureau of Land Management, Colorado State Office, 2850 Youngfield
    Street, Lakewood, CO 80215; (303) 239-3600
U.S. Bureau Land of Management, Grand Junction, (970) 244-3000
U.S. Bureau Land of Management, Grand Junction, (970) 243-6552
U.S. Bureau of Land Management, Pueblo, (719) 589-4975
U.S. Forest Service, P.O. Box 25127, Lakewood, CO 80225; (303) 275-5350
U.S. Forest Service, Grand Mesa, (970) 242-8211
U.S. Forest Service, Poudre Canyon, (970) 498-2770
U.S. Forest Service, Yampa, (970) 638-4516

National Forests in Colorado

Arapahoe and Roosevelt National Forest Headquarters, 240 West Prospect
    Road, Fort Collins, CO 80526-2098; (970) 498-1100
Grand Mesa–Uncompahgre and Gunnison National Forest Headquarters, 2250
    Highway 50, Delta, CO 81416-8723; (970) 874-7691
Gunnison National Forest, (970) 527-4131
Pike and San Isabel National Forest Headquarters, 1920 Valley Drive, Pueblo,
    CO 81008; (719) 545-8737
Pike National Forest, Pikes Peak Ranger District, Colorado Springs,
    (719) 636-1602
Pike National Forest, South Park Ranger District, Fairplay, (719) 836-2031
Rio Grande National Forest Headquarters, 1803 West Highway 160, Monte
    Vista, CO 81144; (719) 852-5941
Routt National Forest Headquarters, 29587 West US 40, Suite 20, Steamboat
    Springs, CO 80487; (970) 879-1722
San Isabel National Forest, La Veta, (719) 742-3601
San Juan National Forest Headquarters, 701 Camino Del Rio, Room 301,
    Durango, CO 81301; (970) 247-4874
San Juan National Forest, Pagosa (970) 264-2268
White River National Forest Headquarters, Ninth and Grand, P.O. Box 948,
    Glenwood Springs, CO 81601; (970) 945-2521
White River National Forest, Rifle, (970) 625-2371

APPENDIX B

PARK ACCESSIBILITY

Colorado State Parks works to make each park as barrier free as possible for the convenience and safety of visitors with limited mobility. All new facilities are constructed with maximum accessibility for all levels of ability. As individual parks renovate and upgrade their existing facilities, whatever can be done to help make the park enjoyable for everyone is being done.

Some visitors to Colorado state parks might require additional information on park access for the physically challenged. Individuals in wheelchairs, those using canes or walkers, parents with strollers, and any other person with mobility impairment may need more specific information on fishing, hiking trails, camping, etc.

The following information lists the primary activities and facilities at each state park. Each park listed has a varying degree of accessibility. This list is meant only as a general guideline. Visitors should contact each park they may be visiting for more detailed information. See appendix A for park listings.

Arkansas Headwaters Recreation Area: Some designated handicap facilities are accessible for fishing, camping, hiking/walking trails, picnicking, rest rooms, and visitors center.

Barbour Ponds State Park: Some facilities are accessible with assistance for fishing, camping, and picnicking. Some designated handicap facilities are available for fishing and rest rooms.

Barr Lake State Park: Some facilities are accessible with assistance for fishing, picnicking, rest rooms, and visitors center.

Bonny Lake State Park: Some facilities are accessible with assistance for fishing, camping, picnicking, swimming, and showers. Some designated handicap facilities are available for camping, picnicking, and rest rooms.

Boyd Lake State Park: Some designated handicap facilities are available for camping, walking/hiking trails, rest rooms, showers, and visitors center. Some facilities are accessible with assistance for fishing and swimming.

Castlewood Canyon State Park: Some designated handicap facilities are available for walking/hiking trails, picnicking, rest rooms, and visitors center.

Chatfield State Park: Some designated handicap facilities are available for fishing, walking/hiking trails, picnicking, rest rooms, showers, and visitors center. Some facilities are accessible with assistance for camping and swimming.

Cherry Creek State Park: Some designated handicap facilities are available for fishing, camping, walking/hiking trails, picnicking, rest rooms, and showers. Some facilities are accessible with assistance for swimming.

Colorado River State Park: Some designated handicap facilities are available for fishing, walking/hiking trails, camping, picnicking, and rest rooms. Some facilities are accessible with assistance for walking/hiking trails, picnicking, and swimming.

Colorado State Forest: Some facilities are accessible with assistance for fishing, camping, picnicking, and rest rooms.

Crawford State Park: Some facilities are accessible with assistance for fishing, camping, picnicking, and swimming. Some designated handicap facilities are available for rest rooms.

Eldorado Canyon State Park: Some facilities are accessible with assistance for fishing, walking/hiking trails, picnicking, rest rooms, and visitors center.

Eleven Mile State Park: Some designated handicap facilities are available for camping, picnicking, rest rooms, and showers. Some facilities are accessible with assistance for fishing.

Golden Gate Canyon State Park: Some designated handicap facilities are available for fishing, walking/hiking trails, picnicking, rest rooms, and visitors center. Some facilities are accessible with assistance for camping, rest rooms, and visitors center.

Harvey Gap State Park: Some facilities are accessible with assistance for fishing, picnicking, swimming, and rest rooms. Some designated handicap facilities are available for picnicking and rest rooms.

Highline State Park: Some facilities are accessible with assistance for fishing, camping, and swimming. Some designated handicap facilities are available for picnicking and rest rooms.

Jackson Lake State Park: Some facilities are accessible with assistance for fishing, rest rooms, and showers.

Lake Pueblo State Park: Some designated handicap facilities are available for fishing, camping, walking/hiking trails, rest rooms, showers, and visitors center. Some facilities are accessible with assistance for picnicking and swimming.

Lathrop State Park: Some designated handicap facilities are available for fishing and rest rooms. Some facilities are accessible with assistance for camping, swimming, picnicking, and visitors center.

Lory State Park: Some designated handicap facilities are available for picnicking and rest rooms.

Mancos State Park: Some facilities are accessible with assistance for fishing and picnicking.

Mueller State Park and Wildlife Area: Some designated handicap facilities are available for camping, picnicking, rest rooms, and showers.

Navajo State Park: Some facilities are accessible with assistance for fishing, picnicking, and visitors center.

North Sterling Reservoir State Park: Some facilities are accessible with assistance for fishing, picnicking, and visitors center. Some designated handicap facilities are available for camping, rest rooms, and showers.

Pearl Lake State Park: Some facilities are accessible with assistance for fishing, camping, picnicking, and rest rooms. Some designated handicap facilities are available for camping and rest rooms.

Picnic Rock State Park: Some facilities are accessible with assistance for fishing, picnicking, and rest rooms.

Ridgway State Park: Some designated handicap facilities are available for camping, walking/hiking trails, picnicking, rest rooms, showers, and visitors center. Some facilities are accessible with assistance for fishing and swimming.

Rifle Falls State Park: Some facilities are accessible with assistance for camping, picnicking, and rest rooms. Some designated handicap facilities are available for rest rooms.

Rifle Gap State Park: Some facilities are accessible with assistance for fishing, camping, picnicking, swimming, and rest rooms.

Roxborough State Park: Some facilities are accessible with assistance for walking/hiking trails. Some designated handicap facilities are available for rest rooms and visitors center.

San Luis Lakes State Park: Some designated handicap facilities are available for fishing, camping, picnicking, rest rooms, and showers. Some facilities are accessible with assistance regarding fishing, picnicking, and rest rooms.

Spinney Mountain State Park: Some facilities are accessible with assistance for fishing. Some designated handicap facilities are available for picnicking and rest rooms.

Stagecoach State Park: Some designated handicap facilities are available for camping, rest rooms, and showers. Some facilities are accessible with assistance for fishing and picnicking.

Steamboat Lake State Park: Some facilities are accessible with assistance for fishing, camping, picnicking, swimming, rest rooms, and visitors center. Some designated handicap facilities are available for camping and rest rooms.

Sweitzer Lake State Park: Some facilities are accessible with assistance for fishing, picnicking, swimming, and rest rooms.

Sylvan Lake State Park: Some facilities are accessible with assistance for fishing, camping, and rest rooms. Some designated handicap facilities are available for picnicking and rest rooms.

Trinidad Lake State Park: Some designated handicap facilities are available for camping, walking/hiking trails, picnicking, rest rooms, showers, and visitors center. Some facilities are accessible with assistance for fishing.

Vega State Park: Some facilities are accessible with assistance for fishing, camping, picnicking, and rest rooms.

INDEX

References to photographs indicated in *italic*

ABOUT THE AUTHOR

Philip Ferranti has hiked the western United States for over 20 years. He has spent much of that time exploring the trails in the Coachella Valley/Palm Springs area. During the summer Philip hikes out of Boulder, Colorado, with the Colorado Mountain Club. Inspired by this organization, in 1992 he founded the Coachella Valley Hiking Club, which is now the fastest growing hiking club in the United States. He has written for *Backpacker* magazine and contributes hiking columns for local newspapers. A career counselor for the College of the Desert and Palm Springs Unified School District and President of Transformation Seminars, Philip also conducts stress management seminars and believes that hiking is "the ultimate and most enjoyable stress management program."

In September 1995, Philip released his first hiking book, *75 Great Hikes In and Near Palm Springs and the Coachella Valley.*

Other titles you may enjoy from The Mountaineers:

Exploring Colorado's Wild Areas: A Guide for Hikers, Backpackers, Climbers, X-C Skiers & Paddlers, Scott S. Warren
Comprehensive guidebook to sixty-two Colorado wilderness areas, national parks, wildlife refuges, and nature preserves.

100 Hikes in™ Colorado, Scott S. Warren
Part of best-selling *100 Hikes in™* Series. Fully detailed mountain hiking guide to Colorado, with detailed trail descriptions, maps, and photos.

Best Hikes With Children® in Colorado, Maureen Keilty
Part of popular *Best Hikes With Children®* Series. Guide to day hikes and overnighters in Colorado for families, including tips on hiking with kids, safety, and fostering a wilderness ethic.

Hiking the Southwest's Canyon Country, Sandra Hinchman
The best dayhikes, backpacks, and scenic drives in Colorado, Utah, New Mexico, and Arizona. Includes distance, duration, difficulty, topographical maps, and more.

The *State Parks* Series
Comprehensive recreation guides including detailed descriptions of natural features, information on activities and facilities, and more!
California State Parks: A Complete Recreation Guide,
    Rhonda & George Ostertag
Oregon State Parks: A Complete Recreation Guide, Jan Bannan
Utah State Parks: A Complete Recreation Guide, Jan Bannan
Washington State Parks: A Complete Recreation Guide,
    Marge & Ted Mueller

Mountain Bike Adventures™ in the Four Corners Region, Michael McCoy
Part of favorite *Mountain Bike Adventures™* Series. Features accurate route descriptions and highlights wildlife, scenery, and historic and natural sites in Colorado, Utah, New Mexico, and Arizona.

THE MOUNTAINEERS, founded in 1906, is a nonprofit outdoor activity and conservation club, whose mission is "to explore, study, preserve, and enjoy the natural beauty of the outdoors. . . ." Based in Seattle, Washington, the club is now the third-largest such organization in the United States, with 15,000 members and four branches throughout Washington State.

The Mountaineers sponsors both classes and year-round outdoor activities in the Pacific Northwest, which include hiking, mountain climbing, ski-touring, snowshoeing, bicycling, camping, kayaking and canoeing, nature study, sailing, and adventure travel. The club's conservation division supports environmental causes through educational activities, sponsoring legislation, and presenting informational programs. All club activities are led by skilled, experienced volunteers, who are dedicated to promoting safe and responsible enjoyment and preservation of the outdoors.

If you would like to participate in these organized outdoor activities or the club's programs, consider a membership in The Mountaineers. For information and an application, write or call The Mountaineers, Club Headquarters, 300 Third Avenue West, Seattle, Washington 98119; (206) 284-6310.

The Mountaineers Books, an active, nonprofit publishing program of the club, produces guidebooks, instructional texts, historical works, natural history guides, and works on environmental conservation. All books produced by The Mountaineers are aimed at fulfilling the club's mission.

Send or call for our catalog of more than 300 outdoor titles:

 The Mountaineers Books
1001 SW Klickitat Way, Suite 201
Seattle, WA 98134
1-800-553-4453